ECONOMICS IN OUR TIME:

Concepts and Issues

Second Edition

DWIGHT R. LEE
Center for Study of Public Choice
George Mason University

ROBERT F. McNOWN
University of Colorado

SCIENCE RESEARCH ASSOCIATES, INC.
Chicago, Palo Alto, Toronto, Henley-on-Thames, Sydney

A Subsidiary of IBM

To Our Parents

Acquisition Editor	Michael Zamczyk
Project Editor	James C. Budd
Editor	Barbara Carpenter
Compositor	Interactive Composition Corp.
Cover Designer	Carol Harris
Cover Photo by	Barrie Rokeach

Cover photo Copyright 1983, Barrie Rokeach

Library of Congress Cataloging in Publication Data

Lee, Dwight R.
  Economics in our time.

  Includes index.
  1. Economics. I. McNown, Robert. F. II. Title.
HB171.5.L3725 1983   330   82-23150
ISBN 0-574-19435-5

Contents

Preface

One reason for the preeminence of economics as a social science is that a broad understanding of the world is possible with the aid of the relatively simple analytical framework provided by economic theory. But too often, students of introductory economics are occupied with so many analytical techniques that they miss the insights a few basic concepts can provide. Therefore, we expose students to a few key concepts and immediately use them to discuss issues. This approach does deny the student an immediate view of many mechanical fine points usually covered in an introductory course. However, a strong case can be made for giving a good overview of the forest before beginning an inspection of the individual trees.

We want to provide the student with an understanding of the economic facts of life in a simple way and how these facts apply to issues that superficially appear quite unrelated. Concepts will, for the most part, be developed as they are needed and used in a simple straight-forward way. Although the analysis is done at the verbal level, substantive concepts are treated without sacrificing accuracy or rigor. The economic reasoning is amply supported with specific examples and facts.

The positive response we received to the first edition of *Economics in Our Time* has strengthened our faith in this approach to introductory economics. Since we rely on contemporary economic issues to illustrate the applicability of economic concepts, a revision after eight years is certainly warranted. While most of the general problems (pollution, regulation, resource management, poverty, etc.) remain the same, specific circumstances have changed and much updating has been necessary. Sentences such as "Imagine gasoline selling for one dollar per gallon" no longer carry the same impact that they did in 1974. Major changes in attitudes and policies toward regulation necessitated major revisions in this material. Every chapter is, in fact, a major revision of the original, although we have strived to maintain the basic structure and approach of the first edition.

We start things off in Chapter 1 acknowledging the pervasiveness of scarcity and the resulting need to make choices and incur costs. The concept of opportunity cost is emphasized, and the role of self-interest as a prime motivating force is treated, along with an extensive discussion of the individualistic precept. The second chapter discusses the enormous informational requirements of a smoothly running economy and how a decentralized market economy consolidates relevant information through prices and applies it to the allocation of resources. The importance of property rights in an economic system is emphasized in this chapter. Market failure is acknowledged here and discussed in the context of specific problems throughout the following chapters: problems that are unavoidable in any economy (resource conservation and discrimination), that are the result of market failure (pollution, education, and poverty) and that result from governmental action (price controls and regulation of industry and occupational entry).

A pervading theme is that government action to correct a market flaw is the substitution of one imperfect mechanism for another. It is our position that most people either grossly underestimate the ability of the free market to desirably regulate economic activity or severely overestimate the ability of the government to perform this regulation, or both. To foster a more complete understanding of the tendency for government regulation to usurp market regulation—even when the social consequences are unfortunate—we include a chapter on the economic theory of the political process. Without an explicit discussion of the social choice mechanism, students are severely handicapped in their attempt to understand some important economic issues, such as occupational licensing and welfare reform.

We think that this book can be used in several different ways, and obviously hope that it will be. Many professors teaching the principles course probably feel that they can present a sufficient amount of curve-bending in class and would like the students' reading material to provide them with interesting, thought-provoking applications of the key concepts. For such a professor, this book could easily serve as main text material. It could also serve as a provocative supplement to one of the more standard principles texts. By tying together and explicitly explaining the supporting economic logic on each issue, we feel that this volume offers some definite advantages over books of readings at the principles level. At the preprinciples level, economic problems courses are offered to give the student some basic insights into the economic process and provoke interest in further study. The book should be useful here because it develops important economic principles and applies them to current issues in an uncomplicated and provocative way.

Despite the fact that only two authors are shown, many people have made important contributions to the final product. We would like to thank William L. Beaty (Sul Ross State University), Robert S. Main (Butler University), John C. Moorhouse (Wake Forest University), Nancy L. Sidener (University of Colorado), R. E. Strain (California State Univ., Long Beach), and Ralph J. Brown (Univ. of South Dakota) for many helpful suggestions on this edition. We also want to express our appreciation to Donna Trenor-Speight and Linda Gathany for their cheerful and competent typing of the manuscript. To our editor, Michael Zamczyk, we owe our thanks for taking charge of this project and overseeing the many tasks that lie between the first drafts and the final product. Finally, we would like to express special appreciation to our wives, Cynthia Lee and Lauri McNown, for their encouragement during the project and the insights they have offered on the issues and arguments presented in the book.

Although the development of this book reflects the efforts of many, we accept total responsibility for the final product.

Fairfax, Virginia   Dwight R. Lee
Boulder, Colorado   Robert F. McNown

chapter 1

The Abundance of Scarcity

1. MOTHER NATURE, THE ULTIMATE SCROOGE

Many are fond of praising the benevolence of Mother Nature, from whom all good things flow. As the source of all material wealth, either directly or indirectly, nature is benevolent indeed. However, it is only with considerable prodding and application of ingenuity that one coaxes the good earth to yield its bounty. As rich as this yield may be with the proper encouragement, even those who are fondest of asserting the generosity of nature are quick to point out that there are limits to this generosity. Exactly what these limits are will no doubt remain a long-standing controversy, but there can be no doubt that they exist.

Nature simply is not as generous as we would like her to be. Everything from environmental concerns to your attempt to improve your income by going to college reflects the stinginess of our home planet. You may object that the fault is not with the stinginess of Mother Nature, but rather with the greediness of Human Nature. Fair enough. But no matter how you look at it, the result is the same. The good things in life are scarce; we cannot have as much of them as we would like.

Even technology cannot save us from the fundamental problem of scarcity. In the last few hundred years, applications of science have considerably bettered mankind's potential for the enjoyment of life. In fact, we have reached the point at which—in most advanced industrialized countries of the world—basic human needs can be satisfied. But this does not imply an end to scarcity. With the satisfaction of more basic needs, people have an increased interest in other goods that enhance their enjoyment of life. Technological advance can increase our production capabilities by a few percent each year, but this slow progress does not come close to eliminating a need for concern about how scarcity is to be dealt with. This gradual progress does permit us to increase the volume and variety of goods available to us, even with a considerable reduction in the workweek, but we are still a long way from a totally automated production of a virtually unlimited output of goods and services.

Technological change often produces basic structural changes that deceive observers into believing it is also eliminating scarcity. We see, for example, that only 2.5 percent of our labor force works on farms in the United States today, as compared with 50 percent in 1870. But as these resources were released from the farm, they were employed in those industries and services where new consumer interests have arisen. Technological change did reduce our need for a large agricultural working force, but insatiable and growing human wants led to its use in other sectors of the economy. While an individual's demand for basic agricultural staples may be fairly limited, consumers have demonstrated an insatiable appetite for many other products. For example, we can observe a strong consumer interest in automobile and jet travel, electrical gadgets, spacious and warm homes, prepackaged foods, nonreturnable containers, synthetic apparel and detergents, decorated tissues, and countless other items somehow associated with the good life. As long as human wants remain unlimited, technological advance will not eliminate the problem of scarcity.

Before you start moralizing about man's disgusting greed, engage in a bit of introspection. Are you satisfied with your present level of consumption, or would you be delighted to lay claim to more goods and services? Careful introspection on the part of just about anyone (casual introspection will do in most cases) would reveal a strong desire for more. This applies even to those whom we would not normally think of as greedy. No matter what your objective, whether personal gluttony or establishing homes for orphans, you will find *more* preferred to *less*. With the possible exception of a few people whose goal is a lifetime of meditating on a rock, the statement, "I don't want much—I just want more," applies to all of us.

So if the desire for more is a fault, we all stand accused. And this desire will never be fully satisfied, because of the "inadequate" wealth surrendered by nature. Mother Nature is the ultimate Scrooge. It is here that we must face up to a dismal reality. We are limited in our ability to convert what nature has provided us into those things we want, but we are unlimited in our ability to want more. Scarcity has always been and always will be the fundamental problem facing mankind.

2. IF THIS, NOT THAT

Dealing with the problem of scarcity dominates the lives of all. Scarcity forces choice, and much of our day is spent making choices in one form or another. Since having everything we would like is clearly impossible, we are constantly forced to choose some items at the expense of forgoing others, although the rejected items may be very desirable indeed. Most of us routinely reject such items as around-the-world cruises, Rolls Royces, alligator shoes, private airplanes, and luxurious yachts. These items are not rejected because they are undesirable or even because they are all financially out of reach. But choosing them would require large sacrifices in terms of forgone opportunities. Buying a new Chevy, adding on a room, having Junior's teeth straightened, and taking a trip to Yellowstone seem even more desirable than driving your Rolls Royce to and from work.

Most choices are routine. They are based largely on past experience and well-established preferences, requiring little conscious thought. When we make our regular trip to the supermarket, we usually don't lament all those things we have to do without because of the necessity of nourishing and indulging our bodies.

There are many instances, however, when the alternatives that are forgone as a consequence of making a decision are more conspicuous. For the most part, cigarette smokers are aware that they are almost certainly giving up several years of life and many illness-free days when they choose to continue assaulting their respiratory and cardiovascular systems with nicotine and tar. Similarly, motorcyclists must be aware of the safety they are forgoing for the advantages of a form of transportation that is not only economical and reliable but also packs a thrill. Certainly students contemplating four or more years of college recognize that the major alternative to college is the income from employment that could be obtained during those years taken up by college study.* Related to the decision regarding a college education is the choosing of a vocation. Here again, the forgone opportunities resulting

---

*The period 1965–70, when a trip to Vietnam was a likely alternative to full-time college study, saw record numbers of young men electing to go to college. It is also interesting to note a strong positive relationship between draft exempt status for those studying for the ministry and the number receiving a call from the Lord. As the alternatives to college became less attractive, college became more attractive for more people.

from a choice are major influences in making a decision. Of course, an individual's abilities and interests are also important in making an occupational choice, since they determine the attractiveness of different vocational alternatives. But an individual may have great interest and talent in many fields. The problem, then, is not simply to pick an occupation in which one has interest and displays talent. The problem is to choose so that the loss from forgone opportunities is as small as possible. People with the widest range of interests and abilities will often have the most difficult time making a choice.

The point is that any time we are forced into making a choice, as we continually are, we incur a cost. Making a choice, by definition, involves denying ourselves some alternative courses of action. And it is the value of the most attractive forgone alternative that is the inescapable cost of any action we choose. This concept of cost, referred to as *opportunity cost,* may appear so obvious that it seems trivial. However, as is often the case with simple concepts, the implications of the concept of opportunity cost are far-reaching and, in many instances, quite subtle.

It will be interesting at this point to examine a couple of seemingly paradoxical situations with the concept of opportunity cost in mind. First consider the case of the modern homemaker, surrounded by labor- and time-saving conveniences that would have seemed absolutely miraculous in Grandmother's day: automatic washer and dryer, dishwasher with a built-in garbage disposal, self-cleaning oven, and self-defrosting refrigerator that dispenses ice cubes and cold water at the touch of a button, to list a few. Now suggest to modern day consumers that they start preparing meals from scratch in the delicious and nutritious way Grandmother did. Probably they will say that there isn't enough time. But haven't we just seen that time is exactly what they should have plenty of?

People always have the time for those things they really want to do, but they are reluctant to do things that are extremely costly. Here we find our modern homemakers' real objection to cooking like Grandmother did. If they spent a large part of their day slaving away in the kitchen, the opportunity cost would be enormous. They would be passing up opportunities that never presented themselves to Grandmother. With much greater awareness of interesting and useful things to do as a result of a good education, with much greater mobility as a result of a reliable car in the garage, and with reasonably delicious, easy-to-prepare alternatives to cooking from scratch waiting at the nearby supermarket, our modern counterparts to Grandmother are perfectly justified in objecting to our cooking suggestion. By objecting, they are attempting to do nothing more than what we all attempt. Faced with many alternatives, the modern homemaker is trying to choose those with the least opportunity cost attached.

Another interesting example is provided by the accomplishments of prisoners. Many have marveled at the dedication and diligence displayed by a number of prisoners who have successfully applied themselves to difficult tasks under extremely unfavorable conditions—certainly a prison environment is not conducive to great accomplishments. The Bird Man of Alcatraz comes naturally to mind: Robert Stroud made truly remarkable advances in the knowledge and treatment of bird diseases. Caryl Chessman became famous as a result of extensive knowledge of criminal law that he acquired while on death row in San Quentin; his skill in directing the legal battles postponed for years his 1960 execution for kidnap and rape. Malcolm X amassed the huge vocabulary that was later to make him an articulate and forceful speaker as a result of hours spent reading one of the few books he could obtain while in jail: the dictionary. Other examples probably come to mind of the single-minded dedication that imprisoned individuals have displayed. Undoubtedly, many different factors were important in each of these cases. However, an important common denominator in all of these accomplishments was the small cost involved. With the very restricted opportunities available to one in prison, little opportunity cost is attached to immersing oneself completely into those tasks that can be pursued. If you want to significantly lower the cost of studying economics, simply arrange to have yourself put in jail for a few days with nothing to read but this book.

It should be clear that the opportunity cost associated with any decision is of major importance in making the choices that we continually face. Unfortunately, we all too often accept arguments that fail to take the other person's opportunity cost into consideration. For example, many people think rent-control ordinances are fair because they supposedly keep the rent charged by landlords in line with their costs. But assume there are two apartment complexes, one owned by Janet Jones and the other by Sam Smith, identical in every respect except one. Jones's mortgage payments are lower than Smith's because she bought her apartment building when prices were lower. From this information, many people (especially those living in Jones's units) would argue that Jones's apartments should rent for less, since her cost is lower. But is this correct? The real cost to Jones is not what she has to pay out in cash every month. Her cost is equal to the income she is forgoing by not selling her apartment building and investing the money elsewhere. This is her opportunity cost. Since Jones and Smith own identical apartment buildings, this cost is the same for both of them, regardless of the relative size of their mortgage payments. Any rent-control ordinance that determined rents on the basis of cost would have to let both Jones and Smith charge the same rate.

The concept of opportunity cost is extremely valuable in developing an intelligent perspective on many important social issues. Many widely held opinions are not supported by careful analysis. For a few examples, consider the following popular positions: the all-volunteer army may be nice, but it is much more expensive than the draft. The operation of the free market encourages racial discrimination unless severe controls are imposed. Big corporations are hiding valuable inventions, such as carburetors that provide astounding gas mileage, in order to protect their profits against lost sales. Letting important natural resources, such as prime timber land, lakes, and rivers, be sold off to private interests would result in their misuse and eventual destruction. As long as human lives are being lost as a result of taking medical drugs that have not been fully tested, measures should be taken to improve the safety of drugs before they can be sold. As long as pollution poses a threat to human life, steps should be taken to reduce it.

The fact that large numbers of people strongly agree with these opinions indicates that many are prone to overlook important implications of the opportunity cost concept. Subsequent chapters will look at these opinions, as well as others, very carefully and critically with the concept of opportunity cost firmly in mind.

3. THE ULTIMATE MOTIVATOR

In the preceding section we discussed the inevitability of continually having to choose from various alternatives. While it was not explicitly stated, it is obvious that the criteria used in making these choices is *self-interest*. We choose those alternatives that we feel will make us as well off as possible; that is, those that have the smallest opportunity cost attached. In choosing a career, we evaluate alternatives in terms of what will be best for us, considering such things as financial rewards, personal satisfaction, difficulty of qualifying for—and pursuing—different careers. In deciding on how diligently to apply yourself whether in school, on the job, or at play, the primary consideration is the connection between your efforts and your rewards. Invariably you will find that your dedication and devotion to the task at hand diminishes as the relation between hard work and personal return becomes more tenuous. This largely explains such things as why people who own their own businesses work longer and harder than do government bureaucrats; why good-looking men spend more time than ugly ones in pursuit of beautiful women; or why most people work much harder for an employer than for their church, even though the church promises much the greater reward. Certainly self-interest is the ultimate motivator.

This is not to say that other people's feelings do not impinge on how we view our self-interest. Certainly an unhappy girlfriend can have a significant impact on her boyfriend's personal satisfaction and vice versa. Neither are we denying that many people's self-interest is to help others. One would certainly find it hard to refute the contention that people such as Albert Schweitzer and Florence Nightingale pursued their self-interest by intentionally helping others. While self-interest can take many forms, in most cases it takes the form of putting personal well-being above the well-being of others.

Many people feel that this pervasive self-interest is a sad commentary on the status of mankind. These people are inclined to believe that only by effecting fundamental changes in man's nature can we hope to straighten out the world. Although "The Impossible Dream" may make a good song, it's not clear that it makes good social policy. Pinning one's hopes on the moral rejuvenation of mankind seems to us unrealistic and, as we hope to make clear, unnecessary.

A more optimistic view of the world comes from recognizing that the inevitable and enormous energy generated by self-interest can be the primary source of good in a free society. Consider for a moment that most people living in the United States today live a life of luxury by standards of a few generations ago. The comforts and conveniences of today's homes, fast and reliable transportation, modern medicines, the availability of large quantities and varieties of food, and entertainment in the form of radio, television, and movies are but a few of the things that make life today more pleasant than ever before. (If you don't believe us, just ask your father or grandfather. They will be happy to tell you how rough it used to be.) Next reflect for a moment on the enormous amount of work that has to be performed by literally millions of people to provide you with the goods and services that benefit you every day. It is entirely safe to say that these countless people exert themselves on your behalf, not because they care about your welfare, but because they care about their own. They are motivated to get as much satisfaction as possible with what they have to offer. The best way to accomplish this is to use their efforts to satisfy the demands of others, because by providing for others they are able to obtain those things that enhance their own sense of well-being.

4. PERSONAL FREEDOM—IT SOUNDS GOOD, BUT

The following important proposition summarizes the preceding section: *In pursuing their own self-interest, individuals unintentionally can do more to enhance the social good than if that had been their primary purpose.* While deciding for yourself how convincing this proposition is, you should be informed that not everyone has found it equally persuasive. Since this idea was first given substance in 1776 by the Scottish philosopher Adam Smith, it has been the subject of a great deal of controversy. Much of this controversy centers on the questions of what we mean by the social good and how much we should restrict the individual's freedom to pursue self-interest. We now examine these two questions.

Closely aligned to the above proposition is the belief that the happiness and welfare of the individual are the primary ends of social processes. In this view, the social good has no meaning except in terms of the well-being of the individuals that make up the society. Many people do not accept this individualistic precept. In their opinion, the "good of the state" or the "public interest" transcends individual welfare, and the individual's primary responsibility is not to himself but to the state. Once this view is accepted and individual welfare becomes subordinate to some higher good, pursuing one's self-interest hardly seems a laudable activity.

If one is unwilling to accept the individualistic view in assessing the social good, we see that our proposition will not be very compelling. Even if one does agree with the individualistic precept, however, there is still plenty of room to disagree on the question of how much freedom the individual should be allowed in the quest for personal gain. Almost everyone will agree that some restrictions have to be put on individual freedoms. It is generally accepted that one individual should not be allowed to profit from others through coercion and threats of physical violence. These are such effective ways of gaining an advantage over others, however, that there are always some who cannot resist the temptation to use them. Of course, those who yield to this temptation run the risk of having society impose severe restrictions on their future actions.

Having agreed that individuals should not be allowed to use coercion and violence against others, are there other reasons to limit people's freedom to pursue their self-interest? Many people say yes.

Some feel that most people are incapable of making intelligent decisions for themselves. Many who feel this way would deny it if asked, "Do you think most people lack the ability to make intelligent choices for themselves?" However, they strongly support policies that impose severe restrictions on people's choices. The primary justification for these restrictions is the belief that people would make foolish decisions if given too much freedom.

A good example is the law in many states that motorcyclists have to wear protective helmets. There is no doubt that wearing a helmet increases the chances of surviving a motorcycle accident. But in the absence of mandatory helmet laws, many motorcyclists choose not to wear them. Why? Because there are many things in life besides safety that people value. Motorcyclists commonly talk about the thrill and sense of freedom they experience from motorcycle travel. Wearing a bulky motorcycle helmet greatly reduces the quality of this experience for many, and they are willing to pay the price—in terms of reduced safety—for the enjoyment of riding without one. Of course, not everyone will agree with their judgment, and many of us may feel strongly that they are being foolish.

But all of us sacrifice safety for thrills, convenience, and savings. Skiing is much more hazardous than sitting in the library with an economics book, but for most people it is a lot more thrilling. Probably all of us have at times sacrificed safety for the convenience of not buckling our safety belts. And there is no doubt that one of those massive 1965 Buicks (the type that looks pregnant) is much safer than the little motorized roller skates that people call cars today. You can have a head-on collision in your Buick with a Toyota and you won't even know it; and neither will the guy in the Toyota. But many people think the savings that come from driving a small car are worth the safety that is sacrificed. Is a motorcycle helmet law any more justified than a law requiring everyone to wear a helmet while skiing, or a law requiring everyone to wear a seatbelt or drive nothing smaller than a Sherman tank?

Another reason often given for imposing restrictions on freedom of choice has little to do with the paternalistic instinct. Many will agree that the best judge of how a given choice will affect the welfare of an individual is that individual. But unfortunately, it is claimed, the values and priorities of most people are not what they should be, and it is society's responsibility to encourage these people to partake of the "finer" things in life. To meet people with such concern about the attitudes and values of others, one need go no further than the minister whose job is threatened because of declining church attendance; the struggling artists or writers who can't find buyers for their creative endeavors, a robust Sierra Club member bemoaning the fact that many people prefer driving into beautiful wilderness areas to backpacking in; the intellectual whose favorite political candidate just went down to a landslide defeat; or the patron of the symphony who is concerned about the viability of this favorite pastime because of poor community support. Undoubtedly, you could expand on this list of examples. Many of these people, if given the opportunity, would be more than willing to "benevolently" impose their values and priorities on others. Fortunately for most of us, this type of benevolent impulse is severely restricted.

However, ways are still found to encourage people to enjoy the finer things in life and to forbid or discourage them from some of the more vulgar pursuits. Governments at one level or another follow conscious policies of subsidizing such things as symphonies, art museums, higher education, trips to national parks, and living a wholesome life on the farm. For the most part, the effect of these policies is to subsidize the activities of the wealthy at the expense of the poor. This should not be surprising, since it is generally higher-income people who enjoy these activities and who have the political influence to obtain government favor. On the other hand, governments actively discourage, through taxation or prohibition, such things as beer drinking, smoking marijuana, pornographic movies, prostitution, rock festivals, and gambling. Why are these things discouraged? The obstacles that many overcome in order to engage in them provide ample evidence as to their enjoyment. It is also difficult to make a strong case against these activities on the grounds that engaging in them interferes with the pursuits of others. It appears that the primary reason the state discourages many such activities is that many people feel the values and priorities of others are not in keeping with acceptable standards.

There is yet another reason why many, if not most, are against personal freedom, at least the personal freedom of others. The freedom of others to enter into activities that we are pursuing makes it much more difficult for us to profit from these activities. There are numerous examples of special-interest groups seeking and obtaining severe restrictions on the rights of others to engage in certain activities. The motive is almost always to protect the incomes of the members of the special-interest group by excluding would-be competitors. Of course, their reasons never sound quite so self-serving.

- According to the American Medical Association, the policy of restricting the number of students admitted to approved medical schools is motivated solely by public concern; the medical profession wants to make sure that the public has nothing but the very best in medical attention.
- In many states laws exist that allow the milk industry to exert strong control over the entry of new dairy farmers and forbid milk from being sold for less than a specified price. The reason for these laws, according to the milk industry (which actively supports them), is to protect the consumer from inferior fly-by-night operators and maintain an orderly market so that the responsible, high-quality producers (those already in the business) can survive.
- Labor unions have been among the most active supporters of minimum-wage laws. This has been cited as evidence that labor unions are concerned with the welfare of all labor, not just that of its own members. However, the effect of the minimum-wage laws has been to restrict the ability of lower-skilled workers not in unions to compete with higher-skilled union labor by offering their services for less.
- Incumbent politicians in the U.S. House of Representatives and Senate overwhelmingly supported the Campaign Reform Act, which provided public financing for political campaigns and imposed tight restrictions on the amount and type of support a candi-

date could receive from private contributors. The effect of this law has been to reduce the opportunity for unknown politicians to marshal the resources necessary to obtain the public exposure that incumbent politicians already have. Obviously, this serves to reduce the competition incumbents have to face. The stated objective of campaign reform was the high-minded one of protecting the political process from the corrupting influence of money and special interests.

We now turn to a consideration of one last reason why many feel that personal freedoms should be restricted. Before doing so, however, it will be helpful to consider three vitally important functions that any economic system must perform. First of all, in every economy some mechanism has to exist for determining what to produce and in what quantities. Since it is impossible to produce everything people enjoy in the quantities they would like, this is obviously an important function. Second, after it has been determined what and how much is to be produced, we need to have some method for deciding on the proper method of production. In this decision the choices are many and the stakes are high. There are obviously many ways to produce most commodities: machinery can be substituted for labor in agricultural production, a dam and a river canyon can be substituted for coal-powered turbines in electrical production, plastics and aluminum can be substituted for brick and wood in construction, computers can be substituted for clerks in providing banking services. Since productive resources are limited, decisions concerning how they are used in the productive process are crucial. Finally, it has to be decided how the goods and services that are being produced are to be distributed among those in the economy, all of whom want more.

These three functions are obviously important, and this is the final reason that many would restrict individual freedoms. They feel it is absolutely insane to allow the capricious impulses of self-seeking individuals, who have little interest or knowledge about most things outside the narrow sphere of their own interest, to determine how these functions are performed. Without some effective checks on personal freedom, it is argued, individuals could go into any productive activity they wished, regardless of the importance of the output. Resources could be used poorly to produce shoddy products, the motive being "production for profit rather than use." Some individuals would undoubtedly prosper, either because of special talents or fortuitous circumstances. These fortunate few would be able to purchase vast amounts of expensive trivia while many of those less fortunate go without basic necessities. In order to prevent these inefficiencies and injustices from becoming the dominant characteristics of the economy, it is seen by many as absolutely essential that we move away from individual freedom and responsibility toward greater reliance on rational economic planning and control by socially concerned experts.

It's easy to understand the appeal of rational economic planning and control. First of all, it is very difficult to comprehend how the alternative—seemingly unorganized, uncontrolled, and unrelated individual activities—could lead to anything but chaos. Second, most of us have a strong confidence in man's ability to control and shape his surroundings in desirable ways through the application of scientifically determined knowledge to specific problems. The remarkable successes that have inspired this confidence have been confined largely to our conquest of the physical environment.* However, it is felt by many that the same rational approach that has led to the control of many physical phenomena can also be used to control our economy for the benefit of all. In other words, if we can go to the moon, we should be able to eliminate poverty, clean up our cities, save our environment, preserve our valuable national resources, and so on.

It is certainly true that many of our opinion leaders—politicians, scholars, scientific specialists, journalists, the clergy, and those in the performing arts—are in favor of more central direction and control in economic matters. When such people express this opinion, it normally carries a lot of weight. These are usually the very talented and concerned, and their background and experiences lend considerable credibility to their utterances.

It is interesting to note, however, that many of our opinion leaders have highly developed and specialized interests. They invariably see the things that they are interested in as crucially important, not only to themselves but to society at large. This is true of the physicist doing research on subatomic particles, the space scientist working on the manned space-flight program, the dedicated ballerina, the expert in ancient Egyptian art, the specialist in urban problems, the physical educator concerned about the nation's physical fitness, the specialist in sex education for elementary school students, and so on. These specialists are often frustrated because the public doesn't seem to appreciate the full importance of their specialties. They are likely to feel that if the uninformed masses were not so free to squander their incomes on frivolous commodities and pursuits, more resources could be transferred into things of real importance. These specialists are no doubt confident that if these allocative decisions were made by intelligent and "rational" planners, their particular specialty would receive the substantial support it so obviously deserves.

---

*It should be noted that some of these conquests have recently been widely recognized as having very undesirable effects on our well-being. This awareness and the associated ecology movement have had the effect of dampening the enthusiasm of many for technological solutions to our problems.

It is clear that this concern that order cannot emerge from unrestricted pursuit of millions of individuals is in direct conflict with our proposition on the pursuit of self-interest leading to the social good. According to the proposition, allowing individuals a large measure of freedom to pursue their self-interest will benefit society more than conscientious individuals whose primary objective in life is to improve social welfare. This proposition may be seen as implying one of two things, or both. One possible implication is that there exists some system of information and control that channels the activities of self-seeking individuals in such a way that the three functions of what to produce, how to produce it, and who receives it are adequately performed. Another interpretation is that the economy is too complicated and individual preferences too private and diverse for do-gooders to be effective. It is extremely difficult for any person or group, no matter how noble their intentions, to avoid unfortunate results when they attempt to make and affect the allocative decisions that the three functions of the economy require.

In the next chapter we are going to consider the question of how well the pursuit of self-interest performs the three critical economic functions. This will be a look into the market economy, how it works, and when it can and cannot be expected to work well.

The following chapters deal with specific issues such as government regulation, the environmental crisis, crime, education, and poverty. The material presented in this chapter and the next will be useful in providing a framework for discussing these issues. One shouldn't be surprised if many popular views are severely challenged in these chapters.

DISCUSSION QUESTIONS

1. Under ideal circumstances, all firms should be making zero profit. Use the concept of opportunity cost to explain why this is true.

2. Do you think there is any way to allocate the output of our economy among all consumers in such a way that they all felt they had their "fair" share?

3. What do you feel is the connection between scarcity and discrimination?

4. Is the concept of opportunity cost useful in explaining the high divorce rate among Hollywood personalities?

5. The three functions of an economy, deciding 1.) what to produce, 2.) how to produce it, and 3.) who gets it, are all related. Explain these relationships.

6. Contemplate for a moment the enormous amount of information and effort required to supply a community with the goods and services absolutely required for its survival. How is the necessary information disseminated to those best able to act on it? What motivation do they have to act on this information once it is provided?

7. If you were obligated to argue in front of a large group that 1.) competition is the result of capitalism, or 2.) competition is the result of scarcity, which position would you choose? What would be your main points?

8. Assume that you own a house with a $200/month mortgage payment, which you are renting out for $260/month. For your own shelter you are renting an apartment for $220/month. Would it be cheaper for you to move into the house you own or stay in the apartment?

9. If you are over 60 years old, having sex on a full stomach can be hazardous to your health. Can you develop an argument that a law against senior citizen sex on a full stomach is in principle different from a law requiring an airbag on all cars sold in the United States?

chapter 2

Order from Chaos

1. THE PROBLEM OF ECONOMIC ORGANIZATION

Consider for a moment the awesome task that our economic system faces. Eleven million business units produce almost $3 trillion worth of goods and services for over 200 million consumers. In the process, the skills of 100 million workers and a multitude of raw materials are used. How do we manage to coordinate the activities of all these firms and induce them to use the appropriate methods of production? Why does it happen that the goods produced are the ones that consumers want? Or does our system fail to accomplish all of this? In fact, given completely selfish and independent action by individuals in this economy, should we not anticipate absolute chaos? In this chapter we want to analyze the nature of the economic problem just hinted at and the means by which the capitalist system attempts to solve the problem.

The basic task of any economic system is deciding how to ration scarce resources among an unlimited number of competing uses. The goal of a rational economic system is to provide a collection of goods and services that corresponds to consumers' or society's desires while economizing on the use of scarce resources. As long as people desire more goods (broadly defined to include leisure time, a clean environment, and the usual material products of industrial society), a well-designed economic system will attempt to squeeze as much satisfaction as possible out of the limited productive materials available.

This requires that a great deal of information about consumer preferences, available resources and laborers, and alternative production techniques be made available to the relevant parties. It also requires that the activities of individual firms and households be coordinated and that incentives to economize on scarce resources be provided. In a market system, this is accomplished through decentralized decision making with individual market prices conveying the appropriate information; firm and household activities are coordinated through markets, and incentives are provided by profits and wage differentials. A pure market system functions without centralized planning. Exactly how this is accomplished and the extent to which the price system is likely to function properly is the primary subject of this chapter.

There is, of course, an alternative to using markets to organize production; this is centralized planning.* One way to appreciate what the price system does accomplish is to consider the dimensions of the task faced by a planning bureaucracy in an advanced industrialized society.

2. THE PLANNING APPROACH

Imagine a society that has done away with the "chaotic" and "exploitative" institution of the market. People no longer sell themselves as commodities in return for life's necessities. Production is no longer subject to the whim or avaricious nature of the capitalists but is now based on social needs.

When the new economic system was first instituted, the government attempted to acquire information on individual preferences by means of a questionnaire. Every year the citizens were required to submit an itemization of their consumption needs for the coming twelve months, so that the Planning Board could make a reasonable decision about what was to be produced. But the itemization was not sufficient, for peoples' desires exceeded the $3 trillion in goods and services that the economy was capable of producing. The planners needed information on the relative intensity of consumers' desires for various products. Also, the questionnaire did not elicit detailed enough information about the particular products individuals wanted.

To rectify this problem the Planning Board developed the Complete

---

*A third alternative is an organization of production and commerce according to social traditions. This form of economic organization is found in most primitive societies but is of little practical importance to modern industrial societies.

Preference Inventory form, which was to provide more detailed information on consumption desires and some measurement of the intensity of these desires. The typical entry looked like this:

Item 4893: Pen
Consume in 1984? Yes _____ No _____
Ballpoint, fountain, or cartridge _____
Color _____
Width _____ Length _____
Weight _____
Fine, medium, or heavy point _____
Retractable head or removable cap _____
Ink color _____
Desired lifespan _____
Intensity of preference:
Relative to other products desired, give intensity rating (1-100) _____
How many of the following items would be necessary to compensate you for not obtaining the item in question?
Pencils _____
Typewriter _____ (use decimal fractions)

The project was wisely abandoned when it was discovered that a complete description of an automobile with accessories would fill 500 pages.

Instead, a body of consumer "experts" was established to decide what the public really needed. Many considered this a major improvement, since individual tastes led to the consumption of many commodities that were deemed unnecessary.

With the problem of collecting information on consumer preferences obviated by the planners' decision on what was to be produced, the Planning Board turned to the question of how production should be organized.

Again a mountain of information was needed. The planners had to have an inventory of the kinds and qualities of raw materials, equipment, and laborers available and information on where these resources were located. They needed to know the productive capabilities of every factory, mine, utility, and acre of farmland, and how an increase in resources available to each plant would affect production in other plants. Particular information on the techniques of production was also collected to make sure that each plant was organized as efficiently as possible.

Given this information and the planners' decision on the output of final goods and services to be produced, it was necessary to decide how production should be organized and give each plant the appropriate directive. Should basketballs be produced with leather or a synthetic material? Should wheat farming use light hand equipment and much manual labor or heavy machinery? Should computers be used for scientific research or for accounting purposes? Where were engineers most needed, and how much of available resources should be used to train more technical personnel? Questions such as these numbered in the millions, and the complexity of the problem forced the planners to rely on individual plant managers to make many of the decisions.

It was decided that the decisions relating to the production processes of each plant—what resources to use, which production techniques to employ—would be made by the individual plant managers, while the Planning Board would coordinate the activities of every firm so that each industry's output would be consistent with the needs of other firms and the final output requirements of the plan. Directives were provided in the form of quotas for each plant.

Plant managers were obligated to meet these quotas in order to retain their jobs. Managers who exceeded their quotas were often rewarded with bonuses or the possibility of advancement. Eager to satisfy the requests of the Planning Board, many plant officials found that they could meet their quota or even exceed it if they concerned themselves less with the quality and variety of product turned out. One over-zealous manager exceeded his quota of underwear by 150 percent; unfortunately, not every interested consumer had a twenty-eight-inch waist. Other producers were able to meet their quotas only by employing very scarce and valuable inputs. Their only concern was producing a maximum quantity of output; there was no reward for an economical use of scarce resources. Quotas simply did not provide sufficient information on what should be produced or how production should be organized in order to economize on scarce resources. Even if plant directors could be motivated to provide society with the correct kinds of goods at a low cost, they did not have the information necessary to carry this out. Was it worth the extra cost to consumers to have longer-lasting jewels in their wristwatches? Did society want to economize on the use of computers in banking operations by employing additional accountants? Did individuals want to pay the additional cost for hardcover books or were paperbacks adequate? No plant manager could make this decision accurately, since he was not provided with the appropriate information on relative scarcities of resources or the actual value consumers placed on the goods his plant was producing.

As a result of these problems, the planned society found that it was not making the most effective use of its scarce resources to satisfy human wants. Productive materials were not being used in those lines of activity where their contribution to society's welfare was the greatest. And, of course, this society brushed aside the problem of collecting and transmitting information on consumer preferences.

The basic point of this illustration is that any large industrial economy faces formidable problems of information and coordination that must be solved if production is to (a) correspond to consumer preferences, and (b) provide maximal output for a given use of scarce resources. If these problems are enormous for a centrally planned economy, how is the allocation problem solved in a market economy, in which no direction from governmental authorities is provided? Without some planning organization, shouldn't we expect the market system to result in complete chaos? The answer, to be discussed in the following sections, is that not only is production nonchaotic, but rather it is likely to be organized on a highly rational basis. To see this, we must analyze how prices and markets serve to organize production in a capitalist economy.

3. MARKET PRICES AND PRIVATE PROPERTY

A rational economic system should organize production so that (a) the goods and services produced are in harmony with individual consumer preferences, and (b) this output is achieved with a minimum use of scarce productive resources. We wish to examine the extent to which we expect a market system to accomplish these goals.

Advanced industrialized economies are dynamic; there are continual changes in consumer preferences, in technologies of production, and in relative scarcities of productive resources. A rationally organized economy must continually respond to these changes to assure an output that corresponds to consumer preferences and is efficient in its use of scarce resources. In a market system, this comes about through changing prices and profits in the various individual markets. Prices convey the appropriate information on relative scarcities and consumer preferences; markets serve to coordinate the activities of individual producers and consumers; and profits and wage differentials provide the incentives for individual economic agents to respond to changing economic conditions.

To comprehend how market prices provide the information necessary to guide appropriate economic decisions, you need to understand the importance of private transferable property rights. In a market economy, most resources are privately owned. The owner of a resource has the right to employ it as he or she chooses or sell it to someone else. One advantage of private ownership is immediately obvious. People have more incentive to take care of things they own than things they do not own. Ask yourself where you are most likely to see graffiti carved into a wall: in bathrooms in private homes or bathrooms in public buildings? You can surely think of many other examples in which people take better care of their personal property than they do of public property—property owned by everyone and therefore owned by no one in particular. In a world of scarce resources, it is no small advantage to provide incentives for people to exercise care in the use of resources.

The second advantage of private ownership comes from the transferability of ownership rights. When resources can be bought and sold, prices for these resources materialize, and these prices provide crucially important information. The owner of land, for example, will generally consider selling it only to the prospective buyer who offers the highest price. And only if the highest bidder offers a price for the land that is higher than the value the owner places on the land will it actually be sold. Therefore, the prices that buyers face in the marketplace reflect the value of resources in their highest-valued alternative use. *The market price of a good is equal to its opportunity cost.*

Prices therefore guide resources into their highest-valued uses. People will only buy something that is more valuable to them than the price they pay for it. With prices equal to opportunity cost this means that people will buy only those items that are worth more to them than the items are worth in their best alternative employment. This is really quite amazing if you think about it. We certainly cannot expect the user of a resource to be informed about all the millions of alternative uses the resource has or even to care about them. The user is primarily concerned with his or her own use for it. Yet the market price of the resource reveals all one needs to know to make a decision that fully considers the value of these alternative uses. Furthermore, the market price provides the individual with the incentive to care about these alternative values and act accordingly.

As production technologies, consumer preferences, and relative scarcities of raw material change, there will be corresponding changes in the opportunity costs of various products. If producers and consumers are to make appropriate decisions in their use of scarce resources, they need to respond to these changing circumstances. Fortunately, market prices will change to reflect movements in the pattern of opportunities. As a result, economic decision makers are able to adjust their behavior so that resources are continually being directed into those activities that have become more valuable and out of those that have become less valuable. The next four sections provide examples of how a market economy motivates the appropriate responses to changing conditions.

4. THE ECONOMICAL USE OF SCARCE RESOURCES

Consider first how the market would respond to a severe depletion of a resource like oil. Since oil has so many alternative uses, there would be extremely strong competition among oil users for this increasingly scarce resource. With many buyers wanting to purchase the limited supply of oil, its price would be bid up. This increase in the price of oil informs firms and individuals that the relative scarcity of oil has increased, and its use should be reduced. But in addition to providing valuable information, the increased price motivates self-interested energy consumers, rather, individuals or firms, to respond in a socially desirable way by conserving their use of oil.

Profit-maximizing firms and budget-conscious consumers would attempt to substitute other forms of energy. Coal, natural gas, and hydroelectric power would be used more extensively. New forms of energy—nuclear, solar, geothermal—would become economically feasible. The higher price of oil would also stimulate research in the development of alternative oil-saving technologies. More trains and cars would be powered by electricity, as more conventional forms of transportation became increasingly costly. In sum, consumers and firms would react to these changes in the structure of prices by reducing all oil-consuming activities.

Oil would continue to be used, but chiefly in those activities where it is socially most useful. Where substitutes do not exist, where oil is extremely productive, and where consumer demand for an oil-using activity is greatest, the higher price would be paid. The higher price paid reflects the higher value of the alternatives forgone, namely, the multitude of activities that were curtailed as a result of the oil scarcity. Oil had to be bid away from people who wanted to drive a car with 500 cubic inches of gas-guzzling machinery, from people who preferred air freight to the slower rail freight, and others.

So the higher price of the resource not only provides information on its greater value or opportunity cost; it also gives consumers and firms the incentive to economize on its use. Firms, in trying to minimize costs, and consumers, in attempting to spread their limited budget over a wide range of wants, will restrict their use of this high-priced resource. This information on the increased scarcity is transmitted via markets through several stages from oil producer to consumer. Additional markets transmit the information on secondary effects—the impact on other energy sources and on consumption of all energy-using activities.

But economical use of scarce resources is only one part of the story. We also require an economic organization to provide a collection of goods that corresponds to consumer preferences. Again, the workings of competitive prices and markets lead to this result.

5. PRODUCTION TO SATISFY CONSUMER WANTS

Before a firm begins to consider what resources are needed for production, it decides what it is going to produce. Assuming its goal is profit maximization, the firm will want to produce in markets where consumer demand is strong enough to yield revenues that more than offset costs. The information on intensity of consumer preferences is summarized in relative commodity prices. Obviously firms are attracted into the production of those commodities whose prices are greater than the costs (measured by input prices) of producing them. With input prices reflecting opportunity cost, this profit motive results in a pattern of resource use that provides more value for consumers than alternative patterns of resource use.

Consider, for example, the recent surge of interest in camping and backpacking. Many new outdoor enthusiasts have entered the market for camping equipment. Sleeping bags, tents, cross-country skis, backpacks, and boots have all experienced a tremendous boom in sales. Retailers, discovering their inventories being depleted, increase the size of their orders; the information on increased consumer demand is thus transmitted to the producers. In order to increase production, they must lure additional resources away from alternative uses; goose down, nylon, skilled workers, and designers are all attracted to this industry by the lure of higher prices. These resources are now worth more to society in the production of camping equipment than in their previous line of activity. But to attract scarce resources into this industry, the higher cost of production will have to be covered by the consumers of camping equipment. This change in consumer tastes in favor of the consumption of these goods will have repercussions in other markets. Other industries using the same materials and skilled labor as the camping-equipment industry will experience rising production costs; their products will show a price increase, and consumers will cut back on their purchase of these goods. With a limited quantity of resources available, it is necessary that the increased consumption of camping equipment be offset by reduced consumption elsewhere.* It is the job of markets and prices to make sure that resources shift according to consumer preferences. This is accomplished by increasing the profit opportunities in those fields where prices rise as the result of increased consumer demand and reducing incentives in industries where the consumers deem the use of scarce resources to be less important.

6. CHANGES IN TECHNOLOGY AND THE ROLE OF PROFITS

A dynamic economy must also react to changes in technology. Inventions and innovations must be fostered as well as incorporated into the

---

*This is really only true for a static economy with no technological progress. Productivity gains may permit us to have increased consumption of camping equipment with some increase, or only a small decrease, in consumption elsewhere. But this increase will be smaller, or the decrease larger, than it could have been without the increased consumption of camping equipment.

system. One of the great virtues of the market system has been its ability to encourage technological changes, for these have contributed to the present state of development of capitalist countries. In a market system, the opportunity to reap profits provides the incentive to develop new techniques and products for commercial purposes. An example of this is the development of the ballpoint pen industry; here we see not only the tremendous profit potential associated with innovation but also the automatic responses of the price system to technological change.

In 1945 Milton Reynolds began production of the first ballpoint pen. Costing 80 cents to produce, this pen retailed for $12.50. Consumer interest was immediately strong, and profits were accordingly large— as much as $500,000 per month on an initial investment of $26,000. But unfortunately for Mr. Reynolds, the huge profits were both a signal and a strong inducement for other producers to enter this line of business. In spite of the threat of patent-infringement suits, other manufacturers of ballpoint pens began marketing their own products. Since Reynolds was selling at a price so high above costs, many firms found they could undercut him, capture a share of the market, and make a healthy profit. By the end of 1946, there were approximately 100 ballpoint pen manufacturers, and prices were as low as $3. By 1948, less than three years after the sale of the first pen, the price fell to 39 cents, and production costs had been reduced to 10 cents.

Notice that the movement of firms into this line of production took place automatically. No research grant from the National Science Foundation was necessary to induce Mr. Reynolds to invent the ballpoint pen—the potential for huge profits was sufficient motivation. No planning agency was needed to direct new firms to begin production of more pens—the observation of a price in excess of cost told potential producers that this was a worthwhile venture. The quickness with which new firms moved in response to the existence of excessive profits, in spite of a possible barrier imposed by the patent laws, provides a striking illustration of the responsiveness of the market system to consumer demands. It is important to note that it is the ability of firms to make profits, often gigantic profits, that gives consumers ultimate control over production decisions. The surest way to leave the consumer powerless in the marketplace would be to have the government tax away business profits while bailing out those firms not able to make a profit. If owners of businesses found that responding to consumer demands generated no more profit than ignoring these demands, they would have neither the motivation nor the resources to innovate and expand the production of those products that consumers value most.

The ballpoint pen example also illustrates how the market system leads to the development and application of low-cost production techniques. With the huge potential for profit in this industry, there was a tremendous incentive for innovation in production techniques. The firm that was able to produce ballpoint pens more cheaply could undercut competitors and expand sales and profits. With such incentives, it is not surprising that production costs were cut by 90 percent within three years. And, of course, once better production techniques had been developed, firms were induced to phase out older methods in order to minimize costs. In highly competitive industries, in fact, the adoption of least-cost production is necessary for survival; if profit margins are low, firms need to be very attentive to their production techniques. But in any case, a profit-maximizing firm will want to minimize costs, and one important component of this goal is choosing a method of production that is of least cost.

7. THE INTERDEPENDENT ECONOMY

For each particular market, it is seen that prices convey information on technology, resource scarcity, and consumer preferences. But more than this, prices transmit information that is needed to coordinate the activities of many diverse but interrelated markets. Fundamental to solving the problems of economic organization is the recognition of the tremendous degree of interdependence in any advanced industrialized system.

The output of automobiles involves the use of workers and raw materials that otherwise could be used in the production of, for example, tractors. The level of tractor production, in turn, affects the amount of wheat that can be produced, and this influences the price of flour and bread. The price of bread affects the quantity of other foods consumed, and so on. Because of complex interdependencies in the economy, a decision or event in one sector of the economy can have far-reaching effects elsewhere. The smooth functioning of an economy requires that relevant information about changing economic conditions be transmitted to all parties affected, and that the actions of all firms and individuals somehow be coordinated.

An illustration of economic interdependence is provided by a little known and seemingly unimportant event: in 1972, the anchovies failed to run off the coast of Peru. Anchovies are an important ingredient in animal feed, and the poor showing made by these fish in 1972 was one factor contributing to the agricultural shortages of the following year. The anchovy shortage was immediately obvious to the producers of animal feed, and they consequently turned to other sources of protein for their products. Animal-feed producers did not have to know *why* there was a shortage of anchovies; they merely had to economize on anchovies in their products that year. Given this information, feed producers became more active purchasers of soybeans, a substitute for anchovies, bidding this protein source away from alternative uses. These other users of soybeans—makers of margarine, salad oil, paint, plastics, soaps—found the beans more difficult to obtain. Again, information on the protein shortage needed to be communicated to these producers so that they could take it into account in their production decisions. With a market system, such information is conveyed by higher soybean prices. Consumers needed to be urged to economize on the consumption of meat, because cattle production required a greater use of the valuable soybean. Continued lavish consumption of meat would require the diversion of soybeans away from its other valuable uses. Through higher meat prices, families were induced to find other sources of nourishment during this period. Few shoppers were aware of the poor anchovy harvest, but they did respond correctly to the situation.

These were only the more direct effects of the anchovy shortage. In addition, farmers were induced to respond to the increased demand for agricultural sources of protein by planting more crops. More land had to be brought under cultivation, and increased production required more machinery and fertilizer. The production of tractors and combines diverted resources away from automobiles and industrial machinery. Increased fertilizer production required greater amounts of natural gas, and, with plants operating near capacity, additional fertilizer plants were needed. The demand for natural gas by fertilizer producers, of course, required the diversion of this resource from other uses, such as heating homes and offices. Some users responded by employing other sources of heating fuel, and the entire allocation of petroleum among its alternative uses was thus affected. The construction of new fertilizer plants required the employment of engineers, construction workers, materials, and so forth, which had to be diverted from other uses. This in turn curtailed the construction of new industrial plants required in the production of other goods.

The indirect and longer-run effects are endless. Without further elaboration, it becomes clear that there exist interdependencies of vast complexity. When a shortage of anchovies in Peru affects the demand for natural gas in Peoria, for example, it is clear that the tasks of economic organization are formidable. But what would be impossible for a planning agency is performed automatically by the market system. The essence of the price system is that the relevant information about economic changes is carried to all parties concerned through market prices and that in addition these prices provide the inducement to act in a manner consistent with the change in conditions. A housewife many not know the first thing about Peruvian anchovies, but she will economize on meat products when their prices rise as a result of the anchovy shortage. A producer of natural gas has little interest in the fact that anchovies contributed to the increased demand for his product by the fertilizer industry, but he is quite willing to respond to the offer of higher prices for gas by the fertilizer producers. The information and incentives needed to coordinate a complex economy are provided by the relative prices of intermediate and final products in the economy.

8. SOME QUALIFICATIONS

The above discussion illustrates how the market system comes to grips with the fundamental problems of information, coordination, and rationing of scarce resources confronting any economic organization. Changes in tastes, technologies, or resource scarcities will set off alterations in relative prices. Consumers and firms will respond to these relative price changes by economizing on their use of scarce resources and by causing resources to shift into lines of greater consumer interest.

But there must be something wrong with this idealistic picture. If production is supposed to correspond to consumer preferences, then how does one explain the "production" of dirty air? And is it not the case that monopolists have the power to charge high prices simply because of their importance in the market, so that prices do not truly reflect opportunity costs of production? Furthermore, this description of a rationally organized economy made no mention of the distribution of incomes; we could be economizing on all of our scarce resources and producing according to individual's preferences, but some people might starve because of inadequate incomes.

Certainly such problems exist; otherwise there would be no point in writing a book on economic problems. While we will consider specific problems in more detail later, it is useful at this point to state explicitly what conditions and qualifications must be assumed for a price system to provide an output that minimizes the use of scarce resources and is in harmony with consumer preferences.

First of all, the prices that firms and individuals face must accurately reflect relative scarcities. This will be the case only if they are owned by someone who demands to be paid a price equal to the opportunity cost of the good. Many of our resources—the oceans, atmosphere, rivers—are not privately owned and hence are used as if they were free goods. A firm producing steel will take into account the costs of coal, iron ore, labor, and equipment that goes into the production of steel, but it will not include the costs to society of air and water pollution, which may result from its production processes. Hence the price of steel understates its true social cost; it does not convey the correct information to other firms and consumers about the true opportunity cost of steel production. People do not receive the correct information or incentives and hence make no attempt to redesign their behavior in a way that would reduce pollution. Problems arising out of this divergence of private and social costs will be analyzed more fully in Chapters 7 and 8, where the issues of pollution and natural-resource usage are considered.

A second condition for the proper functioning of markets is that competition must prevail among buyers and sellers. In some cases, firms have been able to work cooperatively to lessen competition and thereby reap higher profits. When firms act collusively and manage to prevent competition from outsiders, it is possible for them to restrict output and thereby force prices upward. It may be possible, in industries containing but a small number of firms, for the firms to collude successfully and limit output for a short period of time. But it is almost always true that an industry can achieve long-run success at restricting output and increasing price above the competitive level only with governmental barriers to entry. These governmental barriers to entry, which protect existing firms against competition, often come in the form of regulation that is purported to protect the consumer. Chapter 4 develops a theory of social choice that implies a dominant role for special-interest groups in governmental decision-making processes. This analysis is extended and applied in Chapters 5 and 6 to discussions of the effects of governmental regulation of industry and consumer protection.

Finally, correctly functioning markets will in no way guarantee the elimination of poverty or the provision of an equitable distribution of income. In a market economy, individuals receive an income that depends on their ownership of productive resources and the price for which they can sell, hire, or rent them. Some people are owners of valuable commercial plots of land or shares of some corporation; by permitting others to use their land or capital, they are able to draw a handsome income. Most of us are owners of a labor resource. If we develop this resource by acquiring more education or work experience, the return that we are likely to receive will increase. But because different individuals own vastly different kinds and quantities of productive resources, their incomes will be vastly different also.

In fact, there is no reason to suppose that the existing pattern of incomes is desirable according to prevailing ethical or humanitarian standards. For this reason, the government has found it desirable to undertake programs designed either to support incomes directly or to provide individuals with greater earning power. Some of the programs the government has enacted and specific aspects of the problem of poverty are analyzed in Chapters 10, 11, and 12, on discrimination, education, and poverty, respectively.

The remaining chapters, dealing with price controls, (Chapter 3) and myths about capitalism (Chapter 9), serve to illustrate further the functioning of the market system and the results, anticipated or actual, of interfering with market processes. It is seen in Chapter 9 that several common misconceptions about capitalism can be corrected by a more careful identification of economic costs. And in Chapter 3, an appreciation for what the market system does accomplish is gained by examining the performance of the economy in instances where markets have been restricted from functioning freely.

Our purpose in the following chapters will be to analyze particular problems of the market economy and to examine alternative policies that have been proposed or implemented to deal with them. In reading these chapters, one will develop a better understanding of the amazing amount of coordination and order that comes through market inter-action based on private property and freedom of exchange. However, no system is perfect, and problems do exist in a free-market economy. It should be emphasized that some of the problems blamed on the market economy are really the result of scarcity and will exist no matter how the economy is organized. Even an economy that works perfectly will systematically deprive people of many things they want and probably feel that they deserve. But problems will arise in market economies that could be alleviated with appropriate government intervention. Such cases do not, however, indicate that government intervention is desirable. Government processes are also imperfect, and just because the ideal government policy can improve upon the workings of the market does not mean that improvement will come from the policy that is actually implemented. As will be seen in subsequent chapters (beginning in Chapter 3), it is often the case that government "solutions" make things worse rather than better.

DISCUSSION QUESTIONS

1. Many economics texts refer to the economic problem as one of deciding (a) what, (b) how, and (c) for whom goods will be produced. Explain how these questions are resolved in a market economy and in a centrally planned economy.

2. Prices convey information about resource scarcities and consumer demands. Prices also have important effects on individual incomes. Trace the effects on individual incomes (who gets hurt, who benefits) of an increased scarcity of oil; of the invention of the ballpoint pen.

3. Some socialist countries are turning to a greater reliance on markets in allocating resources. What problems of a centrally planned economy is this likely to solve? What problems of a market system are likely to be introduced?

4. Describe how the information of a petroleum shortage is transmitted to interested parties in a market system. How is this done with central planning?

5. A common criticism of the advanced capitalist system is that power becomes concentrated in the hands of a small number of business leaders. Is concentration of power likely to be a greater or lesser problem in a planned economy? Explain.

6. In centrally planned economies, little value is placed on the desires of individuals. The official ideology is that individual desires should be subordinated to the broader concerns of the "public interest." Explain why you would expect more emphasis to be placed on "public interest" and less on individual preferences as the economy becomes more centrally planned.

7. There are literally hundreds of millions of people around the world whose efforts are necessary in making available those things you consume. There are also hundreds of millions of consumers around the world who consume the same things you consume. If all these suppliers decide to produce a little less, or all the other consumers decide to consume a little more, your consumption plans will be frustrated. Yet you are so seldom frustrated when you go into the market (what you want is normally in the store waiting for you) that it never occurs to you that your success completely depends on your plans being consistent with the plans that untold millions of other people are making. How do you think this amazing amount of international coordination takes place?

8. In a centrally planned economy, the economic plan will be formulated in response to political as well as economic considerations. With this in mind, assume that somehow the central planners have access to complete information on consumer preferences, production technologies, anchovy shortages, and so on. If, because some of these economic considerations change, major revisions in the economic plan are called for, what motivations do you think the central planners would have to make these changes? To resist these changes? Even if the central planners wanted to make the changes, how could they communicate the new information they have to the millions of producers and consumers in the economy who ultimately have to act on it?

chapter **3**

Cooperation through Competition

1. THE INEVITABILITY OF COMPETITION

In Chapter 2, we saw in general terms how the price system causes resources and commodities to be moved in response to changing technologies and consumer preferences. In this chapter, we will continue looking at the important role market prices and exchange play in organizing economic activity. The important point to be developed is that the communication that takes place through free-market prices directs individually competitive behavior into a remarkable pattern of social coooperation. In developing this point, we will make use of the simple but extremely useful concepts of *demand and supply*. The analytical framework provided by these two concepts will allow us to understand how it is that a cooperative pattern of behavior emerges from the voluntary decisions of millions of individuals, each motivated by narrow personal concerns and possessing but limited knowledge about the concerns of others.

The social cooperation we will be discussing in this chapter is clearly desirable, but as we will see, it is not inevitable. Social cooperation depends crucially on the institutions of private property and free exchange for the market prices that are necessary to convert competitive behavior into cooperative behavior. While social cooperation is not inevitable, competitive behavior will—because of scarcity—always be with us, regardless of the social institutions that guide economic decisions.

Because of scarcity, we simply do not have the resources to produce all of the things we would like. As a consequence, some mechanism has to exist for rationing resources among alternative uses and users. And regardless of the form rationing takes, people will compete for what is available, since there is never enough to satisfy everyone's desire for more. When people say they find competition undesirable, it is really scarcity that they find objectionable. As long as there is scarcity, competition is inevitable.

While competition is inevitable, it can take many different forms, depending on how commodities are rationed. Some types of competition are productive in that they promote social cooperation and motivate the production of those commodities people value most. Other types of competition are unproductive, motivating activities that do nothing to increase output and often serving to promote social conflict. The important question is not whether competitive behavior should be encouraged or discouraged. That has already been determined by scarcity. The important question is what type of rationing is most likely to motivate productive rather than unproductive competition?

Market prices are one means of rationing scarce commodities. Commodities and labor are directed to those paying the highest price. In general, this leads to very productive competition as people are motivated to train for and seek jobs that make the most of their productive talents and thus pay well. Furthermore, rationing through market price motivates a cooperative interaction among millions of individuals that channels resources into their most valuable uses. How this cooperative interaction emerges from price rationing is the main topic of this chapter.

But other types of rationing should be recognized. "First come-first served" is a common way of rationing goods when they are not priced or when more is desired than is available at the existing price. When rationing takes this form, people compete by getting up early and waiting in long lines. It is not unheard of for this type of competition to degenerate into pushing and shoving contests. There is certainly nothing productive about such competition. Even when people wait in long lines in an orderly fashion, time that could otherwise have been used for enjoyable or productive pursuits is simply being wasted.

Another common way of rationing things that are eagerly sought but unfortunately scarce is through good looks and personality. Some of the most desirable things on your campus are rationed almost entirely on the basis of good looks and personality. As a result, competitive behavior will be seen in efforts to look good and act personably. This is surely a desirable, or productive, form of competition. Those around us are more attractive, pleasant, and interesting because this type of competition takes place.

Violence and threat of violence have a long history as effective rationing devices. In fact, they are so effective that governments have almost universally attempted to reserve the exclusive right to exercise them. When things of value are rationed through violence, competition finds scarce resources devoted to guns, bombs, missiles, and other devices of death and destruction. Obviously, the direct consequences of this type of competition are not productive, and when the instruments of this competition are actually used, the result is destructive. It should be kept in mind, however, that productive activity depends on security against foreign invasion and the protection of property rights. To the extent that this can be accomplished only by maintaining the potential for violence, military strength is indirectly productive. Unfortunately, once destructive potential is available in our world of scarcity, the temptation for countries to use it not only to protect what they already have but to take what others have is hard to resist. Whether necessary or not, most will agree that violence is an unfortunate form of competition.

Rationing by government directive is a much discussed and often implemented means of solving the rationing problem. Many see this as an appealing approach, since it allows government authorities to distribute goods so that people get what they "should" have, not what their incomes allow them to buy. But under this type of rationing, people compete against each other by attempting to persuade government authorities that their "needs" are the most deserving. These attempts include such things as making campaign contributions, lobbying for or against new legislation, hiring lawyers and accountants to discover loopholes in existing legislation, and doing favors for influential political authorities. This competition through political influence is largely unproductive. A large number of intelligent and capable people who could be producing valuable goods and services are instead devoting their efforts to fighting for preferential political treatment.

2. EQUILIBRIUM PRICE AND SOCIAL COOPERATION

In order to begin our analysis of how price rationing leads to productive social cooperation, we must examine how prices are determined in individual markets by the interaction of supply and demand.

Suppose you are at the supermarket, shopping for food for the week. You have a strong liking for meat, particularly the prime cuts, but at the same time certain limitations are placed on your behavior by your income. Checking out the price of porterhouse, you decide that you can afford only one steak this week, and the rest of your meals will feature hamburger and chicken. Perhaps if porterhouse were selling for only $3 instead of $4.75 per pound, you would have purchased two steaks. At the same time, there are other shoppers who will choose to buy no steak at $4.75, although they would buy some if the price were lower. Therefore, if the price were to fall, more steak would be consumed—first of all because existing customers would increase their own volume of purchases and secondly because people presently not buying any steak would then purchase some.

This phenomenon is called a *demand relation*. For a given group of consumers with certain tastes and income levels, a demand relation describes the quantity of a good that will be consumed at various alternative prices. According to the above reasoning, we would expect the quantity of any good consumed in any time period to increase if there is a decline in its price relative to the prices of other products. This is in fact the law of demand. Naturally, the demand relation will change over time as incomes and tastes change. For example, as the result of a persistent increase in incomes in the United States, people demand a greater quantity of medical care, even though its price has increased relative to that of other goods and services. This does not invalidate the law of demand; there is still an inverse relation between price and quantity, but it is a different one from that which prevailed when incomes were lower.

On the other side of these markets are various firms, each deciding how much to produce and sell. In trying to squeeze as much profit as they can out of their enterprises, the firms base this decision on a comparison of production costs and sales revenues at the alternative output levels. It is reasonable to suppose that, for most firms, costs increase as output goes up. Consider, for example, a wheat farmer who wishes to increase the size of this year's wheat crop. With no time to procure additional land, he can still increase his yield per acre by fertilizing and weeding more extensively. There is, however, a maximum yield of wheat which can be extracted from given acreage, and as this maximum is approached, the application of more and more hours of work will yield smaller and smaller increases in output. In terms of costs, this means that each additional bushel of wheat can be produced only at greater costs.

Firms will expand output only if doing so will increase profits. Thus they will provide a greater quantity of goods for the market only if they are offered a higher price to cover the increasing costs of production. If the price of a good is low, there will exist only a few highly efficient firms who find it profitable to produce and sell the good. If the price increases, not only will the original firms increase output, but other new firms will be induced to enter this field of production. This implies that increases in the price of a good will induce a greater quantity of this good to be offered for sale on the market. This relation between price and quantity supplied is called a *supply relation.* A supply relation may also shift over time, for example, as the result of changes in technology or resource prices.

Buyers and sellers of each good come together in *markets,* where the decisions and interests of both interact. Each buyer decides how much to purchase in response to the market price, with more demanded the lower the price. Each seller decides how much to offer for sale in response to the market price, with more being supplied the higher the price. At any one time, the price for a good may be such that buyers want more of it than suppliers are willing to sell, or that buyers want less of it than suppliers are willing to sell. There is, in such a situation, a discrepancy in the decisions of consumers and producers. It is through market prices that this discrepancy is communicated to both buyers and sellers, and cooperative adjustments are motivated that will remove the discrepancy.

Imagine, for example, gasoline selling for 30 cents per gallon. At a price this low, drivers would have little incentive to economize on fuel. They would drive more often, and faster, shift back to larger cars, and thus demand much more gasoline than they do now. Producers, on the other hand, would find it unprofitable to supply more than a bare minimum of gasoline; costs would be reduced by extracting and refining only the most accessible crude oil. More gasoline would be demanded than supplied, and a *shortage* would exist.

Faced with the shortage, buyers would compete against each other by offering to pay more for gasoline. The increasing price communicates important information to suppliers, telling them consumers want more gasoline. It also communicates to consumers that gasoline is in short supply and it should be used more conservingly. The increasing price not only provides this information; it also provides the incentive to act on it. As long as the shortage remains, the competition among consumers will keep the price rising, thereby communicating the information necessary to reduce the shortage. The price continues to rise until it is motivating producers to supply exactly as much gasoline as consumers want. This is referred to as the *equilibrium price.*

Looking at this process from the other side, assume that the price of gasoline is $3 per gallon. People will walk or ride bicycles to work, form car pools, drive more slowly and keep their cars better tuned, switch to smaller cars and motorcycles, and make other adjustments to reduce their use of gasoline. Suppliers, on the other hand, would have a strong incentive to recover less-accessible deposits of crude oil and operate their refineries at full capacity in order to supply a greater quantity of gasoline. In short, more would be offered for sale at $3 per gallon than consumers would want, and a *surplus* would exist.

Rather than let inventories accumulate, gasoline suppliers would compete against each other by reducing the price below $3 per gallon. The falling price informs suppliers that gasoline is relatively plentiful and motivates them to produce less of it. The falling price informs consumers that the product is relatively abundant and motivates them to consume more of it. Competition among suppliers will continue to force the price down as long as a surplus remains. At some point the price will reach the equilibrium price, and consumers will be willing to buy exactly as much as suppliers want to sell.

It is important to recognize that something truly remarkable is accomplished by an equilibrium price. By equating the quantity of a good consumers want to buy with the quantity suppliers want to sell, the equilibrium price is providing all the information and motivation necessary for millions of widely dispersed people to make decisions that are compatible with each other. When you make a simple decision to buy 10 gallons of gas, this decision can be successfully carried out only if it is consistent with the decisions that are being made by all other gasoline consumers and the millions of people who in one capacity or another are involved in the production and distribution of gasoline. These people live all over the world and speak many different languages, and you have but very limited information on the concerns and circumstances that guide their decisions. Yet somehow you are able to implement successfully your decisions on gasoline consumption. And this amazing success is not confined to just your gasoline purchases; it is duplicated over and over again with the thousands of products that all of us purchase every day. Millions and millions of people throughout the world, many of whom are officially enemies, are constantly cooperating with each other by making production and consumption decisions that are mutually compatible. This truly amazing international cooperation comes from the price competition that keeps market prices close to eqiulibrium prices.

As long as markets are open and unrestricted, there will always be the tendency for the market price to move toward the equilibrium price. In the real world, of course, demand and supply relations are always subject to change in response to changes in such things as income, preferences, technology, and new discoveries. This means that the equilibrium price for any particular good will be constantly moving up or down. It is not likely, therefore, that at any one point in time the market price for a good will equal its equilibrium price, and market prices will not motivate perfect coordination and cooperation. But because price competition keeps market prices close to equilibrium prices, we do find a pattern of cooperation among millions of competing individuals that is truly impressive.

Indeed, market prices perform so well in this regard that most of us simply take for granted the amazing task that they perform, never thinking of how dependent we are on the coordination they provide. As with many things we take for granted, the best way really to appreciate the cooperation that comes from unrestricted market prices is to consider what it would be like without them.

3. SHORTAGES AND FRUSTRATION

Just because quantities of goods supplied and demanded tend to be equal under free-market exchange does not imply that everyone is happy with equilibrium prices. These prices will almost surely be considered unreasonably high when buying and unreasonably low when selling. People confronted by $2.50 per pound for hamburger, $1.50 per gallon for gasoline, or $500 per month for a small apartment will be tempted to suggest a straightforward remedy to their plight: a legally imposed ceiling on prices. Many workers will see the wages they are offered as too low to support the standard of living they feel they deserve. It may appear to them that a governmentally established minimum wage above what they would otherwise earn is the best way to improve their situation. When there is widespread discontent because a price suddenly rises rapidly or a politically influential group has a strong incentive to keep some price from falling, we often find the political process responding by controlling market prices. But such controls seldom produce the intended effects. Instead, they prevent people from communicating with each other through market prices and, as a consequence, cause a breakdown in the pattern of productive social interaction and cooperation that comes from free expression through market exchange.

We will first consider the effect of the government imposing a legal ceiling on the price of some good, with the ceiling being less than the equilibrium price. As sure as night follows day, enforcing such a price ceiling will cause a shortage as consumers want to buy more of the good than producers are willing to supply. In August 1971, President Nixon imposed general price controls which, because of inflation, soon held many prices below their equilibrium levels. Predictably, it was not long before shortages were in the news. The horn of plenty appeared on the cover of one of the weekly news magazines, but it was empty. By 1974, almost all of the price ceilings had been eliminated and, with prices able to seek their equilibrium levels, predictably we quit hearing about shortages. Well, almost. We quit hearing about shortages except of energy. Concerns over energy shortages have continued into the 1980s, which is completely expected, since price ceilings on energy products continued into the 80s.

Although price ceilings are supposedly enforced for the benefit of consumers, the effect of price controls is to frustrate consumers. With the price of a product controlled, consumers are not able to buy as much of it as they want. Without the control, they would communicate this frustration to producers through their willingness to pay more rather than do without. But with the price control, this type of communication has been outlawed, and as a result consumers cannot get others to cooperate with them. Price controls are a form of government censorship that is socially disruptive because it distorts the market communication upon which so much social cooperation depends.

An enlightening historical example of the unfortunate consequences of price ceiling is provided by the siege of Antwerp in 1585.[1] The Duke of Parma was besieging the city in an incident destined to become the turning point of the Dutch Revolution. In anticipation of severe food shortages, speculators began accumulating food supplies with the expectation of selling them at high prices in the future. The speculators' purchases of food added to the existing demand and consequently forced prices up. Seeing this and desiring to protect its citizenry from the "extortionist" practices of the speculators, the government of Antwerp imposed a ceiling on the price of food and legislated severe penalties for selling food at any higher price. But the government had failed to recognize that the speculators were performing a valuable service in buying and storing food for the siege. With the ceiling imposed on the price of food, the incentive to purchase and store grain was lost. Nor was anybody willing to risk supplying the city with additional grain by running the relatively weak blockade. Food supplies were rapidly depleted merely because the government had destroyed any incentive to replenish or economize on the use of food. By the use of price controls, the City of Antwerp imposed a more effective blockade on itself than the enemy could have accomplished. As a result, the siege imposed undue hardship upon the citizens of Antwerp and ultimately contributed to the unfavorable outcome, from the Dutch point of view, of the campaign.

4. NONCOOPERATIVE FORMS OF COMPETITION

Price ceilings will not always lead to the loss of a war, but they will invariably and unnecessarily result in waste, increased social hostility, and reduced social cooperation. Price ceilings make it illegal for people to engage in price competition. This necessarily means other forms of competition will become prevalent—forms that are less productive and less conducive to cooperative interaction than is price competition.

First Come, First Served

When price controls are imposed, there is invariably an increase in rationing by first come, first served. Long lines begin forming for the price-controlled products, as competition favors those who get up the earliest and wait the longest. We saw this type of competition in this country during the gas shortages of 1974 and 1979. Because of the shortages created by price controls and government allocation, people were waiting in line for hours in order to buy 10 gallons of gas.

In those countries where price controls are almost universally applied, almost everything is in short supply, and waiting in long lines is a way of life. In the Soviet Union, for example, the average housewife spends 14 hours a week waiting in line. The Soviet press itself has reported that Russians spend 30 billion man-hours annually waiting in line to buy things.[2] That is the equivalent of 15 million people working a 40-hour week year round. Russians seldom go anywhere without a large satchel. When they see a line, they normally get in it before even finding out what is being sold. It is not uncommon for two or three pranksters to start a line in front of a building just to see people start queuing up behind them.

Obviously, this form of competition is enormously wasteful of time, as well as other valuable resources. For example, using a conservative measure for the value of time, the U.S. Department of Energy estimated that $200 million worth of time was being wasted per month in gas lines during the spring of 1979. It was also estimated that 100 million gallons of gasoline per month was being burned idling in gas lines during the same period. This waste, along with the sheer aggravation of waiting in long lines, meant that the real cost of gasoline was much higher than indicated by the stated price. In fact, once the cost of waste is taken into consideration, there are strong reasons for believing that price ceilings increase, rather than decrease, the cost of buying goods.

In addition, the communication and cooperation that take place through first-come, first-served competition is a poor substitute for that which comes from price competition. When consumers are waiting in long lines for a product, they are providing to suppliers information that they want more of that product. But this communication is not effective, because it provides no incentive for suppliers to respond by making more available. Also, waiting in long lines is not conducive to harmonious interaction among consumers. Gas lines in 1979 often transformed the friendly neighborhood service station into an arena of hostility where aggravation was pervasive, fights common, and killings not unheard of. Market clearing prices are a vastly underrated source of social harmony.

Favoritism and Discrimination

When prices are not allowed to ration desirable commodities, we are more likely to find them rationed on the basis of favoritism and discrimination. When markets are free and people are competing through prices, suppliers can discriminate against consumers. They can, for example, refuse to make their product available to people who possess "undesirable" characteristics, while favoring those who have "desirable" traits. But discrimination of this sort will impose a cost on suppliers by reducing the demand for their products, which means lower prices and fewer sales. This cost of discrimination will not eliminate all discrimination, but it will discourage some of it. Impose a price ceiling, however, and the cost of discrimination is eliminated, since suppliers are then in a position of being able to sell more than they want at the highest price they can legally charge. Imposing a price ceiling is in effect telling suppliers that they can discriminate for free. Obviously, a price ceiling will encourage discrimination.

Imagine yourself in the situation of renting 20 units in an apartment complex you own. The advantages of renting only to attractive members of the opposite sex are obvious. You could do this, of course, but only by offering a special rent to those you find attractive; say $250 per month rather than the prevailing market rent of $350 per month. In other words, exercising your preference for beautiful renters will cost you $100 per month on each unit, or $2000 per month. This cost of discrimination will surely increase the attractiveness of the otherwise "not-so-hots" who would also like to rent from you. Now ask yourself: what happens to the cost of discrimination, and your willingness to discriminate, if the law forbids you from charging more than $250 per month?

Your honest answer to this question reflects behavior that is widely observed when price ceilings are imposed. During the gasoline shortages experienced in this country during the 1970s, gas station owners did not make everyone wait in a long line for 10 gallons of gasoline. Those people the owners liked, or who were in a position to return favors, were often allowed to come in after hours for a quick fill-up. At one point, the Department of Energy issued an order prohibiting this discrimination, but it was rescinded as unenforceable.

When products are rationed through favoritism and discrimination, people will compete by attempting to gain influence with those who control supply. Not only is this type of competition largely unproductive, it may put people who have certain ethnic or physical characteristics into a position in which they find it hard to compete at all. Price ceilings make it difficult for those whom we often think of as disadvantaged to benefit from the cooperation that comes from free-market exchange and puts them at an even greater disadvantage. As we will see in Section 8 of this chapter, this is also true of price controls that establish floors on prices.

Lowering Quality and Convenience

Price ceilings will invariably result in lower quality products and less consumer convenience. Under a price ceiling, suppliers will face excess demand for their products. They will not be able to profit legally from this excess demand by increasing price and output, but profit can be increased by cutting cost and selling a lower-quality product. Not only will this be to the advantage of suppliers, it will also further the interest of the consumer. Not being able to communicate through higher prices their desire for a higher-quality product, consumers will find an increased supply of a lesser quality or less-conveniently available product preferred to no increase at all.

Examples of decreases in quality and convenience are easy to find when price ceilings are imposed. A rent-control ordinance was recently passed in Los Angeles. Obviously, apartments are not going to deteriorate overnight, and the casual observer might not notice any reduced quality. But soon after the rent controls were imposed, a survey was taken of firms providing products for the upkeep and maintenance of apartments; it was found that after rent control, business declined 35–40 percent. This clearly means that the service that tenants are receiving from landlords has declined. On the other hand, the reduced maintenance cost may delay decisions to convert apartments into condominiums.

During the 1979 gas shortages there was widespread evidence that some dealers were adding water to their gasoline. Watered gasoline immediately reduces your miles per gallon and will eventually damage your engine and rust your gas tank. During the summer of 1979, garages did a booming business repairing water-damaged engines and replacing gas tanks.

During the same gas shortage, gas station owners cut their cost by greatly reducing the hours they were open. For example, in September 1978, the average gas station in New York City was open 110 hours a week. But in June 1979, this average had decreased by 27 hours a week.[3] Price controls resulted in a significant decline in consumer convenience.

All of these examples reflect a breakdown in the ability of people to communicate and cooperate with each other. Consumers would rather have higher quality and more convenience than they get when price ceilings are imposed. They would be willing to communicate this desire to suppliers through higher prices, but with price ceilings this effective means of communication is outlawed by the government. With freedom to communicate through market exchange, we would never find gas station owners reducing their payroll hours if it meant that the hours consumers spent waiting in gas lines would increase by many times the number of hours the owners saved.

Tie-In Sales

Another common phenomenon under a price ceiling is tie-in sales. By a tie-in sale we mean selling the price-controlled product only to those who also buy another product that is invariably over-priced. The sale of the price-controlled product is tied to the sale of an over-priced product.

An interesting example of tie-in sales occurred during the 1971–73 price controls in the U.S. For a time during this period there was a large shortage of toilets. At the maximum price the government had fixed for toilets, people wanted more than were available. In some cases, the completion of new houses was being delayed for lack of a toilet. This situation provided one hardware chain an opportunity to unload a large inventory of rubber bathtubs it had been unable to sell. With the toilet shortage, the chain was able to sell all of the rubber bathtubs by requiring that anyone buying a toilet also had to buy a rubber bathtub. Also, since the government had not gotten around to determining the "right" price for rubber bathtubs, they were sold at a high price.

Again we find a lack of cooperation. Cooperation in this case would have been producers' providing more toilets, something they would have been happy to do at prices consumers would have been willing to pay. Price competition would have obviously led to this cooperative outcome. But with price competition outlawed, competition took the form of consumers being willing to take a product they did not want in order to get one they did. This is just another example of nonprice competition not being able to motivate the cooperation that comes from price competition.

5. COOPERATING ILLEGALLY

As with any form of censorship, the attempt to restrict communication through price controls will never be completely successful. The policing of price controls will increase the cost of market communication, but never enough to eliminate it. The willingness of consumers to pay more than the controlled price, rather than get fewer units of a product than they want, will be communicated through illegal, or black-market, transactions. Despite the fact that history records many cases where convicted violators of price controls were put to death, there has never been a price-control episode not accompanied by widespread black-market activity. Governments, no matter how repressive, have never been able to prevent consenting adults from engaging in the act of mutually advantageous exchange.

During World War II, the U.S. government controlled the prices of many products, including gasoline. Despite more than 100,000 paid and volunteer "price watchers" scouting for price-control violators, and the strong patriotic support for the war effort, black-market activity was widespread. The Office of Price Administration (OPA), which administered the controls, estimated, for example, that 2,500,000 gallons of gasoline a day were sold on the black market during the war.

Because of the gasoline shortage created by the World War II price controls, the OPA issued gas coupons that consumers had to have to buy gas legally. The idea was to distribute the coupons, and therefore the gas, fairly among all consumers. Of course, consumers wanted more gas at the controlled price than their coupons allowed, and they were willing to pay black-market prices to get it. Gas station owners who sold black-market gas, however, had to acquire gas coupons illegally in order to protect themselves against the OPA inspectors. According to Joseph Valachi, in testimony before the U.S. Senate, the Cosa Nostra (popularly known as the Mafia) made handsome profits during World War II by acquiring gas coupons and selling them to gas station owners. According to Valachi, these coupons were obtained by counterfeiting, burglarizing OPA offices, and, in many cases, simply by buying them from OPA officials.

The existence of black markets allows more communication and cooperation among people than would be possible without black markets. Government sanctions against black-market activity simply makes the market process of cooperative communication more costly than it would otherwise be. Much of the competition among suppliers takes the unproductive form of avoiding detection by the authorities. The resources that suppliers devote to outwitting the authorities are matched by resources the authorities devote to avoid being outwitted. In the absence of price controls, these scarce resources could be used to produce valuable goods and services, rather than being wasted in activities that largely cancel each other out.

6. AN EXAMPLE OF RENT CONTROLS[4]

When price ceilings are imposed, some combination of all of the above alternatives to open-market competition will generally come into play. The example of rent controls in Stockholm, Sweden, is illustrative.

In Stockholm, "temporary" rent controls were established during the Second World War in 1942 (they were not completely removed until 1975). As economic theory predicts, a housing shortage developed, and the city set up an official waiting list to allocate living on a first come-first served basis. By 1963, 315,000 people, or 40 percent of the city's population, were on the official waiting list. Since landlords found it unnecessary to advertise vacancies, the thousands of eager renters in Stockholm found ingenious ways to acquire information on apartment vacancies. A common way was to scan the obituary notices for indications of newly vacated units, and more desperate parties actually bribed neighborhood morticians for such information. A common gift at christenings was a certificate placing the child on the official waiting list. With an average waiting time of eight to ten years, this was not an unreasonable gift.

Of course, people who were in a position to receive favored treatment did not have to wait as long as those with less influence. A survey of newlyweds fortunate enough to have their own housing showed that only 29 percent got their dwellings by waiting on the official list. The remaining 71 percent got their housing through family, friends, employers, or other connections. In other words, landlords tended to discriminate in favor of those who were well placed and against those who were not.

There was clear evidence that the quality of rent-controlled units in Stockholm was allowed to deteriorate. In many cases this decline reached its ultimate as rental housing was destroyed to make way for office buildings that were not covered by rent controls. There were also plenty of cases in which the owners of a rent-controlled apartment required that the renter take it furnished, with the furniture being rented at very high prices. This is, of course, an example of a tie-in sale. Stockholm authorities also constantly had to worry about black-market exchanges, since renters would eagerly pay more than the legal rent to assure themselves of an apartment, and they could normally find a landlord willing to accommodate them.

An additional unfortunate aspect of controls is that their improper functioning is often taken as a sign that they need to be stiffened or extended to other areas. In Sweden, for example, when rent controls slowed the construction of new apartment units, the government attempted to make construction and ownership of new units more profitable by holding down the cost of mortgage funds. In the usual style of control advocates, this was accomplished by placing a ceiling on mortgage interest rates. This, not surprisingly, caused the supply of funds for housing investments to dry up, as investors moved their funds into more profitable, uncontrolled sectors of the economy. In order to compensate for this, the government required that financial institutions place a certain percentage of their domestic loan funds into the housing market. Financial institutions countered this simply by lending a greater percentage of their funds abroad. Undaunted, the government made the final move and imposed restrictions on overseas investments. That the harmful effects of controls could easily be eliminated by their removal is an option that government regulators seldom consider. If your boat is sinking because of a hole in its bottom, your response would certainly be an attempt to plug it up. The typical response from government would be to drill more holes in the bottom, hoping the water would run out.

7. HARVESTING THE POCKETBOOK OF THE TAXPAYER AND CONSUMER

Government efforts to control prices do not always find prices being held below the free-market levels. Government programs and legislation exist for the purpose of maintaining some prices at artificially high levels. But by interfering in the communication that takes place through market exchange, price floors reduce social cooperation and coordination in much the same way as do price ceilings. In this section, we examine the effects of government efforts to establish floors under the prices of important agricultural products.

The stated objective of our farm policy of maintaining high agricultural prices is to aid low-income farmers and provide the incentive necessary to maintain a productive farm population. Interestingly, the primary reason for a high percentage of farmers receiving low incomes is that farm productivity has increased very rapidly over the years. Productivity—the quantity of output that can be produced by a unit of labor—has increased more rapidly in the agricultural sector than it has in the nonagricultural sector of the economy. Because of rather rigid limits on the amount of food we can consume, our demand for food has not increased nearly as much as our demand for other goods as our incomes have increased. This has meant that prices of agricultural products have tended to decline relative to other prices in the economy, as consumers communicated their desire to have nonagricultural production expand relative to food production.

The result has been a dramatic decline in resources devoted to farming. The number of farms, for example, has declined from an historic high of 6.8 million in 1935 to fewer than 2.9 million today. While in 1929 at least 25 percent of the U.S. population lived on the farm, today only about 2.5 percent of our population is so situated. As with most declining industries, however, migration from farming has not been fast enough to prevent farm prices, and therefore farm incomes, from declining relative to nonfarm incomes.

This tendency for farm incomes to decline was given strong impetus during the Great Depression, when all incomes—but particularly those of farmers—fell sharply. Between 1929 and 1933, farm prices fell by 50 percent and farm incomes by 66 percent. In response to this depression of farm incomes, the federal government enacted the Agricultural Adjustment Act of 1933, which initiated a government effort to support farm incomes that continues to this day.

The initial program established price supports for different crops at levels that were deemed appropriate by the political process. If at the support price farmers produce more of a crop than consumers want to buy (which is generally the case, since otherwise the support program would have little effect), the government buys the excess at the support price. Under this program, farmers are clearly not coordinating their decisions with the decisions being made by consumers. The movement of resources out of farming and into more valued employment is retarded, and more agricultural products will be produced relative to the production of other goods than consumers desire.

The price-support program actually did not have a pronounced effect until the 1950s. Until this time, farm prices and incomes had been maintained at levels favorable to farmers by the huge demand created by World War II and the Korean War. But then, with the slackening of foreign demand for agricultural products, the provisions of farm policy legislation began to take hold. The government found it necessary to purchase agricultural surpluses and store them, in order to maintain the prices above their market levels. By the early 1960s, these surpluses had become huge. From 1961 to 1965 the average amount of wheat, for example, being stored by the government was over 1100 million bushels. From 1966 to 1970 an average of almost 650 million bushels of wheat was being stored. At one point it was costing the government $1.1 million per day just to store wheat.

Inventories of agricultural products have declined in recent years, as market prices increased faster than support prices for many products during the mid-1970s, and existing inventories were utilized for school lunch programs and foreign aid or became spoiled. The government has also attempted to reduce the accumulation of inventories by emphasizing price support programs that restrict farm output. The acreage allotment program became the chief instrument of U.S. agricultural policy in the 1960s. Under this program farmers wishing to take advantage of government price-support programs must agree to limit the amount of acreage they place under cultivation. During the 1960s an average of 60 million acres—almost 20 percent of total farm acreage—was kept out of production through this and similar programs.[5] The objective is to restrict the level of output enough to maintain high prices without governmental accumulation of surpluses.

The acreage allotment program has not been very successful in realizing its objective. First, farmers are directed only to cut back on the use of land. With a high supported price, they will attempt to increase output by more intensive cultivation of the land they are free to use. While low-cost production techniques may call for large quantities of land relative to other inputs, this program will induce farmers to employ more labor and machinery than is most economical. Scarce capital and labor resources will be overutilized in the farming sector and diverted from use elsewhere in the economy. An undesirable side effect is that farmers are encouraged to overuse environmentally harmful fertilizers and pesticides in squeezing a maximum output from their land. At the same time that one agency of the government is restraining the use of damaging fertilizers and pesticides, another is encouraging their use through a combination of crop price supports and acreage restrictions. Second, the land that farmers choose to remove from production is naturally the least productive. The more intensive cultivation of the smaller acreage will mean that the reduction in output will be considerably less than the reduction in land under cultivation. In fact, in the case of wheat, acreage under cultivation was reduced from 80 million acres in 1953 to 55 million acres in 1960, while output actually increased from 1.2 to 1.4 billion bushels! This came about not only because of the more intensive use of fertilizers, tractors, and insecticides, but also because at the same time the government was limiting farm acreage, it was spending millions of dollars on research and spreading information to increase productivity.

As taxpayers and consumers, the nonfarm public is paying billions of dollars annually to maintain agricultural price-support programs. In the late 1960s, taxpayer support of farm incomes was more than $5 billion per year. Add to this the cost to consumers—approximately $5 billion per year—for higher food prices which result from the price support programs, and we get a total transfer of income from the nonfarm to the farm sector of about $10 billion per year.*[6] In more recent years, this cost has been reduced somewhat as market prices for agricultural products have increased. It has been estimated that in 1978/79, farm programs cost taxpayers $1.44 billion and consumers $5.85 billion annually.[7]

Despite these huge transfers to farmers, the incidence of poverty among farmers is still much greater than among nonfarmers. In the late 1970s, well over half of the total number of farms generated sales of less than $10,000, with average net income of less than $3500. The fact is, poor farmers receive very little from farm programs. A farmer's subsidy depends not upon his level of income, but rather upon the volume of agricultural output he is capable of producing and selling. If the government supports the price of wheat, for example, at 20 cents per bushel above the free market price, the farmer who sells 10,000 bushels obviously receives ten times the subsidy of the farmer who sells only 1000 bushels. Thus we should not be surprised that the largest farmers receive the largest subsidies.

In 1978, farmers with less than 70 acres of crops received an average of $363 dollars from price-support programs. Farms with more than 2500 acres averaged $36,005 from the government. Those farm families that are considered poor receive only about 10 percent of the government agricultural subsidies, while the nonpoor farmers receive the remaining 90 percent. A token effort was made in 1977 to prevent the big farmers from getting such a large share of the subsidies when Congress passed a law limiting payments to individual farmers at $40,000. However, the law specifies payments to persons, and large farm owners have easily circumvented the intent of the law by distributing ownership of the farm over several members in the family or by incorporating their farms. In 1978, 52 farming corporations collected more than $100,000 each.[†]

Our agricultural program is not just a nice welfare program for wealthy farmers; it is a welfare program that is supported dis-

---

*It should be pointed out that farmers do not receive everything that taxpayers and consumers lose because of inefficiencies that are created by the program. For one thing, thousands of federal employees serve as intermediaries between the taxpayer and the farmer, and they take their cut of the action. The number of these federal employees is growing despite the fact that the number of farmers is declining. Only 19,500 persons were employed by the U.S. Department of Agriculture in 1920, when the farm population was approximately 31 million. By 1975, employment in the Department of Agriculture had soared to 121,000 while farm population had declined to under 9 million.

†We are talking here about direct payments from the government. These figures do not include the additional income farmers receive through the higher prices paid by the consumer.

proportionately by the poor. A large part of a low-income family's expenditures go for basic foods, and the prices of these foods are kept artificially high by our agricultural program. During 1978–79, the price support programs increased the price of wheat by 17.5 percent, the price of peanuts by 40 percent, the price of milk by 11 percent, and the price of sugar by 88 percent.[8] Obviously, our farm program was not designed to assist the disadvantaged.

8. AN HONEST DAY'S UNEMPLOYMENT FOR AN HONEST DAY'S WORK

The federal minimum wage law is another important example of a policy that prevents some prices (in this case wages) from declining to their equilibrium levels. The first minimum wage law in the United States was adopted in 1938 for the purpose of requiring employers to pay their workers a wage no lower than a minimum standard. The standard in 1938 was 25 cents per hour, supposedly high enough to assure that every worker received a wage adequate to sustain a decent and healthy existence. Since 1938, the minimum wage law has been amended many times to extend coverage to new occupational groups and to increase the legislated minimum. The logic behind minimum wage legislation is straightforward: if wages are substandard, simply make substandard wages illegal. Unfortunately, this logic has little going for it except wide acceptance and good intentions. Simple economic analysis predicts that the effect of minimum wage legislation is to hurt the very people it is supposed to help by reducing their ability to communicate through market exchange.

If a price—in this case the price of labor—is set above the market equilibrium price, those supplying the good or service will be eager to make more of it available than buyers are willing to accept. There is no reason to expect the effect of minimum wage legislation to be any different. Workers making more than the minimum wage will not be directly affected. But low-wage earners—the unskilled and teen-agers—will find that there are not as many jobs as they would like to have at the minimum wage. Because of their low productivity, some of these workers will not provide their employers with sufficient output to justify the minimum wage. Competition for the consumer's dollar will require that employers faced with high-cost, low-productivity workers substitute less-expensive, productive resources—machines for example—for unskilled workers. As the cost of any factor of production, including labor, is bid up, firms will have to economize on its use if they expect to be able to price their products at the levels the consumer will pay. Although it may appear that it is the firm that is firing unskilled workers when the minimum wage increases their cost, it is really consumers who are firing them.

So economic analysis predicts that unemployment will increase among the unskilled, primarily teenagers, when minimum wages are imposed. With more teenagers being interested in working than will be able to find jobs, many will be willing to take a lower wage rather than remain unemployed. But the minimum wage law makes it illegal for them to communicate this information to firms and, ultimately, to consumers, who would be willing to employ them at the lower wage.

The evidence strongly supports the view that the minimum wage increases teenage unemployment. Over the period 1955 to 1981, the minimum wage was increased from 75 cents to $3.35 per hour—a greater percentage increase than that of the average manufacturing wage over the same period. In the late 1940s, the teenage unemployment rate hovered under 10 percent. Since that time, the teenage unemployment rate has increased significantly, going over 20 percent in some years, in spite of the fact that the unemployment rate for adult males declined during the 1960s. Even though the Carter Administration backed a minimum wage increase in 1977, it acknowledged that its estimates indicated that the increase would cause about 90,000 workers (mostly teenagers) to lose jobs by 1981.

Another unfortunate effect of the minimum wage is that it allows employers to discriminate against potential workers at no cost. In an unrestricted labor market an employer can certainly discriminate against workers, but doing so will reduce the effective labor supply and increase the wage that has to be paid. With the unemployment created by a minimum wage, however, employers will find more people willing to work than can be hired. Since no one can legally offer to work for less than the minimum wage, it costs the employer absolutely nothing to discriminate against minorities, women, or any other group. The minimum wage law eliminates the cost of discrimination and will, according to economic analysis, cause an increase in discrimination.

This means that the minimum wage law will further handicap the very people it is supposed to be helping. In their effort to find part-time or summer employment, teenagers from more affluent and influential families are less likely to be discriminated against than teenagers from poor families who need employment the most. With the minimum wage making it impossible for the poorer teenager to offset this disadvantage by offering to work for a little less, the minimum wage favors the wealthy teenagers. This is consistent with empirical research which indicates that teenagers from high-income families are more likely to obtain minimum wage employment than teenagers from low-income families.[9]

Minority teenagers are particularly disadvantaged by the minimum wage. The unemployment rate among black teenagers has increased dramatically over the past three decades, and Walter Williams, a black economist at George Mason University, puts much of the blame on the increasing minimum wage. In 1948 the minimum wage had not been raised in a while and was largely ineffective because of the inflation during World War II. The unemployment for 16–17-year-old blacks was 9.4 percent in 1948, lower than the 10.2 percent unemployment rate for 16–17-year-old whites. By 1976 and nine minimum wage increases later, 40.6 percent of 16–17-year-old blacks were unemployed as opposed to 19.7 percent of 16–17-year-old whites. Table 1 provides more detail.[10] Obviously, fluctuations in economic activity affect year-to-year changes in these unemployment rates but cannot account for the unmistakeable trends since the late 1940s.

A common response at this point is that, without the minimum wage law, many would not be able to earn a decent living. This may be true, but several things need to be recognized. First, making it more difficult for someone to get a job does not make it easier for them to earn a living. Second, in particular cases where poverty is a problem, there are much better ways of addressing this problem than an across-the-board minimum wage requirement (see Chapter 12). Finally, relatively few people who are looking for jobs covered by the minimum wage are the sole supporters of a family. Most are teenagers interested in a little extra spending money or work experience.

The importance of work experience should be emphasized. For many young people, particularly minority youth, the public schools have

TABLE 1

Teenage Unemployment Rates by Race (Males)

Year	White 16–17	Black 16–17	White 18–19	Black 18–19
1948	10.2	9.4	9.4	10.5
1950*	13.4	12.1	11.7	17.7
1955	12.2	14.8	10.4	12.9
1956*	11.2	15.7	9.7	14.9
1960	14.6	22.7	13.5	25.1
1961*	16.5	31.0	15.1	23.9
1963*	17.8	27.0	14.2	27.4
1965	14.7	27.1	11.4	20.2
1967*	12.7	28.9	9.0	20.1
1968*	12.3	26.6	8.2	19.0
1970	15.7	27.8	12.0	23.1
1974*	16.2	39.0	11.5	26.6
1975*	19.7	45.2	14.0	30.1
1976*	19.7	40.6	15.5	35.5

*Indicates a change in the minimum wage law.

failed to prepare them for productive employment. Their best hope for developing productive skills is through work experience and on-the-job training. Many of these young people would be willing to work at a very low wage for the opportunity to acquire such experience and training. This is no different from a student's willingness to attend college for four years. In both cases, an advantage is seen in reducing one's income—when one is young and has less financial responsibility—in return for a higher income potential in the future. The minimum wage denies many young people the opportunity to make this exchange. If it were national policy to ensure that disadvantaged minority youth remained disadvantaged throughout their lives, few policies would be more effective than the minimum wage.

If it is true that the minimum wage law hurts the very people it is supposed to help, who supports this law and why? The group that has most consistently pushed for increasing the level and coverage of the minimum wage is organized labor. This may appear strange, since the wages of almost all union members are well in excess of the minimum wage. But consider the fact that union workers are able to improve their bargaining position by reducing the ability of unorganized and less-skilled workers to compete for jobs by offering to work for a lower wage.

It is unions not just in the U.S. that are strong supporters of the minimum wage. In South Africa, job-reservation laws have until recently been effective at reserving many jobs for whites only. As these job-reservation laws began breaking down because of both external and internal pressures, white-dominated South African labor unions suddenly started pushing minimum wage legislation for blacks. One explanation for this sudden interest in black wages is that white union officials in South Africa suddenly developed a throbbing concern for the well-being of blacks. Another, and to us a more plausible, explanation is that minimum wage legislation was seen as a way of preventing blacks from effectively competing for jobs traditionally held by whites.

We must begin to realize that government attempts to control prices, whether by establishing price ceilings or price floors, invariably have unintended and unfortunate consequences. This realization comes from an understanding of how market prices allow people to engage in productive and cooperative communication with each other. Little good—and much harm—can come from government interference with this communication process.

DISCUSSION QUESTIONS

1. The text points out that workers who are laid off because of a minimum wage law may find employment elsewhere but that this

will force wages down in these other lines of employment. It was also asserted that unions favor minimum wage laws because they will reduce competition from low-wage workers. Is there some contradiction here? Explain.

2. In the late 1960s, farm subsidies were being provided at the rate of $5 billion per year. Would it have been possible for anyone at this time to purchase farm land with the expectation of reaping huge profits from this subsidy? Explain.

3. If rent controls were removed from residential units in New York, rents would undoubtedly increase. Would they increase immediately to a level which is higher, lower, or the same as the level of rents that would have prevailed if no rent-control program had ever existed? Explain. What does this suggest about the difficulty of removing controls once they have been imposed?

4. Legal price controls often lead to black markets, where goods are bought and sold at illegal prices. Given that such exchange takes place voluntarily, is there moral justification for the government to punish those engaging in black-market activities?

5. Explain why you believe a price ceiling would increase, rather than decrease, the price of a product.

6. A price ceiling increases discriminating practice of suppliers against consumers. Will a price ceiling also increase the cost of discrimination consumers practice against suppliers? Why or why not?

7. It is often argued that price controls on natural gas help poor people by keeping the price low. Explain why this will probably not be the case even if poor people are able to get as much natural gas as they want at the controlled price.

8. Given that competition is inevitable and that the ability to compete successfully will vary among individuals regardless of the form competition takes, do you believe it is even possible for government programs to have significant success in equalizing incomes?

chapter 4

Public Choice: When It Is Smart to Be Ignorant

1. EVERYBODY WANTS IT, BUT NOBODY WILL PAY FOR IT

In discussing how the free market works, we have been assuming that when consumers desired something strongly enough, it was profitable for someone to provide it. For most goods and services, this is the case. The fact that people desire ballpoint pens, designer jeans, massages, automobiles, tropical fish, and underarm deodorants is all that is required to guarantee that they will be provided, because the desire for these items is coupled with a willingness to pay for them. Unfortunately, this is not true for some desirable goods and services. It is quite easy to think of things that everyone would like to have, but for which no one will voluntarily pay a single cent. Let's consider an example.

Suppose a small town of 5000 has grown up along a river that periodically overflows and floods the community. Although flood damage is somewhat unpredictable, let's say that each person in the town would be willing to pay $50 to avoid floods or threats of floods. If a dam could be constructed for $100,000 that would eliminate floods entirely, it would surely appear to be a desirable investment. Each individual in the town could receive a service—flood control—that they value at $50, for only $20. Quite a bargain. But no one can be expected voluntarily to pay $20 for $50 worth of flood prevention. Why not? The answer to this question becomes clear once we recognize an important difference between a desirable commodity such as flood control and most other useful goods.

With most goods, the more one person consumes, the less of the good there is for anyone else to consume. The more hamburger you eat, the less there is for someone else to eat. The more housing you occupy, the less there is for others to occupy. Commodities that have this characteristic are referred to as *private goods*. There is little possibility that you will be able to benefit from the private good that someone else purchases for his or her own use. If you desire the services from such goods, you are obliged to purchase them for yourself.

The dam in the above example is obviously not a private good. If you live in the town protected by the dam, the fact that many other people also benefit from the flood prevention service in no way reduces the benefit you receive from this service. When a good is characterized by the fact that once it is provided individuals cannot be selectively excluded from its benefit, and one person can consume it without reducing its availability to others, we refer to it as a *public good*. Commonly thought of as public goods are national defense, clean air, a well-defined legal system, and, of cource, flood protection.

We should now be able to see the difficulty in trying to get any one individual in our town to contribute toward the construction of a dam. Each person knows that if the dam is built, he will receive the benefit whether he supports the project or not. If people could be excluded from the benefit of the dam, a private party would build it, knowing that individuals would each rather pay their share of the cost than be denied the flood protection. But since it would be impossible to exclude anyone living in the town from the benefit once the dam was built, no private company could expect to be compensated for building it. Any attempt to organize the community to build the dam will be an uphill battle. Most people will be content to sit back and hope that someone else does the job. Each individual realizes that if he works hard to organize the group and contributes his share of the cost, it will come to nothing unless everyone else cooperates. But he also realizes that if everyone else cooperates, he can be a free rider; the dam will be constructed whether he does anything or not. So no matter what the rest of the community does, the smart thing for each individual to do is nothing. This explains why the "let George do it" attitude is such a pervasive one.

We see that if everyone does what is individually rational, the result will be collectively irrational. If everyone attempts to be a free rider, the dam will not be built, and everyone in the community will be worse off as a result. This type of dilemma has typically been avoided by individuals allowing themselves to be collectively coerced. For example, we collectively permit ourselves to be forced to drive on the right-hand side of the road, stop at red lights, and pay for some public projects. When everyone is forced to pay for the dam, it is guaranteed that it will be built and everyone will be better off. This is a strong justification for the existence of government agencies with the power to coerce. Without the existence of such agencies, many desirable public goods would never be provided.

2. THE ABUSES OF COERCIVE POWER

Clearly the power to coerce is a power that can be employed usefully, but it can also be abused. Some restrictions must be placed on the government's power to force the populace to finance projects. In a democratic society these restrictions are normally exercised by the public through their voting behavior. The public can express their preference for public goods in the ballot box. These votes, it is hoped, will provide governmental agencies with accurate information. This information should identify those projects that will convey benefits that exceed their costs. Once this information has been transmitted, government officials, interested in responding to the desires of their constituencies, will impose the necessary taxes and provide the desired public goods. The hope of a democracy is that the information conveyed by voters will lead the government to use its coercive power to provide only those public goods and services that are justified from a cost and benefit perspective.

This form of public choice would obviously work well in our town with the flood problem. Given the opportunity to force everyone else to contribute to the dam, each individual would also be willing to obligate himself to contributing his share. Since each person's share of the cost is less than the benefit, we can expect a vote on the dam to pass unanimously. In this situation, the information that the voters transmit to the government leads to the correct decision. But before we jump to overly optimistic conclusions about the efficiency of the democratic process, let's recognize that we have considered a very unusual situation. We have considered a situation in which everyone has the same benefit and pays the same cost. We also considered an all or nothing project. How large the dam should be was not considered. Unfortunately, most public choices are more complicated than this.

It would be unusual to find an issue on which everyone agreed. On most issues, some people will be in favor and others will be opposed. If our previous example were more realistic, we would have to recognize that many people in the town probably live well out of the flood plain, and the dam would provide no benefit to them. These people would be against any flood-control project for which they had to pay. But if the government waited until everyone agreed before doing anything, it wouldn't have much to do. Majority rule seems a reasonable solution to the problem. If more than half the people in a community desire a public project, the government will almost always respond to this desire. Majority rule seems a natural one to follow, if for no other reason than because it is familiar to all of us. But a reasonable argument can be made for it. The majority rule is the only one that keeps the smaller group from imposing its will on the larger group. With less than a majority required to pass a public project, a smaller number of people supporting the project could force a larger number to go along against their will. On the other hand, with more than a majority required, a smaller number against the project could deny it to a larger number in favor of it.

Regardless of the rule used, any public choice will normally find a part of the group benefiting while the whole group pays. The result is that government projects have a strong tendency to be too large and overfunded. Any project should be expanded only as long as the additional benefit from expansion is greater than the additional cost. If the group benefiting from the project also pays for it, we can be sure that expansion would cease, once the additional benefit fell below the additional cost. But this isn't true when the benefiting group doesn't pay the full cost of its project. Additional benefits from enlarging the project will still be greater than the additional cost *the group pays*, and the project will be expanded further. There's nothing surprising about this. Most people will consume more of a good or service if they can get someone else to help pay for it. This is true whether the someone else helps pay for it voluntarily or involuntarily.

A more realistic version of our flood-control example would have demonstrated this tendency for public projects to be overfunded. There are many different types of dams that could be constructed, with more expensive dams providing more flood protection. Let's assume that those living in the flood plain are in the majority and therefore control the decision. If these people had to pay the entire cost of the dam, we would expect construction to proceed only as long as an additional dollar spent on the dam would reduce flood damage by more than a dollar. But with the whole community paying, those in the flood plain will want to enlarge the project even when another dollar spent reduces flood damage by less than a dollar. Not all of the additional dollar spent is their cost, but all of the reduced flood damage is their benefit.

3. WE NEED IT

The opportunity for one group to benefit at the expense of others through governmental projects has not gone unnoticed. Groups with special interests have been quick to realize the advantages of getting everyone to chip in a little to support the things they feel are important.

Of course, special-interest groups are not usually so blunt as to suggest that they should receive tax money for their personal benefit. They have found a much more effective strategy: obtain government subsidies for their pet projects by arguing that it will benefit everyone in the community. Interest groups are not at all bashful about their claims. Not only will their project benefit everyone, but it is something that we all "need." When we hear these arguments, it pays to be skeptical.

What does it mean to say that we need something? Taken seriously, it means a threat to our existence if we forgo the recommended commodity. Yet we often find our need for a product related to its cost: the lower the price, the greater the "need." Notice how many times the word *need* is used by people who are arguing for things that others will have to pay for. It's amazing what a person will "need" when someone else is picking up the tab.

4. PSEUDOPUBLIC GOODS

A natural question to ask a special-interest lobbyist is this: "If your project is so desirable, why do you have to come to the government to get it funded? If everyone needs a good or service so much, why aren't they willing to pay for it?" (in which case some enterprising entrepreneur will be glad to supply it). Most special-interest advocates will have a couple of answers for this. They will argue that most people aren't aware of all the benefits they will receive from the project, or that the project is a public good and deserves support on that basis.

The first answer should persuade very few. If you don't benefit from a private good, it's because you don't care enough to purchase and consume it. Of course, there are always people who feel that you aren't too bright if you don't like the same things they do. But how to spend your money is your concern, not theirs.

If the lobbyist claims public good status for his or her proposal, some questions have to be asked. Does the project convey important benefits to the community at large? Is it impossible to deny anyone these benefits once the project is completed? These are strict requirements, and we might expect few projects to qualify for government support as public goods. But you would be amazed at the number of projects that are funded at public expense because they are supposedly public goods.

For example, many big cities have built large sports arenas, largely at taxpayers' expense. Supporters claim that a sports arena, with the major league teams that usually go with it, brings recognition and fame to the city. Furthermore, the argument goes that this will benefit everyone who lives in the city, whether they ever go out to the old ball game or not, because they will be living in a more prestigious community. And this should justify coercing everyone in the city to contribute to the sports arena.

Clearly, this is a weak argument. The people who receive the primary benefit from a sports arena are those who frequent them to watch ball games. It's easy to prevent a person from receiving this benefit if he or she doesn't pay at the gate. The assertion that everyone would benefit from the arena whether they go to the games or not has to be questioned. A sports arena will generate growth and congestion that many will find undesirable. To these people, paying for a big sports palace makes about as much sense as paying for an unnecessary root-canal treatment.

It's probably true that some people who never go to a sporting event may feel a little bit better just knowing they can or knowing that their city makes national news occasionally for something other than a rising crime rate. But does this justify commandeering funds from everyone in the city to build a sports arena? What about fine restaurants? Certainly fine restaurants enhance the reputation of a city. Many people are happy to know that one is near by, waiting to serve them, whether they ever visit it or not. But most people would find a proposal to publicly finance restaurants a little farfetched. If desirable side effects justified government subsidies, well-kept yards, hair styling, pretty dresses, face-lifts, car washes, toothpaste, deodorants, smiles, ice cream parlors, and athlete's-foot medication would all qualify for a handout.

Regardless of the desirability of requiring the public to pay for certain things, it should be recognized that special-interest groups expend a lot of effort to get subsidies for those things from which they receive enjoyment and profit. Many of these efforts have been successful; the sports arena example is only one of many. The more "cultured," and usually wealthier, members of many cities have managed to obtain government support for symphonies, operas, ballet, and the performing arts in general. The stated justification for requiring everyone to pay for entertainment that caters primarily to the tastes of the rich is similar to that given for subsidizing sports arenas. Supposedly, everyone in a community will benefit, even those who prefer to sit home with a can of beer and watch all-star wrestling on tv.

Most cities have somehow decided that everyone benefits from golf courses, whether he or she plays golf or not. Consequently, people in many communities find themselves contributing to public golf courses and subsidizing golfers. The only complaint by golfers is that the public is not sufficiently sensitive to their "needs." According to a news report that appeared in the Los Angeles Times: "Los Angeles needs 24 more golf courses, according to a report submitted to the City Recreation and Park Department by the National Golf Foundation. Their survey discovered that there are 160,000 golfers in the Los Angeles area, and many of them do not play golf as often as they would like because of the lack of courses."[1] One wonders how many more courses these 160,000 golfers would need if instead of being subsidized by the 6,000,000 or so Los Angeles residents that don't play golf, their greens fees were raised to cover the entire cost of providing these courses.

Many more examples could be given of special-interest groups trying to drain a subsidy out of the public trough for goods and services that benefit them primarily. Just follow the proposals and requests that come before meetings of your locally elected officials. You will probably be surprised at the number of "socially concerned" people who have identified some urgent public "need." Many of these urgent "needs" will be provided for with the help of public subsidies. While some version of the public good argument will normally be given to justify these subsidies, few projects will pass muster as public goods. Most of these projects receive funding at public expense because they benefit individuals and groups that exert a lot of influence on public decision makers. Most of those things that are asserted to be public goods are more accurately termed pseudopublic goods.

5. YOUR VOTE DOESN'T COUNT

One may be wondering at this point why special-interest groups are so successful. Many very effective special-interest groups contain only a small percentage of the total population. It certainly isn't a large percentage of the population that attends the opera or ballet. Why doesn't the majority vote against having their hard-earned money confiscated to support projects that provide them with little or no benefit? Looking at this question will give us additional insight into how public choices are made.

It would clearly be inconvenient to have the entire electorate vote on every issue that came up. The cost of polling everyone is a substantial one. A natural way around this problem is to have periodic elections to elect representatives from different geographical areas. These elected representatives collectively make the decisions on most public issues.

Ideally, if those representatives don't vote on the issues in a way that pleases the majority of their constituencies, they will be voted out of office in the next election. In this way, each voting citizen has an indirect vote on all issues without the expense of a large number of voterwide elections.

Representative democracy, as briefly described above, has been a successful mechanism for making social choices in many countries. But there are some important differences in the way it is ideally supposed to work and how it actually does work.

One of the keys to an efficiently working democracy is a concerned and informed electorate. Everyone is supposed to take time to study the issues and candidates and then carefully weigh the relevant information before deciding how to vote. Although an informed citizenry is desirable from a social point of view, it's not clear that individuals will find it personally desirable to become politically informed.

Obtaining detailed information about issues and candidates is a costly endeavor. Many issues are very complicated, and a great deal of technical knowledge and information is necessary to make an informed judgment on them. To find out how candidates really feel requires a lot more than listening to their campaign slogans. It requires studying their past voting records, reading a great deal that has been written either by or about them, and asking them questions at public meetings. Taking the time and trouble to do these things—and more—is the cost that each eligible voter has to pay personally for the benefits of being politically informed.

What are the benefits of being politically informed? Basically, there are two. Some people simply enjoy being informed. These people will be willing to make an effort to acquire some information on public issues just for the sake of knowledge. The other benefit from being informed has nothing to do with satisfying intellectual curiosity. By being politically informed, individuals have the knowledge to influence social decisions in directions that will yield them the greatest benefit. Unfortunately, this does little to motivate most people to become informed, because it isn't much of a benefit. The probability of one person's vote having any effect on an election is practically zero. With thousands voting in local elections and millions voting in state and national elections, each citizen is safe in assuming that his or her vote really doesn't count.

So, for most people, the costs of becoming politically informed are noticeable, while the benefits are negligible. As a result, most people limit their quest for political information to listening to the radio on the way to work, conversations with friends, casual reading, and other things they normally do anyway. Even though most people in society would be better off if everyone became more informed, it isn't worth the cost for most individuals to make an effort to become informed themselves. You will receive the benefits from the awareness of others whether you study the issues or not. And if no one else becomes informed on the issues, you are not going to change things noticeably, no matter how politically aware you are. So political apathy is not the result of moral decay or lack of patriotism in our society. It's simply the result of individuals acting rationally. This phenomenon, which is easily recognized as another example of the free-rider problem, has been referred to by some observers as rational ignorance.[2] In other words, as far as most political issues are concerned, it is smart to be ignorant.

The implications are very interesting. For one thing, legislators have an easier job than they otherwise would. With the public at large poorly informed on complex issues, elected representatives are under less pressure to be informed themselves. They will be able to score points with the constituents back home for policies that give the appearance of solving problems, whether they do or not. Since the effects of many policies are hard to predict, even by knowledgeable experts, we can expect a great deal of legislation to be passed that aggravates the problem it was intended to solve. In fact, we have already seen examples of such legislation in the discussion of price controls and minimum wages in Chapter 3.

Lack of political awareness on the part of the public also makes it easier for politicians to get away with exaggerated claims and promises—false and misleading advertising, if you will. Whether we are dealing with a politician promoting candidacy or a salesman promoting a used car, there is a tendency to exaggerate the truth if it will help convince the consumer to vote for, or buy, the product. An informed group of consumers is probably the most effective way to keep this tendency under control. The more consumers know about a product, the less advantage can be realized by advertising it falsely. And the fact is that most people spend more time and effort sizing up the alternatives when they buy a used car than when they vote for a political candidate. Polls consistently indicate that the majority of the people of voting age do not even know who their congressional representatives are, much less how those representatives stand on specific issues. When people buy a used car, they at least kick some tires and take a test drive; more often than not, they have their mechanic check it out. They are motivated to become somewhat informed because, as opposed to a political election, the decision they make on a used car is the decision they are going to have to live with. This reduces the benefits that a used-car salesman can realize from gross misrepresentation, though it does not eliminate it entirely. But don't expect to hear the outrageous whoppers from used-car salesmen that politicians tell routinely.

There are obvious advantages to be realized if citizens became more informed politically. Unfortunately, there doesn't seem to be any easy or desirable way of overcoming the problem of rational ignorance. As we have already mentioned, rational ignorance can be explained by the free-rider phenomenon, and the customary solution to this type of problem is for everyone to submit to coercion. But this approach is not practical in the case of political awareness. Do we really want to force everyone to become politically well informed? And if we do, how are we going to determine when an individual is adequately informed? Unfortunately, most of us find a close correlation between how much the other guy agrees with us and how well informed he is. Clearly, pushing very far in the direction of having the government require and test political awareness could lead to abuses that would easily offset the benefits of having a more informed society. About as far as we have gone in this direction is to require that all students receive a minimum amount of education with mandatory courses in history and civics. Of course, one of the big topics in most high school civics courses is the importance of the individual vote.

6. SPECIAL-INTEREST POLITICS AND CONTROLLING GOVERNMENT

We don't want to leave the opinion that everyone is politically apathetic. This obviously isn't the case. Many individuals have a great deal of motivation to become well informed and politically active in support of particular issues. We have seen that many times a relatively small number of individuals will receive the bulk of the benefit from a particular social choice, while the society at large picks up the tab. Clearly, such individuals will have strong motivation to organize a political pressure group. In this way, they can influence key decision makers and have a far greater impact on the outcome of a social decision than they would with just their one vote. Also, members of a special-interest group will find it relatively easy to organize and act as a unified team. This possibility exists because a common purpose motivates the members, and their numbers are relatively small. Of course, the free-rider phenomenon can be a problem even in special-interest groups. But the smaller the group and the narrower the objective, the easier it is to organize and get everyone to contribute their share. Also, the benefits of effective action may be so great to some members of the group that it pays them to work for the group's objective, even if other members fail to carry their load. It is not surprising that special-interest groups are often able to bring a great deal of political pressure to bear on certain public decisions.

But what about those not in the special-interest group? They will pay the bill if the special-interest group is successful. Why can't the majority of citizens effectively counter the political power of a minority group? The answer to this question lies in the fact that the majority makes up such a large group. If a special-interest group is successful in getting everyone else to pay for something that benefits it, the cost will be spread over such a large number that the amount that any one person will have to pay is negligible. There isn't much motivation for an individual citizen to spend time and effort to resist an interest group, even if it were guaranteed that this resistance would be effective. This motivation vanishes completely when the previously discussed impotency of the individual voter is considered. Consequently, we can expect little resistance to the political pressure exerted by special-interest groups to expand government programs.

When an issue comes up that benefits the few at the expense of the many, the elected representatives will be solicited by the few but will hear little or nothing from the many. Each representative knows that a favorable vote on the issue will be recognized and appreciated by those in favor of it and will go unnoticed by those paying the bill. Since getting re-elected and obtaining political IOUs are obviously important to elected representatives, it isn't hard to predict that special-interest groups will be very effective at influencing their voting behavior.

The other side of this coin is that it is difficult to reduce government programs once they are in place. Government programs that arise because of the influence of special interests will generally be perpetuated by the influence of special interests. The elimination of such a program will deny a few significant benefits while saving each general taxpayer but a few dollars in taxes. This explains why it is so difficult politically to reduce government spending, even though the majority of the voters favors such a reduction in general. When people argue for cutting government spending, they invariably have in mind government programs other than the ones that benefit *them*. So any attempt to reduce government spending by isolating one program at a time will meet strong resistance from those benefiting from the program under review and receives little support from the millions of taxpayers who will save but a few dollars each if the program were eliminated.

This suggests that the best hope for controlling government is by presenting a political package that calls for a simultaneous reduction in many programs. No special interest will be willing to sacrifice its program if it expects to be required to continue paying for the programs of others. But if government has grown to the point where people feel that they are not getting their money's worth for the taxes they pay, then many groups will be willing to see their program reduced—if it means some savings on the taxes paid to support everyone else's programs.

An analogy that is not too overdrawn may be helpful here. If most ships are productively transporting goods, the few that are pirates can do very well living off the efforts of others. However, if everyone becomes a pirate, the booty will be small, and all would be better off if everyone went back to shipping goods. But no one will start shipping goods again as long as everyone else remains a pirate. Clearly, the way out of this situation is to get a general agreement requiring everyone to give up piracy.

An example of this principle in action occurred during the early months of the Reagan Administration when President Reagan was attempting to get the Congress to reduce spending on social programs. The opponents to the spending cuts wanted to break up Reagan's budget proposals into specific program areas, with each being voted on separately. Those in favor of the budget cuts insisted on voting on all of the proposed cuts as a package. As a package, the budget cuts were approved. Considered separately, they would have almost certainly been voted down.

7. THE UNFORTUNATE CONSUMER

One area in which special-interest groups have tended to exert political pressure is in legislation to restrict competition. Competition among producers is the great protector of consumers. Competition constantly forces producers to make products that are as pleasing as possible to consumers and to sell them as cheaply as costs permit. If one producer attempts to compromise on quality or to charge a price higher than justified by cost, his or her sales and profits will decline. There are other producers always anxious to expand their sales and profits by offering the customers a better deal than "the other guy." Those firms that are best able to satisfy the desires of the customers will thrive, while those that find themselves rejected will be eliminated.

While competition is good for the customer, it leaves a lot to be desired as far as producers are concerned. There's little chance for large profits when competition is active. Even when a company comes up with a product that's cheaply produced and for which customers are willing to pay a lot, large profits will be short-lived. Others will be quick to respond to profit opportunities by providing the same, or similar, product at a lower price. Recall the ballpoint pen example in Chapter 2. Competition forces firms to be constantly on their toes, looking for better ways of satisfying customer desires, if they expect to survive. So it's not surprising that while businesspeople give the virtues of competition a lot of lip service, most of them can immediately think of several "good" reasons why their particular business should be protected from "too much" competition. Businesspeople are quick to realize the benefits they would reap if somehow they could eliminate some of the competition they face.

Acting by themselves, there is little a group of business owners can do to keep out unwanted competition. But, unfortunately, businesses have had a willing ally in their fight against competitive pressures. The goverment has been all too willing to pass and enforce laws that protect established firms from competition. For example, laws exist that limit the number of taxis, liquor stores, and banks that many cities can have. This reduces the competition that established firms in these businesses face, and as we will soon see, reducing competition increases the prices you pay. We have laws that restrict the flow of thousands of foreign goods into this country. This allows domestic producers to charge higher prices than they otherwise could. For example, it has been estimated that trade restrictions on sugar are costing the American consumer approximately $1\frac{1}{2}$ billion dollars annually.[3]

The benefits of restricting competition in a given industry go to a relatively small and easily organized group of people. This group will be highly motivated to spend time and effort to influence legislation in their favor. For example, there are approximately 10,000 sugar producers in the United States, and the average annual gain each receives from government trade restrictions on sugar is more than $40,000. On the other hand, each consumer buys literally thousands of different items. A price increase on any one of them will have little effect on his or her overall budget. Continuing with our sugar example, trade restrictions on sugar annually cost each of the 230 million American consumers only $6.25 on the average. Because of this, it is extremely difficult to organize consumers to effectively counter special-interest producer groups. Competition can be viewed as a public good, and any attempt to organize consumers to maintain it comes face to face with the free-rider problem. This explains the widely observed fact that government policy tends to be slanted in favor of producers at the expense of consumers.

This neglect of consumer interests by the government has been used as a justification for pushing legislation specifically designed to protect the consumer. Consumer protection legislation is not new. The consumer movement is only part of a long history of efforts to counter business-oriented legislation by giving the consumer some legislative muscle. Unfortunately, this attempt has not been a very successful one. Much well-intentioned legislation designed to benefit the consumer has had exactly the opposite effect. In the next chapter, we examine the results of some consumer protection legislation from the perspective of how it has actually worked, not how it was intended to work.

DISCUSSION QUESTIONS

1. Many colleges and universities require students to pay fees that are used to support various campus activities, ranging from the gay liberation movement to the sports and recreational programs. Would you be prepared to argue that these mandatory student fees are justified because they are used to support public goods? Can you think of any other justification for making support for these activities mandatory? What kinds of problems do you think you would encounter if you attempted to organize a campaign to make support of campus activities voluntary?

2. Can you think of any reasons why providing for public goods will result in more social conflict and controversy than providing for private goods?

3. What would be an argument in favor of a two-thirds or three-fourths majority rule in certain political decisions?

4. The text points out that the pervasiveness of the free-rider problem and the high costs of organizing large groups tend to make large groups relatively weak political pressure organizations. What distinguishes a labor union from other large groups, so that unions are a powerful political force in our society?

5. The most important factor behind a good harvest is the weather. Yet there is little or no effort to teach techniques of weather modification in agricultural colleges. Why do you believe this to be the case? How is this fact related to the widespread political ignorance that one observes?

6. If a government agency were established to protect consumers against the profiteering of pencil manufacturers, what group in the economy do you think would be most likely to influence the decisions made by this agency? What do you think would be the long-run effect on pencil consumers? On pencil manufacturers?

7. The implication of some of the discussion in this chapter is that unlimited democracy can be abused. Give some examples of the unfortunate consequences of empowering the government to do whatever a majority of the voters want done. In what ways does the U.S. Constitution restrain democracy?

chapter 5

Protecting the Consumer against Low Prices and Lifesaving Drugs

1. COMPETITION: FACT OR FICTION?

Consumer protection is provided by active competition among producers. When this competition exists, producers are forced to respond to the desires of consumers. When many producers are actively trying to get the jump on each other by providing a better product or a lower price, the consumer is king or queen. And the producer who ignores them does so at his own peril.

But can we sit back and rely on competitive forces in the marketplace to protect consumers? Many people say no. While acknowledging the desirability of competition, many feel that it is naive to believe that much competition actually exists among producers. To these people, competition is a myth that describes a world somewhere between Fantasyland and Frontierland in that make-believe realm of Disneyland. And there are some very compelling arguments to support their position.

For one thing, effective competition is seen by many as a self-destructive force. The firms that are most efficient at satisfying the desires of consumers do in fact drive out the less efficient firms. But what is the logical conclusion of this phenomenon? Eventually a few firms, and possibly only one, have driven all other firms from the industry. Once this happens, there is little effective competition. Consumers have little choice in picking among producers. They either take the product and pay the price offered by the few existing firms, or do without. This type of self-destroying competition is prevalent when the average cost of production decreases as production increases. As a firm becomes larger and its per unit costs drop, it becomes easier to lower price and drive competitors out of business. When average production cost drops over a large range of output, cost considerations may make it undesirable for more than one or two large firms to supply the entire demand for a product. This leads to a natural monopoly situation, with costs lower than they would be if many firms were attempting to supply the product. But, unfortunately, there will be little or no competitive pressure for these cost savings to be passed on to the consumer.

While competition among producers is usually thought of as requiring a large number of sellers, consumers will benefit from active competition even when the number of producers is limited. As long as there are a few sellers of a product (an oligopoly), competition, if present, will prevent any one firm from really taking the consumer for a ride. Unfortunately, businessmen who find themselves faced with a few persistent competitors have been quick to discover the advantages of cooperating with each other. By coming to a gentleman's agreement regarding price and market shares (forming a cartel), they can avoid the competition that forces them to pass much of their profit on to consumers in the form of lower prices. This tendency for sellers to enter into collusive agreements has long been recognized. In 1776 the Scottish philosopher Adam Smith observed: "People of the same trade seldom meet together, even for merriment and diversion, but the conversation ends in a conspiracy against the public, or in some contrivance to raise prices."[1] Again, it would seem that competition cannot be depended on to provide meaningful protection to the consumer.

Even when there is a large number of producers, each dependent on the whims of the consumer, the effectiveness of competition has been doubted. The consumer has to have a great deal of information if he is to be sure of making the right decision when purchasing a product. Many products are extremely complicated, and it is extremely difficult to judge their relative quality. How many people really know if a Sony Betamax is better or worse than a comparable model from Sharp? Furthermore, the complicated technology inherent in many products makes it difficult for consumers to determine the risks to health and safety to which the user is exposed. Because it is difficult for the average consumer to identify an inferior product, many feel that an opportunity exists for producers to compromise on quality or safety without reducing price.

Also, with many different stores selling the same products, it is difficult to know whether you are getting the best possible price. New products are constantly coming out as a result of new technologies or someone's inventive genius. And unless the consumers have reasonably good information on product prices, as well as on the products themselves, they will be severely handicapped in their effort to direct their purchasing power toward those producers who are offering them the best deal.

The most common source of information about products is provided by advertising. A great deal of valuable information about products, where they are available and what they cost, is constantly being made available to consumers through advertisements. But advertising is believed by many to hamper effective competition. It is argued that advertising establishes strong brand loyalties, and this makes it difficult for new firms to enter a particular market.* And with the threat of new competitors reduced, the existing firms are in a better position to take advantage of the consumer.

These considerations have convinced many that because relying on competition to protect consumers is not very effective, government must regulate business to protect the consumer. But there are good reasons for believing that competition is a stronger force than the above discussion might indicate. Before making a decision on how effective competition really is, we should first consider some additional arguments.

2. COMPETITION FIGHTS BACK

There can be no doubt that competition eliminates the inefficient producer. This survival of the fittest can lead to a strong market position for a few firms that grow very large as weaker rivals fall by the wayside. It should be recognized, however, that most firms survive because somehow they are able to offer the consumer a better deal than less viable firms. The important question is, "How will the consumer be treated by the few remaining firms after they have achieved a dominant position?" Can we expect a large firm to take a cavalier attitude

---

*In Chapter 9 additional aspects of advertising will be discussed, such as the creation of wants and the psychological manipulation of consumers.

toward its customers once it captures a large share of the market? Not if that firm wants to maintain its position. If price becomes high enough, or quality low enough, renewed competition will arise, eagerly providing the consumer a more desirable alternative.

Even if a firm doesn't face competition in the same product market, it has to recognize that there are many substitutes for its product. If the price of steel gets too high, people will start using more aluminum, wood, and plastic as substitutes for steel. Heating oil, natural gas, coal, and wood are all substitutes for electricity. Instead of buying an automobile, an individual can substitute a motorcycle, bicycle, bus tokens, or a home closer to work. Although it has been argued that petroleum is a "necessity" in our society, we have seen in recent years that consumers have been able to conserve in their use of this resource in response to higher prices. Many other examples could be given. Obviously, some substitutes are better than others, and there may be no perfect substitutes for a given good or service. But as the price of one product goes up, consumers will switch to alternatives. The argument that effective competition is restricted by the number of firms in a given industry is misleading. Even if you owned all the movie theaters in the country, you couldn't afford to ignore the well-being of your customers as long as television, sports arenas, romance novels, bowling alleys, and lovers' lanes offer entertainment alternatives to the public.

Large firms can be anything but complacent about customer satisfaction, judging by the difficulty firms have in maintaining their status as business giants. How many people remember Central Leather Company? It's not exactly a household name. But Central Leather was the seventh largest company in the country in 1909. Unfortunately for Central Leather, plastics came along and provided consumers with a good leather substitute for a lower price. American Woolen used to be a huge company with a large share of the textile market. But American Woolen fell from grace when synthetic fabrics made their appearance, giving the consumer an alternative to woolens that wore well, looked nice, and saved money. Pullman Company, a producer of railroad passenger cars, was right behind Central Leather in terms of size in 1909. But along came the automobile and the airplane. As a result, Pullman was the 185th largest company in the country in 1972, according to *Fortune* magazine. Other forgotten industrial superstars of the past include American Molasses and American Locomotive. Nor are examples of withering industrial giants limited to the past. Consider the problems of Lockheed and Penn Central and the current plights of Chrysler and International Harvester, all once large corporations in industries with few competitors. With constantly changing tastes and technologies, no firm can insulate itself against the desires of the consumer. The firm that appears to control the market today may find itself an obscure has-been in the future because of new technologies or the whims of the fickle consumer.

There are strong reasons to believe that competition is likely to prevail when only a few firms dominate a market, despite the advantages of collusion mentioned in the preceding section. A collusive agreement will work to the detriment of the consumer only if strictly adhered to by all producers. If one producer violates the agreement by charging a lower price, those who attempt to maintain the agreed upon price will find their customers deserting them. As a result, they will be forced to lower their prices. The motivation for a firm to break the agreement and lower price is a strong one. The agreed-upon price will certainly be well above the per-unit cost of production, so a profit can be made on each unit even at a lower price. In addition, the first firm that makes small price concessions to its customers will increase sales tremendously. This, along with the fact that collusive agreements are illegal, explains why producers have always had a difficult time enforcing agreements to keep each other from competing for the favor of the customer. This is not to say that collusion among firms is impossible; there is historical evidence that in industries dominated by a very few firms, collusive agreements can be maintained for some time. However, as we will see later in this chapter, effective collusion is less likely to occur in open, unregulated markets than in regulated industries.

But do most customers have enough information to evaluate the quality and safety of products? Fortunately, producers will find it difficult to pass off an inferior product to consumers, even if few consumers take the time or trouble to check quality before buying. A consumer may not be able to determine the quality of a complicated item before buying it, but he or she will certainly be able to judge its performance while using it. And a dissatisfied customer is not going to make the same mistake with the same company. The firm that tries to sell an inferior product at a high price won't last long. Even in the short run a firm will have difficulty unloading inferior merchandise. It isn't necessary that every consumer check carefully for quality before buying. Few companies can afford to ignore the business of those who are careful shoppers. Careful shoppers make up a much larger share of the market than you might expect. Montgomery Ward and Sears Roebuck buy enormous quantities of many different products. Their business depends on these products' meeting certain standards, and these retailers make sure that they do. Sears, for example, has testing laboratories whose functions are to reduce the risk of inferior goods being sold to their customers. Hertz and Avis are large purchasers of new automobiles every year, and they certainly don't qualify as careless shoppers. Many individual purchasers consult publications like *Consumer Reports* and *Consumer Bulletin* before buying items ranging from electric blenders to automobiles. And every consumer benefits from these cautious shoppers. If a firm makes an inferior product for the nonchalant shopper, it will immediately lose the business of the careful one.

The widespread belief that advertising reduces competition by making it difficult for new firms to enter a profitable industry is not supported by careful analysis. Suppose a new firm comes along with a better product or a lower price. Only by providing the consumer with information about its product and price can such a firm hope to break into an established market and effectively compete with existing ones. Advertising gives firms the means to inform the consumer about new products. Therefore, advertising encourages competition by reducing a major barrier to entry: lack of consumer information.

Compare prices in areas where products can be advertised with prices in areas where they cannot. Professor Lee Benham, of Washington University, St. Louis, investigated the price of eye examinations and eye glasses in different parts of the U.S.[2] He found that prices were lower where advertising was least restricted. In Texas and the District of Columbia, where only mild restrictions were placed on advertising by optometrists, eye exams and glasses had an average price of $29.97. In California and North Carolina, where optometrists were not permitted to advertise at all, the average price was $49.87.

A similar study conducted by the staff of the Federal Trade Commission used trained consumers to test the effect of advertising on prices and services in optometry. In states and cities where advertising for such services was restricted, the average eye exam and pair of glasses cost $94.58 as compared with $71.91 in places with no such restrictions. Furthermore, in cities permitting advertising, the average cost of the basic package purchased from an advertising optometrist was $10 cheaper than from one who did not advertise.[3]

Some casual observations support the view that advertising is primarily aimed at introducing new products. Advertising expenditures are normally a much larger percentage of sales for new products than for established ones. For example, drug manufacturers commonly spend 80 to 150 percent of the first year's revenue from a new drug to advertise it. Obviously, this cannot be continued for long. It appears that advertising is more effective in getting consumers to switch to a new brand than it is in establishing strong brand loyalties.

Competition in the real world, while it doesn't provide the ideal degree of consumer protection, does make the consumer's life more enjoyable than it would be in the absence of competition. We can expect a great deal of competition to continue among firms because of the enormous power the consumer wields. This power takes the form of over two trillion dollars of disposable income (income available after taxes are paid) that the consumer is free to direct toward some firms and away from others, as preferences dictate.

3. LEGISLATING CONSUMER PROTECTION

Despite the arguments in the preceding section, the consumer protection provided by free market competition is not considered adequate by many concerned people. There seems to be a persistent and pervasive feeling that business has the upper hand in dealing with their customers and generally takes advantage of them. There are two easily identified reasons for this feeling. First, there is an almost universal tendency for people to feel that the prices they pay are too high and that the compensation they receive is too low. So even if we have a competitive market working with the smoothness of textbook examples, we could expect that most would still feel they were being overcharged and underpaid. There would still be those who think that consumers need additional protection.

Second, there have clearly been instances in which business firms have taken advantage of consumers and countless examples of ineffective, shoddy, or unsafe products. Businesses have been found colluding to fix prices. Numerous innocent consumers have been bilked into purchasing baldness cures and potentially harmful elixirs. Thousands are maimed or killed on our nation's highways and in their workplaces each year. It is only natural to want these evils to be eradicated from our society.

Because of the widespread feeling that business has been cheating the consumer, a lot of political mileage has been made supporting "consumer protection" legislation. This legislation typically has taken the form of industry regulation. Ever since 1887, when the Interstate Commerce Act established the Interstate Commerce Commission (ICC) to regulate the transportation industry, the standard response to abuses or alleged abuses resulting from business behavior has been to regulate the offending industry. We now have the Food and Drug Administration (FDA), established in 1931, whose mission is primarily to control the quality of drugs and cosmetics that are sold to the public. The Federal Communications Commission (FCC) was established in 1934 to regulate the broadcasting industry. The Civil Aeronautics Board (CAB) was established and empowered in 1938 to regulate the commercial air transportation industry. In the 1970s the Occupational Safety and Health Administration (OSHA) and the National Highway Traffic Safety Administration (NHTSA) were authorized to reduce hazards at the workplace and on the nation's highways, respectively. The purpose of these as well as other regulatory agencies is to protect the public by establishing certain standards of business conduct and enforcing them. These standards cover things such as pricing policy, quantity and quality of the product or service provided, and entry into the regulated industry.

These commissions and agencies were founded with the high expectation that they would improve the balance of power between the consumer and business in those areas where it was felt that business had the upper hand. The typical feeling has been that the agency is a diligent and effective overseer of business, with the public interest its sole concern. It is almost always assumed that consumers are better off with these agencies than they would be without them. When the competitive market is not performing ideally, there is a strong tendency to compare the actual performance of an imperfect market with the imagined performance of a perfectly functioning regulatory agency. It is not hard to predict how such a comparison will come out. Seldom, if ever, will the actual compare favorably with the ideal.

Any meaningful attempt to determine whether consumers are in fact better off has to consider the actual performance of regulatory agencies and commissions. But before looking at this performance, it will be interesting to fall back on the discussion in the previous chapter for some insight into how we would expect a regulatory agency to perform.

4. WHO'S REGULATING WHOM?

Many times a regulatory agency owes its existence to public outcries for protection from maltreatment. With strong support from the public and an enthusiastic staff dedicated to the cause, we can expect the new regulatory agency to apply a great deal of pressure to the industry being regulated. The first few years of the agency's existence usually find it forcefully requiring the regulated industry to act in accord with the public interest. But things begin to change before long. The benefits of the agency's work are spread over the general population, a large and diverse group. The benefit of effective regulation to any one consumer is small, since consumer purchases are spread over thousands of different products. Also, consumers know that they will receive the benefit of effective consumer regulation whether they support the regulatory agency or not (the free-rider problem again). Consequently, the public's interest and support tend to diminish, no doubt hastened by the faith that consumer abuses will be corrected now that the regulatory agency has been established. The original leaders of the agency relinquish control to others. The new leaders, who didn't share in the fight for reform, have less devotion to the cause. With enthusiasm diminishing for the agency both from within and without, much of the original zeal for protecting the consumer is lost.

Meanwhile, what is happening on the other side of the regulatory fence? The regulated industry realizes that it will receive a great deal of benefit if it can circumvent what it considers undesirable regulation. Being a relatively small and homogeneous group, the industry soon learns to act in unison to frustrate the agency's regulatory attempts. The agency soon learns that the path of least resistance involves maintaining an open-minded attitude toward the industry's point of view. Eventually the situation evolves to the point where the agency is actually accommodating the industry. This accommodation is encouraged by the fact that officials in the regulatory agency (particularly those who have demonstrated great ability by their "fair" and "reasonable" decisions) are often able to obtain high-paying jobs in the regulated industry. This path to a higher-paying job is well traveled. Follow the careers of a selection of high officials in regulatory agencies after they have left their posts. You will not have to look far before finding a company president who came up through a regulatory agency.[4]

The above pattern is not a totally accurate description of how all regulatory agencies evolve. Industries related to the one directly subject to the regulation discover that their interests are affected by the agency's decisions, and they too may begin to exert influence on the regulatory agency. The objectives of these related industries and those of other affected interest groups may conflict with the desires of the regulated industry, so that the regulatory agency is subjected to the wills of competing interests. In such instances the outcome of the regulatory process may be difficult to predict. For example, in holding the price of natural gas below market equilibrium levels, the Federal Power Commission has been assuring cheap gas not only to households, but more significantly to oil refineries, power companies, and other industrial users of natural gas. A surprising beneficiary of natural gas price controls is the group of pipeline companies, with even greater benefits from the controls than the savings accruing to individual households.[5]

But regardless of how a particular regulatory agency evolves, there is strong evidence that these agencies often end up serving the interest not of the consumer but of the affected industries. This is widely acknowledged by those who have studied the regulative process, even those who have been strong proponents of industry regulations to protect the public. In a *Playboy* interview in October, 1968, Ralph Nader said: "I originally came to Washington with a great deal of hope that the regulatory agencies would champion the consumers' interest, but it didn't take me very long to become disillusioned. Nobody seriously challenges the fact that the regulatory agencies have made an accommodation with the businesses they are supposed to regulate—and they've done so at the expense of the public."

If the life cycle of regulatory agencies discussed above is not generally accurate, the discrepancy may well be the absence of the initial stage of vigorous regulation to protect the consumer. Many times a regulatory agency is, from its very beginning, used by those whom it is supposed to regulate. An interesting piece of evidence for this point is an 1894 letter written by President Cleveland's Attorney General, Richard Olney, to Charles Perkins, president of the Chicago, Burlington, and Quincy Railroad. The purpose of the letter was to discourage Mr. Perkins from lobbying for the dismantling of the newly constituted Interstate Commerce Commission. Attorney General Olney wrote: "The Commission, as its functions have now been limited by the courts, is, or can be made, of great use to the railroads. It satisfies the popular clamor for Government supervision of the railroads, at the same time that the supervision is almost entirely nominal. Furthermore, the older such a commission gets to be, the more inclined it will be found to take the business and railroad view of things. It thus becomes a sort of barrier between the railroad corporations and the people and a sort of protection against hasty and crude legislation hostile to railroad interests. . . . The part of wisdom is not to destroy the Commission, but to utilize it."[6]

As discussed in the last chapter, many industries have been very effective at influencing legislation in their favor and at the public expense. These are the industries most likely to find themselves regulated for the public's protection. But for the same reasons that these industries have been effective in influencing legislators, they have also been effective in influencing officials in regulatory agencies. The regulated industries have been able to use the regulatory agencies to do things they could never have done otherwise. Collusion among firms and uniform pricing are commonplace in regulated industries. Such behavior would quickly be branded illegal in a nonregulated industry. A firm in most regulated industries has to request permission to reduce price. And the request will usually be denied, being interpreted by the regulatory agency as "unfair" competition. The result is that prices in regulated industries are often much higher than they would be if active competition were allowed. Supposedly one of the purposes of regulation is to maintain and protect competition, but it has had just the opposite effect. Protecting competition has been interpreted by regulatory commissions to mean protecting competitors. This means forbidding an efficient firm from lowering price and attracting customers away from less efficient firms.

But if prices are so high, why aren't a lot of new firms attracted into the industry? In fact, many firms are eager to enter regulated industries, but regulatory agencies normally control entry. As a result, regulated firms have been protected against the type of competition that forces business to be responsive to the desires of the consumer.

People who advocate regulation of business to protect consumers are fond of talking about the power of big business and the abuses of this power. But the power of regulatory agencies, with their ability to use the police power of the state, is enormous in comparison with the power of business. We have already indicated that this power has been abused. With this in mind, we turn to some specific evidence on the question of how the regulation of business has affected the well-being of the consumer.

4. SOME EVIDENCE

A good example of how the power of regulatory agencies has been used in practice is provided by the Civil Aeronautics Board (CAB). Fortunately, it is possible to evaluate the performance of the CAB by looking at how airlines operate in the U.S. without CAB regulation. The CAB has no authority over airlines that operate entirely within the boundaries of a state. Because California is a large state, with a heavily populated corridor between San Diego and San Francisco, a major air travel market exists strictly within its borders. Intrastate airlines in California are regulated by the California Public Utilities Commission (PUC). But the PUC has exerted little control over California airlines. It does little to limit entry, and through 1965 it automatically approved requests for fare reductions. In contrast, the CAB has exerted strong regulatory power over price, entry, and exit.

Comparisons between the intrastate airlines in California and the CAB-regulated airlines are revealing.[7] Intrastate carriers in California charge consistently lower fares than those in comparable CAB-regulated markets. Coach fares in California markets during the last eight months of 1965, for example, were 32 to 47 percent lower than would have been the case had CAB regulation been used in these markets. In 1938, when the CAB was established, sixteen U.S. airlines were in existence. From 1938 until the recent moves to deregulate the airline industry, the CAB had not permitted any new airlines to enter the trunk (long haul) service market. Between 1943 and 1950 the CAB did try a local service experiment and issued local service certificates to twenty-one new airlines. However, these airlines were given explicit instructions not to competitively challenge the existing trunk carriers. In comparison, sixteen carriers entered the intrastate market in California during the period 1946 through 1965. Projecting this California experience to the entire U.S. market indicates that, without CAB regulation, somewhere between 100 and 200 carriers would have provided scheduled interstate passenger service in the U.S. between 1946 and 1965. Only twenty-four to thirty-five carriers actually operated during this period.

One might expect this protection of the airline industry to have resulted in higher profits for the interstate airline companies. However, this is not the case. Not permitted to compete for customers through fare reductions, the interstate carriers offered costly services to draw customers from other lines. Planes were often flying well below capacity as airlines offered more frequent flights, fancier meals, and other amenities. Higher wages and salaries for airline employees also drained away some of the earnings that would have been realized from the high fares. Consequently, the interstate carriers experienced lower rates of return on invested capital than Pacific Southwest Airlines, the most successful intrastate carrier in California.

It is not surprising, therefore, that effective political support for deregulation of the airlines could be mounted. During the past several years there has been a phased deregulation of the airline industry which will culminate in 1984 with the abolition of the CAB. In the interim, price competition and the rising cost of jet fuel have resulted in substantial fluctuations in airline fares, and there has been freer entry by competing airlines into established routes. Contrary to the dire predictions of opponents of deregulation, there is no evidence that the health of the industry or the services provided to the customers have suffered during the past several years. During 1977, 1978, and 1979 average fares changed by 5.8 percent, minus 1.9 percent, and 5.3 percent, respectively, at a time when consumer prices generally were rising much more rapidly and fuel costs were increasing at a substantially higher rate. By reducing the percentage of empty seats, the airlines have been able to cut costs of operation to at least partially offset the rise in fuel costs, and, despite the moderate fare increases of the 1977–1979 period, profit rates of the airline industry during those years improved over those prevailing during the early 1970s.[8] The loosening of previous restrictions on entry and fare changes has apparently benefited both consumer and producer interests in this case.

The Interstate Commerce Commission (ICC) provides a good example of how a regulatory agency is more effective in protecting firms in an industry than in protecting the industry's customers. The function of the ICC is to regulate ground transportation in interstate and for eign commerce. The prime justification for its establishment in 1887 was to prevent consumer abuse by the railroads. As pointed out earlier, the railroads quickly found out that they could use the power of the ICC to their own advantage. Paul MacAvoy has made a careful study of the ability of the railroads to successfully collude and maintain pricing conspiracies, both before and after the Interstate Commerce Commission was established.[9] It was found that railroads in the northeastern United States were not able to collude successfully before the establishment of the ICC. A railroad would break collusive pricing agreements, by giving secret rebates, and thereby gain customers at the expense of its competitors. Until the ICC came along, there was no effective way to punish such a "cheater." But the ICC, among other things, made it illegal to give secret rebates. The result was that freight rates were as much as 20 percent higher in the seven years after the ICC was established.

With the spread of the national highway system a new form of competition threatened to undermine the railroads' protected position. The high cost of railroad shipping and the minimal capital requirements involved in trucking enabled long-haul trucking companies to expand into a highly competitive industry. Under the urgings of the railroad industry, trucking was brought under the regulatory umbrella of the ICC, in spite of the fact that trucking was a naturally competitive industry. Under the authority of the Motor Carrier Act of 1935, the ICC has imposed an avalanche of regulations on the trucking industry, leading to severe inefficiences for truckers serving interstate markets. Traditionally, trucking companies have been granted permission to serve only particular routes carrying specified products. This meant that the trucks would often have to return from a delivery empty, and, in some cases, the trucks were not certified for shipment along the most direct route. A company holding the charter for shipment between Los Angeles and New Orleans and between New Orleans and Boston, for example, was not automatically permitted to make deliveries directly between Los Angeles and Boston.

Naturally, we would expect such regulations to lead to higher costs for the regulated truckers, with these costs being passed on to the consumer of trucking services in the form of higher prices. The evidence is consistent with our expectations. A basis for contrast is available because certain agricultural products are exempt from ICC regulations. In the early 1960s a study was made comparing the costs and revenues per intercity ton mile for 25 exempt trucking companies in the mid-Atlantic area with regulated trucking companies operating in the same general region.[10] The nonregulated carriers' costs averaged out at less than one-half the average costs for the general freight carriers regulated by the ICC. Revenues per ton mile were 58 percent lower for the unregulated carriers than for the regulated general freight carriers.

Additional evidence of the effects of ICC regulation is provided by cases in which deregulation has occurred. In 1952 truck transportation of poultry was deregulated. From a study by the Department of Agriculture it was found that, within five years, freight rates for fresh-dressed poultry declined by 33 percent, and the rates for frozen poultry fell by 36 percent. Not only did freight rates drop substantially, but as the study also pointed out, the quality of service improved.

Competition in interstate trucking has been curtailed by a combination of legal rate-fixing cartels and ICC-controlled restrictions on entry into the industry. Trucking firms join rate-fixing bureaus which set the fares for particular shipments. Independent truckers must appeal to the ICC for deviations from these rates. In addition, every trucking firm operating in regulated markets has been required to own a "certificate of public convenience and necessity" carrying the right to service a particular route and product. Such certificates were issued in limited numbers, and they could be bought and sold. Since these certificates were entitlements to enter a highly profitable business, it is not surprising that they carried a sizable premium. In some cases, these certificates have been owned by firms that engaged in no trucking operations themselves, but merely leased the rights to other operators. The primary beneficiaries of these restrictive arrangements have been the owners of the certificates and the laborers employed by the regulated trucking companies. The aggregate value of the certificates outstanding in 1972 has been estimated to be between two and three billion dollars. Comparisons of wages paid to employees of regulated and nonregulated carriers suggest that earnings in the regulated sector are approximately 30 percent higher than in the nonregulated sector.[11]

As we might expect, regulated trucking firms and their employees have strongly resisted efforts to deregulate the industry. However, following the precedent of the CAB, the ICC has taken steps toward loosening the entry restrictions and weakening the power of the rate-fixing bureaus. The Motor Carrier Act of 1980 effectively ratified the action taken by the ICC toward deregulation of the trucking industry. It is still too early to discern the effects of these changes on the trucking operators or their customers.

6. THE NEW FACE OF FEDERAL REGULATION

Up to this point our discussion has focused on regulations designed to protect the consumer from unfair pricing policies by business. There is some evidence from the CAB and the deregulation of trucking that such regulatory activities are now being eyed in a much more critical light. At the same time that there has been a retreat from pricing and entry regulations, which worked to the producers' benefit, there has been a tremendous growth in regulatory activities designed to protect the health and safety of workers and consumers. Federal agencies are now taking strong measures to encourage safety on the job and on our highways, to protect consumers from unsafe and ineffective drugs, and to guard the air we breathe and the water we drink from noxious pollutants. It may appear that we have entered an entirely new phase of regulation, in which the broader interests of society are truly reflected in the process of regulation. It is hard to see how anyone could object to strict enforcement of laws designed to protect the public from unsafe cars, dangerous working conditions, or chemical poisons in the form of drugs or pollutants. Let's take a look at the performance of the agencies that serve as the watchdogs of working conditions, automobile safety, and the drug industry.*

7. DOES IT MATTER WHY YOU DIE?

Thalidomide was a new and very effective sedative introduced in the late 1950s. It was thought to be so free of undesirable side effects that it was widely marketed without a prescription in Germany and with a prescription in England. But soon it was discovered that birth defects were much more prevalent among children of women who had used thalidomide. Well over 5000 deformed babies were eventually blamed on the use of this drug.

Partly in response to the thalidomide disaster, in 1962 the Food and Drug Administration (FDA) was given increased authority and control over the licensing of new drugs in the U.S. Before a new drug can be sold to the public, the FDA has to be convinced beyond all reasonable doubt that it is safe and effective. At first glance it appears that we have finally found a regulatory agency that is actually working for the consumers' benefit. But let's not be too hasty; first glances can be deceiving.

There can be no denying the benefit associated with making sure that drugs are safe before people use them. But, as with any other benefit, drug safety can only be obtained at a cost. Because of this cost, it is just as possible to have too much drug safety as it is to have too little. We can reduce the likelihood that an unsafe drug will be sold to the public only by increasing the likelihood that a lifesaving drug will be withheld from dying patients. The only way of knowing for sure that a drug is safe and effective against a human disease is to allow humans to use it. On the other hand, the only way to be absolutely sure that a new drug will not harm humans is to prohibit the use of all new drugs. Clearly this would be ridiculous, because the additional cost in human life and suffering will exceed the additional benefit long before complete safety is achieved.

As a result of the much stricter requirement for new drugs since 1962, potentially useful drugs have a smaller chance of ever being made available in the U.S. If current regulations had been in force when penicillin was discovered, it is doubtful that it could have been

---

*The protection of our environment will be addressed in Chapter 7.

used. It would probably have remained in the testing laboratory while hundreds of thousands died of infection, because every hamster or guinea pig that receives consecutive injections of penicillin will die within a few days. A drug expert at the University of Rochester, Dr. William Wardell, claims that denying the public just one drug as valuable as penicillin would cause more harm than all the unsafe drugs have caused since modern drugs were developed.[12]

When a useful drug does make it through the maze of FDA regulations, it is only after a long delay. During the 1950s and early 1960s, prior to the enactment of the 1962 amendments, an average of 25 months elapsed from the initial stages of development until the time a new drug was marketed, and the average cost of this process was $500,000. By 1978 the average time for development and approval of a new drug was eight years, and the cost had increased over one-hundred fold to $54 million.[13] Parke, Davis and Company got a license for its Benylin expectorant in 1948 by submitting a fact report of 73 pages. Twenty years later it took 72,200 pages (167 volumes) for Parke, Davis and Company to get a license for the anesthetic Ketalar.

Defenders of the FDA's policies argue that to a large extent the greater delays are simply the result of an exhaustion of the "easy" drug innovations. However, comparisons of drug use and development in the U.S. with that of European countries indicate that this is not the case. Other countries have proceeded with the distribution of numerous drugs that have been withheld or delayed from distriubtion in the U.S. Rifampin, a strong "new" antibiotic, was being used as early as 1968 to treat tuberculosis in Italy. Papers presented to the American Lung Association indicated that Rifampin was effective against TB in cases where existing antibiotics failed. Only after 50 other countries were allowing use of the drug did the FDA permit it to be sold in the U.S. in 1971. While it is difficult to know how many lives would have been saved by an earlier adoption of Rifampin in the U.S., it is known that 119,000 Americans were being treated for TB during the 1968–1971 period, and 17,000 of them died. Close to 80 medicines being used in Great Britain from 1962 to 1971 could not be purchased legally in the U.S. Moreover, many of these medications were rated by British physicians as better than anything available in the United States at the time.[14]

Not only do current FDA drug standards keep existing drugs from being available, they have also discouraged innovation and production of new drugs. From 1951 through 1962 an average of slightly more than 41 brand-new drugs were made available to the public each year. This average was actually increasing, with a yearly average of 43.5 new drugs being introduced from 1959 through 1962. After the strict 1962 FDA requirements, this average dropped immediately and substantially. From 1963 through 1966 an average of only 17 new drugs were introduced each year. From 1963 through 1970 this average dropped to 15.3.[15]

Patients suffering from rare diseases are the most likely to be deprived of effective treatment under the present system. With development costs so high, firms will not be willing to undertake the huge development and testing costs if the market for the product will be small. A rare form of encephalitis, for example, afflicts primarily children and is responsible for approximately 150 to 200 fatalities per year. A drug known as isoprinosine, used in 35 other nations, has been found to arrest the degenerative effect of this disease in 75 percent of the cases. While the drug has been subjected to nine years of testing and the evidence of damaging side effects is nil, the U.S. firm requesting approval for distribution has failed to meet the stringent FDA requirement of "controlled" tests for efficacy.[16] While it is possible to identify cases in which an existing drug has been delayed in its distribution and make some assessment of the suffering that has resulted, we can only speculate about the potential medicines that might have been developed had strict FDA rules not impaired the incentives for innovation.

Unfortunately, the effects of regulatory delays have not been limited to drugs applicable to rare diseases. For the treatment of heart disease, practolol, a so-called beta blocker, is available in Great Britain. Clinical tests have shown that practolol reduces the mortality of heart-attack patients by 40 percent during the two years following release from the hospital. Applying this statistic to the U.S. data indicates that were this drug available in the U.S., deaths by heart attack could be reduced by 10,000 per year.[17] The costs of withholding such a drug from the U.S. market have obviously been staggering. Finally, in 1981 a beta blocker called timolol was approved for use in the United States to treat heart-attack victims, years after similar drugs were available in Sweden and Great Britain.[18]

It appears that drug safety has been pushed too far by the FDA. With present practices, the human suffering that is prevented by keeping dangerous drugs off the market is more than offset by the human suffering that results from not being able to obtain safe and effective drugs. Rather than giving the FDA the authority to deny everyone in the country a given drug, wouldn't it be more sensible to simply provide information about drugs? Consider a situation in which an individual has a terminal illness against which legally available medication has been impotent. Such an individual would most likely be delighted to try a medication that has a chance of being effective, even though it hasn't been sufficiently tested according to the FDA. Who should be the one to make the decision on such an experimental drug—the patient whose life is on the line or a bureaucratic agency?

Many drugs are both beneficial and harmful at the same time. The FDA is currently keeping the drug guanoxan off the market, a drug that reduces dangerously high blood pressure when other medications fail but causes liver dysfunction in some patients.* But given this information, there can be little doubt that the decision to use guanoxan can best be made by individual patients and their doctors on a case-by-case basis. The FDA has in effect dictated that many people should suffer and die from the effects of high blood pressure rather than take a chance on harming their livers.

If individuals were given more freedom in their choice of drugs, even with information available on the safety of drugs, undoubtedly many people would be harmed by unsafe drugs. But people are also harmed because they have the freedom to drive automobiles, ride bikes, smoke cigarettes, go skiing, and heat their homes. The freedom of choice implies the freedom to accept risks.

If people are permitted more freedom to decide whether or not existing information indicates a drug is safe enough for their particular case, dangerous drugs will be quickly identified. It would take only a relatively few cases with disastrous results to give us useful feedback on an unsafe drug. Deaths and deformities could be quickly traced to the use of the drug. The public outcry and publicity would provide a strong warning that the drug should be avoided. Unfortunately, no such feedback mechanism exists when a useful drug is being withheld from the market. Thousands can suffer and die because a little known drug is buried under an avalanche of FDA regulations and there will be no public outcry. There is no signal that tells the FDA to make available drugs that could benefit large numbers of people. This no doubt goes a long way in explaining why the FDA is much too cautious in licensing new drugs. This regulatory agency is not protecting the consumer or the industry it regulates; it is protecting itself. The FDA knows that if it lets one drug out that deforms or kills, the public, the press, and a whole host of congressmen will be on its back. But the FDA also knows that it can up tie a lifesaving drug for years in bureaucratic red tape and get little or no adverse reaction. The blame for those who die and suffer needlessly will not be placed on the FDA.

8. NEW FRONTIERS OF REGULATORY CONCERN

As with the 1962 amendments to the Food and Drug Act, federal regulatory involvement in other areas of public health and safety has been

---

*Guanoxan has been used in England since 1964. In many cases it is the only known means of reducing seriously high blood pressure, and if side effects from this drug do occur, they can be reversed.

spawned by increased public awareness of a serious problem and a political desire to do something about it. There is probably little doubt in the minds of most Americans that regulation of health and safety is a necessary and valuable government service. Nearly 50,000 people are slaughtered yearly on our nation's highways. Injuries on the job accounted for 14,000 deaths and 2.2 million disabilities in 1970, the year of the establishment of OSHA. To deal with these problems, a number of regulatory agencies have been given control over industrial products and processes covering most sectors of the economy. While all will recognize the desirability of lower accident rates on the job and on our highways, it is not at all clear that the policies of the concerned agencies have been effective in achieving these goals.

The performance of OSHA in regulating on-the-job safety and health reveals a great deal about the problems inherent in such agencies. There is a need felt by the staffs of such agencies to show tangible evidence of constructive action and a desire for immediate payoffs from their programs. Within OSHA this has taken the form of setting performance standards and specific equipment requirements rather than broader directives to businesses to reduce the risks of accidents and health problems. In its haste to do something about job safety, OSHA adopted approximately 4400 "interim standards" within a month of its creation. This certainly made it clear to the Congress and the public that OSHA intended to pursue aggressively the job of assuring greater worker safety. However, OSHA has paid considerably less attention to the problems of workers' health, an area likely to show little immediate payoff, since reduced exposure to health hazards will begin to have observable effects only after years have passed.

The costs of some OSHA safety regulations have been enormous, but there is little evidence of a significant reduction in accident rates resulting from OSHA policies. One extremely costly program, for example, has been the regulation of noise levels. A study commissioned by OSHA estimated the nationwide cost of the 90-decibel standard originally adopted by OSHA to be $10\frac{1}{2}$ billion dollars. More stringent protection against hearing impairment in the form of ear plugs and covers could be purchased by individual workers or their employers for only 43 million dollars, but the option of personal protection equipment is not a viable alternative under OSHA's approach to job safety. Coke-oven standards adopted by OSHA in 1975 were estimated to cost between 230 million dollars and 1.3 billion dollars *annually* for a safety program that affects only 22,100 workers.

Certainly the protection of life and limb is something on which we are willing to spend considerable resources. Given that we are spending billions of dollars in the form of physical-equipment purchases and modifications, it would be nice to know that we are getting some return in the form of lower accident rates. Unfortunately, there is little evidence indicating that OSHA has had a significant impact on job-related accident rates. Studies comparing injury rates for OSHA inspected and noninspected plants have failed to detect a significant difference in injury rates between inspected and noninspected firms, and half of these studies indicate a perverse (positive) effect of inspection on accident rates. A study of accident rates focusing on industries targeted by OSHA for special attention showed no significant effect of the targeting program on accident rates in comparison with rates that would have been projected in the absence of this program.[19]

An alternative to the standard setting and inspection approach of OSHA would be the levying of penalties on employers in accordance with the number and severity of accidents experienced at their plants. This would reduce the problem of inspection and give employers an immediate and direct incentive to reduce accidents. Furthermore, firms would be able to adopt whatever safety measures individual experience indicated were the most effective means for reducing accident rates, whether in the form of equipment modifications or simply worker training and awareness programs. If we place a high value on the protection of workers' lives and bodies, a rather high penalty should be assessed on any injury or death. As long as the cost of reducing accidents is less than the penalty, profit-seeking employers will provide safer workplaces. Careless employers will bear the costs of their disregard for their workers' safety, will not be able to compete with safer low-cost (low-penalty) producers, and will either be forced to clean up their acts or get out of business. Such an approach would not only do more to increase worker safety than does the existing method of detailed regulations and inspections; it could be implemented effectively with only a fraction of the personnel now employed by OSHA. Unfortunately, this fact explains why there would be considerable political pressure against any move toward the straight penalty approach to employee safety.

9. STILL UNSAFE AT ANY SPEED?

A surprising instance of costly but apparently ineffective regulation is the mandatory installation of automobile safety devices. Since 1966, in anticipation of the enactment of mandatory standards for 1968 car models, U.S. automobile manufacturers have included as standard equipment seatbelts, impact-absorbing steering columns, penetration-resistant windshields, and other safety devices. There is overwhelming evidence that these devices (particularly seatbelts) have been effective in reducing the number of deaths per automobile accident. Studies indicate that fatalities to car occupants involved in accidents have been reduced by as much as 25 percent as a result of these devices—and this despite the fact that seatbelt usage is far from universal.

Such evidence, however, ignores factors other than safety equipment that are relevant to the determination of the level of traffic injuries and fatalities. To consider the effects of driver behavior as well as safety equipment on traffic fatalities, Professor Sam Peltzman of the University of Chicago studied the primary determinants of traffic deaths prior to the years in which safety devices became standard equipment in U.S. cars (before 1966). By estimating the effect of such driver characteristics as alcohol consumption, vehicle speed, and age on the highway death rate prior to 1966, he was then able to project into the period of mandatory standards the fatality rates that would have prevailed each year *in the absence of safety equipment.* His projections indicated that the actual rate of highway deaths during the 1966–1972 period did not differ markedly from the projected rate based purely on driving characteristics.[20] Apparently, despite the engineering and medical evidence on the effectiveness of the safety devices, actual fatality rates have differed little from what would have occurred in the absence of mandatory safety equipment. This seeming paradox can be reconciled only when one recognizes that changes in driving behavior and driver characteristics that have accompanied the installation of safety equipment have offset entirely any reduction in auto fatalities which would otherwise have been achieved.

Although these results may be astonishing to most people, some degree of offsetting behavior on the part of drivers is entirely predictable, according to economic analysis. Individual drivers are constantly making conscious or unconscious decisions involving the trade-off of risk for convenience. Drivers will be less careful about maintenance of their automobile's safety (tires, brakes, etc.) and will drive with greater speed and carelessness if the costs of doing so are reduced relative to the perceived benefits. When cars are equipped with mandatory safety devices, this reduces the drivers' expected cost of fast or careless driving, and they will trade some of this mandated safety for a little more convenience. Also, as additional safety features increase the cost of automobiles, people are more likely to switch to cheaper but more dangerous forms of transportation, such as motorcycles. Perhaps it is surprising that such changes in driving practices have totally offset the potential gains from the safety equipment, but it should come as no surprise that there has been some decrease in safe-driving behavior and some shift to riskier forms of transportation.

10. IT TAKES MORE THAN GOOD INTENTIONS

When we observe a problem, it is natural to want to do something about it. In the realm of socio-economic problems stemming from business operations, the typical reaction to perceived evils is to establish some regulatory agency to set things right. As we have seen, there is a tendency for certain types of regulatory agencies to serve the interest of industry rather than the general public. In other cases, well-intended regulations fail to address effectively the problem at hand. The structure of the regulatory organization in some cases provides little incentive for the balancing of costs and benefits, leads to the adoption of policies that emphasize apparent action and short-run results, and encourages the use of centralized standards and rules, rather than decentralized decisions. While it is easy to imagine the ideal regulatory agency, we seem to be far from being able to construct one that benefits the public.

Unfortunately, governmental concern for the consumer's well-being does not stop with the regulation of business. In the next chapter, we turn our attention to another form of government regulation that has been justified on the grounds that the consumer needs more protection than will be provided by the competitive market.

DISCUSSION QUESTIONS

1. Suppose you were setting up a trucking firm and were able to purchase a "certificate of public convenience and necessity" permitting your firm to service a particular route. Under the regulatory regime that existed before deregulation of trucking, would you expect to be able to make abnormally high profits? Why or why not?

2. Given that the rate at which new drugs have entered the U.S. market has fallen sharply since 1962, why have the profit rates of established drug manufacturers not been adversely affected? Which drug firms are likely to benefit from restricted rates of drug innovation? Which are likely to be harmed?

3. In the absence of governmental regulation is there any incentive for business firms to provide on-the-job safety? Explain.

4. From the industry's point of view, why is the regulation of price without restrictions on entry not sufficient to preserve high rates of profits? In a growing market, would businesses prefer to have control over prices or control over entry?

5. Often economic regulation creates conditions that make it difficult to remove the regulation. Give an example of this, based on material in this chapter.

6. Recently the president of a large cosmetic firm made a statement supporting more government regulation of the cosmetics industry citing "inferior" products being sold by many new firms entering the industry. Would you give the president high marks for being socially concerned? Why or why not?

chapter 6

Let the Protected Beware

1. CHANGE: INEVITABLE AND UNPREDICTABLE

There's one thing we can be sure of: things will change. Technology will change, allowing many items to be produced better and more cheaply. New products will be developed, complementing the value of some existing products and services, while rendering others obsolete. Growing awareness of previously unperceived constraints, such as the recent environmental concern, will reorder our priorities and cause us to re-examine existing criteria of efficient and desirable production. Tastes and attitudes will change, increasing the importance of many activities and products while reducing the importance of others.

The most casual reflection will generate many specific examples of these types of changes. Electronic calculators are now easier and faster to use, can perform more calculations, and are more portable than anything that was available a few years ago. In addition, the current models are cheaper than anything previously available. The advent of the electronic computer drastically reduced the demand for book-keepers but created an entirely new occupation that has seen phenomenal growth, computer programming. The technology that now makes home computers available at affordable prices will soon be changing how we prepare our income tax, plan our meals, and study for final exams. The rapid increase in the price of gasoline sent the large car the way of the dinosaur as motorists switched to greatly downsized high-mileage cars. With the increasing difficulty for young couples to buy a large unattached house, townhouses have become increasingly popular. Since it is now possible to show the latest full-length movie on your home television set, theatres are finding fewer customers, and we now see several small theatres clustered together showing different movies, rather than one large theatre showing only one movie.

We all know that things are going to change, but none of us knows how or when. None of us had any idea 10 years ago how changing technologies, tastes, attitudes, and life styles would shape the society we find today. Not even the "experts" can boast of a high batting average in predicting the future, and those who can claim some success owe their accomplishments more to good luck than to superior insight. Moreover, *new* knowledge, which fosters economic change, by definition cannot be predicted.

The trend that technology will take depends largely on existing technology and scientific knowledge; therefore, it should be about as predictable as any component of social change. Despite this fact, the record hasn't been very encouraging. H. G. Wells, not a bad prophet, commented in 1902, "Aeronautics will never come into play as a service modification of transport and communications."[1]

The National Research Council published a report in 1937 on technological trends and national policy that failed to foresee antibiotics, atomic energy, jet propulsion, and radar. Yet all of these technologies were either in practical use or under development within five years of the report.[2] There is no reason to believe that the crystal balls being used by today's experts are any better than those available in 1937.

2. THE DESIRABLE RESPONSE TO CHANGE

Mobility in the labor force allows people to respond effectively to change. As we have already noted, when tastes and technologies change, some products become more desirable while others become less desirable, new products are made available, and different skills and productive techniques are required. As these changes occur, it is clearly advantageous to have some mechanism that will channel workers toward those jobs that produce the goods and services most desired.

One possibility is to let the "experts" assign individuals to particular training programs and jobs in the hope that employment will mesh properly with the current as well as the anticipated state of affairs.

However, there are several drawbacks to this approach, not the least of which is the "expert's" demonstrated fallibility in anticipating the future state of affairs.

For the most part, individuals in market economies can prepare for and pursue any occupation of their choice. That choice is based on self-interest. Different occupations have different educational and aptitude requirements. They also have different compensations, psychological as well as financial. Individuals, being experts on their personal likes and dislikes, abilities, aspirations, and motivations, choose an occupation that they feel can be pursued with least cost (remember, the cost of choosing a particular occupation is the value of the forgone opportunity of pursuing the best alternative employment).

Now consider what happens when a change occurs that alters the relative values of goods and services. Some people will be fortunate enough to find themselves well established in favored occupations. They will find more and more individuals or firms seeking their services, each willing to offer added compensation in order to secure their services. The result will be rising incomes and better working conditions for those with the newly sought-after skills.

Others will not be so fortunate. They will find the demand for their services stagnating or declining. Many will find their incomes declining as a result of a smaller wage rate or fewer hours worked—possibly both. Still others will be terminated and will be unable to obtain any employment in their chosen occupation.

The response to this situation is clear. Many of these individuals will find it in their best interest to move out of their present jobs and into those occupations benefiting from rising demands. This is not to say that everyone who finds his or her job relatively less rewarding will switch employments. Obtaining a new job requires such things as obtaining information on specific openings, acquiring new skills, providing information to prospective employers on your talents and availability, and moving to a new location. The costs associated with these activities can be high. However, some workers will find the advantages of a change more than worth the temporary cost. Others will be in the process of preparing for a career, and more future employees will move into those jobs favored by increased demand.

This shift in employment is a desirable phenomenon from the social point of view, although it is motivated not by social concern, but by personal self-interest. The effect is to increase the number of people providing those services that have become more valuable. This shift in employment will continue until the attractiveness of entering the expanding employments is no greater than the attractiveness of other employments. This will come about as a result of increased competition among workers in the areas of growing demand and reduced competition in those employments that have experienced declining demands. As already mentioned, it is not necessary that everyone change jobs in response to changing demands. It takes mobility on the part of only a small percentage of the total labor force to bring about the desirable reallocation of labor when demand changes. Those who do change jobs are those who find it least costly to do so. This is obviously desirable, since it means that satisfying the increased demand in one area is done with a minimum sacrifice of other desirable goods and services.

The information that it is desirable for some workers to shift jobs is given in the form of changes in wages, working conditions, and the general desirability associated with different jobs. But information would not be enough. The increased rewards associated with some jobs and the decreased rewards of others provide the motivation as well as the information needed to move workers in desirable directions.

Having workers with the proper skills in jobs that service the needs and desires of the people is certainly a crucial requirement for the well-being of a society. We have outlined the workings of a mechanism that accomplishes this quite well, with self-interest, not social concern, being the driving force. It is interesting to compare this mechanism with the alternative of letting the "experts" decide the relative importance of different tasks and giving them power to direct the appropriate number of people, through conscription or other coercive means, into or out of different employments. We leave it to the reader who doesn't find either procedure satisfactory to come up with a workable third alternative.

3. A PREDICTABLE RESPONSE

As we have seen, changes in tastes and technologies will increase the importance of some occupational skills. Those who possess these skills will find themselves in enviable positions. Because more and more people are competing for their services, they will find their incomes rising. These fortunate individuals will find that they have more money to spend for better vacations, nicer automobiles, larger homes, more expensive clothing, and so on.

Unfortunately, good things don't last forever. While the fortunate ones are adapting to their improving standard of living, others will be considering adjustments also. Observing the increasing incomes and lavish living of those in the high-demand occupations, others will, as we have seen, start moving into these attractive jobs. These newcomers will increase the supply of workers with the desirable skills, and this will reverse the income rise experienced by those originally possessing those skills. The response of incumbents in the expanding occupation is predictable. They will view the newcomers not only as threats to their improving standards of living but also as undesirable from society's standpoint. The entering workers will be called self-serving opportunists with no concern for the public, poorly skilled and inexperienced, simply trying to line their pockets by taking advantage of the public's increased demand for particular goods and services. The original members of the occupation will, particularly if they are organized in professional associations, see it as their duty to stem the flow of those entering the occupation. By doing so, they will perceive themselves as preventing the inexperienced and unskilled from preying on an uninformed public, and also maintaining the high incomes that are so essential if the highest caliber individuals are to be attracted into the occupation.

Let's consider for a moment the charge that the new workers are opportunists who possess inferior skills. In large measure, this accusation is true. Certainly the actions of the new entrants are motivated by self-interest, not an overactive social conscience. Whether one refers to this rather pervading motivation as an "intelligent reaction to the situation" or "opportunism" depends on whose actions are being discussed—yours or someone else's.

It is generally true that the newer members of the occupation will lack the skills and abilities of the established members. There shouldn't be anything surprising about this. Neither is there anything undesirable about it when the alternative to newer and less-skilled workers is considered. With an increase in the demand for the services of an occupational group comes higher prices, unless the supply of these services is increased. Many of those desiring a given service will prefer an opportunity to obtain a less-experienced worker at a lower price to the alternatives, doing without or paying for the very best. This is no different than giving people the opportunity to choose from automobiles that are grossly inferior to the Rolls-Royce, an opportunity most people are happy to have.

While we can agree with the charges made against the newcomers, it is hard to see these newcomers as serious threats to the public interest. To the contrary, the public is the prime beneficiary of this reallocation of labor into high-demand occupations. A more realistic interpretation is that the charges are the natural reaction on the part of those who find their incomes threatened by increased competition. By reacting negatively to this competition, they are displaying the same type of self-interest that they find so undesirable in the new entrants. But as opposed to what they say and may sincerely believe, it is *their* self-interest that is potentially detrimental to the best interests of the public if it leads to efforts to restrict competition.

Preventing workers from entering attractive occupations is difficult. It is almost impossible for an occupational group to protect itself from the competition of newcomers without special help. Unfortunately, many occupational groups have obtained the necessary help from governments.

4. THE RISE OF PUBLIC CONCERN

Obviously, it would not be an effective ploy for an occupational group to appeal for protection from competition with the argument that their incomes would be higher without such competition. This approach would do little to generate the public support needed to get legislation passed that would restrict the flow of new workers into an occupation. A much more effective approach has been found. Many occupational groups have found that the best way to enhance their self-interest is to argue that certain laws need to be enacted for the public's protection. Because of the technical knowledge required to distinguish the experts from the quacks (so the experts argue), some control over the entry into important jobs must exist to prevent unscrupulous, unethical, and incompetent workers from taking advantage of the public. It isn't hard to find examples of occupational groups whose "public concern" is matched only by their feeling of importance to society.

5. CONTROL OF THE EXPERT, BY THE EXPERT, FOR THE EXPERT

Until the end of the 19th century, few occupations (except the practice of law and medicine) required a license. Casual observation will indicate that this is no longer the case. The following is a *partial* list of those occupations that have been licensed by state law:

- junk dealers
- garage operators
- bail bondsmen
- automobile dealers
- coal dealers
- brick masons
- parking lot attendants
- theatre ticket hawkers
- radio operators
- stockyard commission agents
- veterinarians
- librarians

- threshing-machine operators
- dealers in scrap tobacco
- egg graders
- guide-dog trainers
- pest controllers
- yacht salesmen
- tree surgeons
- well diggers
- potato growers
- hypertrichologists (removers of unsightly hair)
- dock workers
- beauticians
- barbers
- plumbers.

Almost without exception, the demand for occupational licensing comes not from a mistreated public but from the occupational groups. It would be difficult to find an occupational group that hasn't made an attempt to become a licensed profession. During one session of the New Jersey legislature, arguments were heard for licensing bait fishing boats, beauty shops, florists, insurance adjusters, photographers, and master painters. None of these arguments was presented by members of a public who had suffered from incompetents working in these occupations. A bill was introduced in the California legislature that would have licensed astrologers. This bill was motivated, not by complaints from the public, but by the concern of a California astrologer that quacks were entering the field. This particular licensing attempt failed. While public-spirited astrologers failed in their effort to protect the public in California, tree experts have been more successful elsewhere. Tree experts have been licensed in several states at the urging of tree experts. The purpose of licensing tree experts, as stated with a straight face by the Chairman of the Illinois State Tree Expert Examining Board, is "to protect the public against tree quacks, shysters, and inexperienced persons."

We do not want to imply that those advocating the licensing of their occupation are not sincere in their belief that everyone will be benefited by such a licensing requirement. These individuals are undoubtedly earnest in their desire to do good. But as Thoreau once wrote, "If I knew for a certainty that a man was coming to my house with the conscious design of doing me good, I should run for my life."

If entry into an occupation is going to be controlled, who has the expertise to determine competence in that occupation? Obviously the general public can't have anything to say about this. It is their supposed inability to distinguish between the experts and the quacks that made licensing necessary in the first place. It seems only natural that those with experience should be the ones to decide whom and whom not to allow into a licensed occupation. Without exception, as far as we know, once an occupation has been licensed, those who have already demonstrated their competence simply by being employed in the occupation are automatically granted a license. This is true even in those rare cases when licensing results from public complaint about the levels of competency and honesty exhibited by those in the occupation.

Once licensing has been established, those currently employed in the occupation will establish a procedure for keeping out the unqualified. Therefore we should expect a direct connection between the admission requirements of a licensed occupation and the skills necessary to perform adequately in that occupation. Most licensing procedures do, in fact, impose training requirements that relate to the proper performance of the occupational skills. The public generally doesn't have to be concerned about whether those who satisfy the licensing requirements are inadequately trained. In fact, licensing requirements are so stringent that it would be difficult to find someone originally in the occupation who could satisfy them.

For example, consider the preliminaries necessary to obtain a barber's license in many states. Aspiring barbers must take classes that cover such topics as the scientific foundations of barbering, bacteriology, hygiene, histology, histology of the hair, skin, nails, muscles, and nerves, chemical aspects of sterilization and antiseptics, and skin, hair, gland, and nail diseases. This requirement usually requires graduating from a barber school, which generally involves 1000 or more hours of instruction. In Arizona, aspiring barbers must complete 1250 hours of instruction at a certified barber college. This is 50 hours more than is generally required at most law schools. Completion of this program of instruction is not sufficient for licensing, as an additional 18 months of apprenticeship are necessary before the candidate may attempt the qualifying examination. Failure of the examination results in the candidate repeating six months of apprenticeship.[3]

An obvious effect of such practices is the protection of the incomes of existing professionals through restriction of the number of competitors. Two less obvious, but possibly more significant, effects of occupational licensing are discrimination against minority groups and impeding geographical mobility of workers. An analysis of the examinations for cosmetology (beautician) licenses in Missouri and Illinois found that blacks had a 30 percent lower chance of passing a written examination than did whites, even after controlling for such other factors as years of general schooling, sex, and age.[4] Nor did this study find any evidence that the written exam was a reasonable indicator of ability as measured by a practical examination.

Geographical mobility of professionals is reduced by licensing requirements in states that do not practice reciprocity. In dentistry, for example, a majority of states will not honor licenses to practice that have been granted by other state licensing boards. While such restrictions could be justified in professions requiring state-specific knowledge, such as the law, it is difficult to see how such reasoning would apply in dentistry. Not surprisingly, it has been found that nonreciprocity in dentistry has impaired incentives for dentists to migrate and has been successful in raising the average fees charged for dental services in states that refuse to honor out-of-state licenses.[5] The resulting higher incomes of dentists in nonreciprocity states is suggestive of the real motivation behind such restrictions.

Excess training and state-specific licensing programs restrict labor mobility and result in higher prices for consumers, while protecting the incomes of the incumbents in licensed occupations. However, there are other requirements that have little or nothing to do with the ability to perform adequately in the occupation. High ethical standards are a universal requirement for membership in licensed occupations. Few would argue against high ethical standards. But in practice, how are ethical requirements interpreted and used by licensed occupations?

A common ethical taboo is individual advertising. It is considered strictly unethical for doctors and dentists to advertise their services. The canon of ethics in the legal profession prescribes the size of the type that may be used on attorney's professional notices and signs. Members of the funeral industry have determined that advertising the price of funerals is unethical.

One is justified at this point in asking why advertising should be an ethical issue at all. A typical response is that allowing professionals to advertise would encourage manipulation of clients and misrepresentation of services by unscrupulous practitioners. For a better insight, consider an important function performed by advertising. Advertising, particularly price advertising, provides an effective way for new members of an occupation to let the public know that their services are available at reasonable rates. This is certainly an advantage to someone trying to establish a practice. Also, the public benefits, since price competition is encouraged. Recall the discussion on advertising and the price of eye examinations and glasses in the previous chapter. It's not hard to guess how the established members of an occupation, the ones who determine what ethical conduct is, will view the efforts of newcomers to compete away their customers with lower prices.

The use of ethical standards to serve the established members of an occupation is not always so subtle. A mortitician in San Francisco was expelled from the occupation for unethical conduct. He was offering $150 funerals when the going price was $500. The official opinion of the

American Bar Association has been that the "habitual charging of fees less than those established by minimum fee schedules may be evidence of unethical conduct."

It is easy to find examples of other requirements that are even less related to occupational performance than are the ethical requirements. In the State of Georgia, one has to submit evidence of a negative Wasserman test in order to apply for a commercial photographer's license. It's not clear how this safeguards the public—unless it is believed that acquisition of a photographer's license will increase one's sexual contacts. As far as we know, there is no evidence to support this belief. Unless you signed an oath to the effect that you were not a Communist, you couldn't have qualified for a veterinarian's license in the state of Washington in 1956. Apparently even animals have to be protected from Communist propaganda. The non-Communist restriction has been used by many licensed occupations. A 1952 Texas statute forbids Communists from becoming pharmacists. In Indiana a Communist cannot get a professional boxing or wrestling license.

The primary effect of occupational licensing is to benefit the members of the occupation at the public's expense. Once a licensing requirement is established, the experts are able to eliminate not only a great deal of undesirable competition but also competition from the "undesirable." The result is higher salaries and more desirable colleagues for the incumbents, restricted choices for many qualified individuals, and higher prices for the public.

Despite the above criticisms of occupational licensing, isn't it true that some occupations are so important and the public's knowledge so limited that regulation is needed to ensure competence on the part of practitioners? In the next section, we are going to look at an occupation about which this is almost universally believed to be the case.

6. "IMPROVING" MEDICAL CARE BY REDUCING THE SUPPLY OF DOCTORS

When it comes to our own health or that of our families, few of us would care to gamble with substandard medical care. The American Medical Association (AMA) has fought successfully over the past 70 years to restrict the number of medical schools, and hence the supply of doctors, in order to maintain standards of quality among medical professionals. The medical profession claims that the U.S. has a health-care system that is second to none. This top ranking may be justified only if quality is measured by cost.

Effective licensing of physicians and control of the supply of doctors by the AMA began in 1910 with the endorsement of a report on medical education commissioned by the prestigious Carnegie Foundation. State-by-state adoption of the recommendations of the Flexner Report, as this document came to be known, terminated the independent status of the medical schools, leaving them at the mercy of the accrediting arm of the AMA. While, legally, accreditation of medical schools is up to the individual states, approval by the Council on Medical Education of the AMA has meant the difference between life and death for a medical school. With almost complete control over the number of medical schools, the AMA indirectly determines the number of graduates and therefore the number of candidates eligible to sit for a medical licensing exam.

Although the public defense of AMA control over medical schools has been that this control protects the citizenry against unqualified physicians, there is little reason to believe that such was the initial effect. Physicians already practicing medicine were permitted to continue their profession, even if they had been graduated from a discredited institution. There was not, nor is there today, any attempt to weed out incompetents through periodic re-examination. As in other professions, medical licensing serves to protect those already in the club.

The ascendency of the AMA led almost immediately to a substantial reduction in the number of medical schools and medical students and a noticeable shift in the composition of medical school graduates. A former head of the Council on Medical Education and Hospitals describes this change in a manner that imputes to the AMA a motivation other than pure altruism:

> In this rapid elevation of the standard of medical education . . . with the reduction in the number of medical schools from 160 to 80, there occurred a marked reduction in the number of medical students and medical graduates. We had anticipated this and felt that this was a desirable thing.[6]

The number of schools subsequently declined to 69 in 1944,[7] but more insidious was the concentration of this decline in particular groups. The number of black medical schools declined from seven to two over this same period. The percentage of physicians who were black peaked at 2.7 percent ten years after the publication of the Flexner Report and declined to about half that percentage 1969.[8] The actual number of female physicians was lower in 1940 than at the time of publication of the Flexner Report.

Supply restrictions have undoubtedly contributed to the high cost of physicians' services and lifetime incomes of doctors. It has been estimated that an individual's investment of time and money in a medical education pays a return of 24 percent. A medical school admission is worth between $50,000 and $125,000 in lifetime earnings over what an individual might otherwise expect with a bachelor's degree.*[9] To some extent the large monetary incomes of physicians are offset by longer working hours, a higher probability of military service at relatively low pay, progressive income taxation, and differences in life expectancy.[10] However, the fact that doctors work long hours and pay high taxes provides little consolation to patients who face steep fees for physicians' services.

To some extent, the high cost of doctors' services leads to the substitution of other services that are not in such restricted supply. People suffering some malady will seek out such alternatives as home remedies, over-the-counter drugs, health foods, chiropractors, and faith healers. By raising the cost of treatment by an M.D., and thus leading people to rely on questionable substitutes, restrictions on the supply of physicians tends to reduce the overall quality of health care in this country.

It can also be argued that the AMA's control over the profession has retarded the advancement of medical knowledge and practice in this country. The Flexner Report promoted a particular form of medical education modeled after the program at Johns Hopkins University. Alternative approaches to medical education were suspect and not likely to receive AMA endorsement for accreditation. The type of control that is exerted over doctors once they enter practice discourages them from engaging in any medical practice or medical research that isn't generally accepted by the profession. The importance of maintaining an approved status with the local county medical society is a strong deterrent to attempting anything that deviates from the conventional wisdom. While this may be a "safe" approach, it isn't one that fosters the maximum advance in medical knowledge. Many, if not most, of the advances that have occurred in science and applied fields have been the result of individuals attempting something new, often at the expense of being ridiculed by the more respectable members of their field.

A good example of how the pressure to be the "right" kind of doctor has impeded new and potentially useful medical practices is provided by the resistance to the use of acupuncture in this country. Although acupuncture has been known of for years, until as recently as 1972 any physician suggesting its use would have been ridiculed seriously by the profession. It was not until the summer of 1972 that the use of acupuncture was reported in United States' hospitals. It would be difficult to find a licensed physician who will treat a patient with acupuncture,

---

*These estimates are discounted present values, which take into account the timing of the expected lifetime earnings stream as well as its magnitude. A medical doctor, for example, must forgo four years or more of earnings before receiving large annual earnings from practicing medicine.

although many feel that in some cases it can be a very useful medical technique. Because of this, many patients desiring acupuncture treatment have turned to Chinese acupuncturists, many of whom have medical degrees from Chinese universities. A large number of these patients report relief for the first time from assorted ailments, even though they have undergone years of conventional treatment. Despite the satisfaction expressed by the patients, these Chinese acupuncture clinics have been shut down in many areas, on the grounds that the acupuncturists are practicing medicine without a license.

Even orthodox practitioners from abroad face serious obstacles to licensing in the United States. Five states in the U.S. have refused to grant medical licenses to foreign physicians, and several additional states specify particular specialties for which licenses will not be granted to foreigners. Seventeen states require more clinical experience of foreign-educated physicians than they do of those trained in the U.S.[11]

But despite obstacles, increasing numbers of foreign doctors have been licensed to practice in the United States. Approximately one out of every six doctors currently practicing in the United States received training outside the United States and Canada. This trend has not gone unnoticed by the AMA. In their efforts to impose further restrictions on the licensing of foreign doctors to practice in the United States, concern is being expressed about attracting doctors away from other countries where they are more desperately needed. While this may be a legitimate concern, it is easy to doubt that it is the AMA's primary motive for wanting to restrict the entry of foreign doctors into the United States.

Not only does the AMA exert tremendous control over entry into the medical profession, it maintains a great deal of control over physicians once they do enter practice. The source of this control comes primarily from the ability of the AMA to keep a doctor from having access to hospital facilities. Hospitals are also approved by the Council on Medical Education and Hospitals. As in the case of medical schools, AMA approval is a life-or-death matter for a hospital. If a hospital is to be able to survive the competition, it has to have the services of low-paid interns. Medical licensing laws generally require intern experience in an approved hospital before admission to practice. With rare exception, only approved physicians are permitted to practice in approved hospitals. Since approved hospitals are the only ones available, being an approved physician is quite important. Generally speaking, obtaining this approval requires that a doctor be a member in good standing of his or her county medical society.

Needless to say, doctors find it to their advantage to conduct themselves in a manner that is considered proper by fellow doctors, the other members of the county medical society. This situation obviously provides an effective way of making sure that the behavior of individual doctors conforms to the proper ethical and professional standards. For example, newcomers, no matter what their past status in the profession, have to serve a probationary period when they join many county societies. The reason for this practice is readily understood: doctors new to an area will have the greatest temptation to cut prices or engage in other highly "unethical" practices designed to take business away from the established practitioners.

Physicians also find membership in a county medical society a decisive advantage in protecting themselves against malpractice suits. A doctor in good standing with his society will normally find an ample number of expert witnesses available to testify in his defense if he is charged with malpractice. The plaintiff, however, will not have such an easy time obtaining the services of expert witnesses. There was a case reported in 1946 concerning a surgery patient who was unable to obtain an expert witness in a case where the surgeon failed to remove a sponge from the patient before sewing him up. Doctors who are not in the good graces of their local society will find the situation exactly reversed. This undoubtedly explains why society members are able to purchase malpractice insurance at a much smaller cost than nonsociety members. If you are thinking of a malpractice suit, make sure your doctor isn't a member of the local medical society.

But without medical licensing, what means are there to protect the public from incompetents? First, notice that medical licensing doesn't protect people from inferior medical treatment. Because of the shortage of well-trained doctors, many people end up not receiving any medical care at all or seeking out the services of those with less training than the AMA considers mandatory. The rapid increase in the number of chiropractors and osteopaths is not unrelated to the restrictions the AMA has imposed on entry into the medical profession.

The best way to protect the public from inferior medical care is to increase the supply of well-trained doctors. This could best be done by breaking the AMA's hold on medical schools and hospitals. We would expect to see an immediate increase in the number of medical schools if their survival did not depend on the approval of the AMA. This increase would be the natural response to the large number of people who desire to enter the medical profession, many of whom are now frustrated in their efforts. This would result in an increase in the number receiving medical training.

The AMA would argue that without its approval being required, the quality of many new medical schools would be poor. It is true that many would not meet the high standards which the AMA now imposes on medical schools. Consequently, we would expect large differences in the quality of those trained in the different schools, with some being more qualified to practice medicine than others. The logical question at this point is what controls should there be to ensure that only the competent will be allowed actually to practice?

Consider for a moment this situation: the only requirement for practicing medicine is that the practitioner has to make public his or her qualifications. Fraudulent misrepresentation of one's qualifications would be a criminal offense. Many aspiring doctors would still go to the finest medical schools and become highly trained specialists. Some would take less training and become general practitioners, many with training comparable to that of current general practitioners, but many with less training. Others would become chiropractors, osteopaths, acupuncture specialists, and so on—again, some having more and better training than others. Still others would get little training at all and become faith healers, witch doctors, and medical astrologers. We can be sure that many veterinarians would attempt to broaden their practice to include human as well as animal patients.

How would consumers react to a situation such as this? It is a safe bet that they would exert some effort to check into the qualifications of a doctor before entrusting their bodies to him or her. Even under the present arrangement, people usually don't pick their doctors completely at random. Unfortunately, the AMA has been able to create such a mystique about physicians that many people just assume that all of them are totally competent and make no effort to check on their abilities. Any objective evaluation would demonstrate a wide range of competence among physicians. Remember, once doctors have been admitted to practice, there is little effort made to re-examine the currency of their medical knowledge, no matter how long they practice. Without a licensing requirement, the value of checking into the qualifications of a doctor would become much more obvious. It would become worthwhile for newspapers or other local media to check into the credentials of the local practitioners and provide their audiences with detailed information relating to the competence of these doctors. This is only one possibility. Undoubtedly, other sources of information would become available once the usefulness of this information became apparent.

Doctors would be under added pressure to provide excellent medical care at reasonable rates once licensing was dropped. Without the AMA having the power to restrict the number entering the medical profession, doctors would be faced with much more competition, and physician's fees would be lower. Incompetents would soon be discovered, and the lack of clients would force them into other endeavors. Without the AMA's control over the hospitals, the importance of being approved by the county medical societies would diminish, as would the present reluctance of doctors to serve as expert witnesses against other doctors in malpractice suits. While it can be argued that this would lead to abuses, at least from the doctors' point of view, there can be no doubt that it would make doctors more careful about sewing up patients before removing sponges and other assorted paraphernalia.

Even though the elimination of medical licensing would increase the pressures on doctors to perform competently, it would almost certainly result in an increase in the range of competence in the medical profession. But with information available on the abilities and performances of different doctors, this wider range of competence is desirable. It would give the public a wider range of quality from which to choose. Individuals will have the option to choose lower-quality medical care at modest fees or much higher-quality service at higher fees. Certainly a wide range of quality is recognized as desirable when one is choosing stereo equipment, automobiles, ballpoint pens, houses, clothes, home appliances, power saws, and many other items. For example, many prefer to realize the savings that go with purchasing a smaller, poorer-quality car so they can adorn themselves in the latest fashions. Some will argue that this isn't wise, since small cars are much more dangerous to drive than bigger, more expensive ones. Despite the fact that there is never a shortage of people around who know what's best for you, it's your preferences that are important when making purchasing decisions. We are all better off when we have a wide range of quality and prices from which to choose.

If a wider range of quality and prices existed in medical care, as it would without the licensing requirement, we would expect to see people taking advantage of the additional options that would be available. For example, if someone needed his appendix removed, he could seek out either the services of a surgeon trained at the prestigious Johns Hopkins Medical School or one trained primarily as a veterinarian. Even though the removal of the AMA's entry restriction would reduce the price of all medical care, the savings associated with the latter choice would be considerable. We can be sure that many would still choose the Johns Hopkins surgeon. But we can be just as confident that many will choose the veterinarian.

Before you say only a fool would let a veterinarian carve on his body just to save a few dollars, you might ask yourself if this is any different from driving a small compact or riding a motorcycle because the expense of a large car is too high. This is certainly taking a risk that could be avoided by spending a little more money. The fact is that all of us do things that involve substantial risks, simply because they are enjoyable or because the safer alternatives are more expensive or less convenient. As an example, what percentage of the population do you think uses across-the-shoulder seat belts? It's approximately 10 percent, despite the fact that wide-spread use would save thousands of lives every year.

If we let the AMA make the decision as to the type of medical care we get, we'll continue to have nothing but Cadillac doctors. If the public could make this decision, we would still have Cadillac doctors, but we would also have Chevy, Volkswagen, Honda, and even Schwinn doctors, as well.

One can agree with the main points of the above discussion and still legitimately argue that the requirements for entering medical practice should be more demanding than simply making known one's qualifications. Very likely there's an entrance policy somewhere between that which the AMA has established and the one just discussed; and it would be preferable to either extreme. However, barring a national policy of enriching entrepreneurs with M.D. degrees, there is no possible justification for allowing the AMA to continue its stranglehold on the medical profession. A policy of essentially free entry into the medical profession would be much better than what we have now.

Licensing by the medical profession has been almost universally endorsed by the public. If strong controls can be justified for any occupation, they can be justified for the practice of medicine. Conversely, since a case can be made for eliminating the control by the AMA over the medical profession, how much better the case must be for eliminating the control by committees of barbers, plumbers, bricklayers, beauticians, well diggers, egg graders, and tree surgeons over entry and practice in their respective occupations.

DISCUSSION QUESTIONS

1. Economists claim that some unemployment is not only inevitable but desirable as well. Based on your reading of this chapter, how would you justify the desirability of some unemployment?

2. It is often argued that automation will eventually eliminate almost all jobs, and unemployment will become a larger problem through time. Considering the pervasiveness of scarcity, what do you think of this argument? Some people say that automation eliminates some jobs but creates others. How would you modify this statement with what you learned from the first two sections of this chapter?

3. Discuss the similarities, as you see them, in the effects of industry regulation discussed in Chapter 6 and occupational licensing discussed in this chapter.

4. What advantages do M.D.'s have in increasing their incomes by restricting entry into their profession that Ph.D's in economics and most other academic disciplines don't have?

5. Discuss the statement, "Self-interest leads to social good when it is pursued in the market place, but has the opposite result when pursued through the political process." Give examples that support this view. Can you think of examples that don't support it?

6. How do you think an M.D. who strongly supports the free enterprise system would respond to our discussion of the AMA?

7. With all due respect to your campus health center, the professionals there are probably not as competent as those at the Mayo Clinic. Yet the next time you feel poorly you will surely check with the campus doctor, not fly off to the Mayo Clinic, even though what you have may be potentially fatal and need the quickest and most expert attention. Why is this? Would you feel better off if your campus clinic were closed down and you had to go to one of only a few prestigious medical centers when you want medical treatment?

8. What is the worst thing that you think could happen if you were not being protected by the licensing restrictions on barbers and beauticians? Could it possibly be as bad as a punk-rock haircut?

chapter 7

Pollution, Private Property, and Politics

1. THE TWO-BY-FOUR-TO-THE-FOREHEAD APPROACH

You may have heard the story about the farmer who couldn't get his mule to obey orders. In desperation he asked a neighbor for help. The first thing the neighbor did was belt the mule across the forehead with a two-by-four. When asked why he did this, the neighbor explained that before you can teach a mule anything, you first have to get its attention.

The same principle applies when trying to make a point to an unreceptive audience. Getting their attention is often the most difficult step. Certainly this approach might be effective when it comes to generating concerns over environmental pollution. Some of the things we are doing to our environment definitely qualify as real attention getters. As a result of heavy concentrations of chemical pollution in the Cuyahoga River near Cleveland, the river has actually caught fire. Large quantities of toxic waste, much of it containing known carcinogens, is dumped into our waterways every day. Thousands of tons of potentially choking hydrocarbons are being discharged every day into the atmosphere over cities like Los Angeles, Denver, and Houston. It is widely believed that industrial pollution is responsible for acid rains that are killing almost all of the fish in many of the lakes in the northeastern U.S., eastern Canada, and some parts of Europe. Some scientists predict that thermal pollution from burning fossil fuels could eventually increase the earth's average temperature enough to melt the polar ice caps, raising the sea level and thus submerging coastal cities like New York and Boston.

2. TOO MUCH OR TOO LITTLE POLLUTION?

Unfortunately, after stories of these environmental outrages have captured our attention, what action we should take remains a mystery. For one thing, there is nothing in the above stories that, by itself, dictates that anything should be done. While most of us undoubtedly react negatively to tons of toxic waste being dumped into the Niagara river, there is no conclusive data that indicate whether too much or too little is being dumped into it. Let us explain.

The use of our environment provides us with all that we have—including life itself. The oxygen in the atmosphere sustains our life. It also fuels the combustion that keeps us warm and powers our automobiles and airplanes. Our water, so necessary for life, is also essential in the production processes that generate the goods and services on which we all depend. A list of the desirable uses of our environment could be expanded indefinitely. If such a list were expanded, it would not be complete without mentioning the use of the environment for waste disposal. Every productive act we engage in or benefit from—whether breathing in and out, growing wheat, or generating electricity—creates unwanted byproducts that necessarily have to be discharged into the environment. The environment's ability to assimilate these wastes is no less important than its ability to generate oxygen.

Fortunately, the assimilative capacity of the environment is enormous. Many forms of waste are readily dispersed by wind and water and are broken down through bacterial action and decay. This assimilative capacity is an extremely valuable resource, and the extensive use of it has been an important factor in the growth of our country and the well-being of its people.

Unfortunately, the assimilative capacity of our environment is limited, as are all other resources. Even those wastes that are readily assimilated can overload the environment when dumped in large enough quantities, causing serious environmental disruptions. Also, many waste products either can't be broken down by natural processes or they decompose very slowly. Aluminum cans, glass bottles, DDT, certain radioactive isotopes, and many plastics are examples of the latter.

Because the assimilative capacity of the environment is limited, using this resource is no different from the use of any other resource: it has a cost. When a firm uses a river to discharge waste from its production process, it is reducing the usefulness of this river for alternative uses such as swimming, drinking, fishing, or assimilating the wastes of a downstream firm. These represent opportunities that are forgone because of the firm's discharges into the river. And it is the value of the most important of these forgone alternatives that determines the cost associated with a firm's use of the river as a waste-sink. This is nothing more than another example of opportunity cost. There is an environmental opportunity cost associated with any activity that dumps wastes into the environment. This is true whether we are talking about an oil refinery dumping sludge into a river, an electric-generating plant discharging nauseous smoke, or a person smoking in a crowded classroom.

On the other hand, we can reduce environmental pollution only at the cost of sacrificing desirable activities and products that cause pollution. To say that we all value a cleaner environment gives no guidance whatsoever in deciding whether or not the environment should be a little bit cleaner, or a little bit dirtier. Surely we all want a cleaner environment. But we also want more housing, entertainment, medical research, fine wines, fast-acting detergents, warmth in the winter, air conditioning in the summer, convenient and safe transportation, attractive clothing, and the list goes on and on. The relevant question is, what is the appropriate combination of environmental purity and all of the other desirable things we enjoy, given that we can have more of one only at the cost of sacrificing some of the others?

It is not easy to answer this question. But it is immediately possible to say something about the desirable combination that would be described as appropriate. This combination will not contain as much of anything as we would ideally like. Ideally we would consume each product up to the point where one more unit was worth nothing to us. But because of the sacrifice involved in expanding our consumption of clean air, gourmet food, or whatever item you care to consider, it will never make sense to continue consuming it until the additional unit is worth zero. So even if we were enjoying the appropriate level of environmental quality, there would remain, at least at times, unpleasant and unhealthy levels of environmental pollution.

This raises the question: just because we have more pollution than we would ideally like, is there any reason for believing that we have too much? Isn't it just as possible that we are not suffering from enough pollution in that the additional production possible with more pollution would be worth more than the benefits sacrificed in environmental quality?

This is a serious question, and it cannot be answered with appeals to horror stories about the environmental and health hazards that come from existing levels of pollution. As accurate and horrible as such stories may be, they consider only one side of the coin—the side that tells us about the benefits from reducing pollution. In order to make an informed judgment as to whether or not there is too much pollution, we have to know something about the costs of reducing it. Unfortunately, as we will see, the costs and benefits from reducing pollution are difficult to dermine. This does not mean, however, that we cannot reach an informed judgment on the question of the appropriateness of current pollution levels. On the basis of standard economic analysis, we can say that we are suffering from excessive pollution. The concern over the quality of our environment is well founded.

3. THE MESS AND THE MYTHS

Before effective measures for reducing pollution to appropriate levels can be determined, it is essential to understand the underlying causes of excess pollution. We find no shortage of answers. Most people who are concerned about the environment have strong views on the causes of environmental decay.

There are those who see the fundamental problem as mass ignorance. If people only knew about the polluting, energy-consuming process that is required to produce the detergent to make their whiter-than-white wash the envy of the neighborhood, they might hesitate to use it. They would surely be persuaded to revert back to old-fashioned, but environmentally neutral soap if they were additionally informed that their detergent contains a benzene that can be transformed into carbonic acid, a poisonous material that kills fish and other aquatic life.

There are others who see a more deeply rooted problem. They feel that people's lack of concern for other living organisms explains their polluting behavior. The factory owners who generate air pollution are certainly aware of the damage they are imposing on others. The problem is that they are too calloused to care about anyone's welfare but their own. To those who feel such insensitivity is the primary cause of our problems, the salvation of our environment and ourselves is seen to depend on some type of cultural or spiritual revolution: If people can be made more sensitive to others and to nature, then effective environmental action will be forthcoming.

Many are convinced that the fundamental cause of pollution is a system of production based on private ownership, capitalism, and greed. When production decisions are in the hands of those who will do anything for a profit, we have to expect our forests to be ravaged, our waterways to be polluted, and our atmosphere to be fouled. Those with this point of view are likely to believe that only through the abolition of private property, coupled with rational central planning—with production for use and not for profit—can we expect to save the environment.

Another commonly heard argument is that our great affluence is the major cause of our problems. With more and more products being produced, larger quantities of production byproducts have to be discarded. The result is that our environment is being used increasingly as a dump. Only a wealthy country can afford such polluting luxuries as two and three cars per family, jet travel, air-conditioned houses, and disposable paper towels. Those who see affluence as the fundamental problem are likely to call for a society poorer in material wealth but richer in terms of the really important things, such as a clean and natural environment.

Another cause that is often identified is modern technology. Reliance on synthetic fabrics, nitrogen fertilizers, electric appliances, high-compression automobile engines, plastics, and many other items has increased the use of technologies that have a strong impact on the environment. In this view, either discarding or drastically altering our current technology is a necessary prerequisite if environmental quality is to be improved.

Finally, we hear from those who put the primary responsibility on an increasing population. Those who blame population argue that every child who is born in the United States will consume and pollute millions of gallons of water, demand hundreds of thousands of kilowatt hours of electricity, and burn up thousands of gallons of gasoline. Providing for this consumption places a tremendous burden on the environment, and those who advocate population control feel that easing this burden will require strong measures aimed at arresting population growth.

There is a certain element of truth in all these points of view. There is also a certain element of myth. The myth arises from the tendency to view them as the fundamental causes of our environmental problems.

It's certainly true that there is a great deal of ignorance about the environmental impacts of our actions. And the more knowledge we have about our ecosystems, the better. But it seems naive to expect people to incur voluntarily a great deal of personal expense and inconvenience to protect the environment, even if they are aware of the destructiveness of their behavior. It might be argued that this simply demonstrates the callousness of people and points to the need for fundamental changes in their attitudes toward others. Describing the human race as calloused and insensitive may be useful in some contexts, but it doesn't go far in explaining why people continue to dirty the water and air. Even the most concerned and sensitive environmentalists drive automobiles, use incandescent lighting, and wear synthetic fabrics—all actions that contribute to our environmental problems.

It can't be denied that businesses being run for profit have been substantial contributors to our pollution problems. But recognizing this is certainly not the same as providing a justification for junking our system of private ownership and free enterprise and replacing it with a system of production directed by central authorities. To the contrary, it is private ownership and production that provide the best framework for solving our pollution problems. Abolishing private property would result in more, not less, environmental decay. In fact, as we shall see, the major reason for the problems we are currently experiencing is the absence of private ownership rights to some of our most important resources. Ample evidence of the failures of central planning to protect the environment is provided by the Soviet Union.* A powerful governmental agency can rape the environment on a much grander scale and with less concern than can practically any private firm, as any Sierra Club member who has ever locked horns with the Army Corp of Engineers or the Bureau of Land Management can tell you.[1]

Certainly, affluence and technology, which tend to go together, are important considerations in a discussion of pollution. It takes wealth and know-how to generate waste in the quantity we do in the United States. However, it is much more reasonable to use our wealth and technology to clean up the environment than to attempt a cleanup by reducing our affluence and technical ability. And certainly, poverty is no guarantee of a clean environment—indeed, quite the opposite. In most underdeveloped countries filth runs in the streets, and the advice "don't drink the water" is worth heeding.

In some ways, however, those who blame our wealth and technology for our environmental problems are absolutely correct. With improved know-how, it has become possible to do something about pollution. Undesirable situations aren't usually thought of as problems until there seems to be some possibility of changing them. Dying of old age, for example, is recognized as a fact of life that well-adjusted people simply accept—not because it's desirable, but because there doesn't seem to be anything that can be done about it. However, if medical research demonstrated the feasibility of maintaining health indefi-

---

*The problems of protecting the environment in socialistic countries will be discussed further in Section 8.

nitely, death from old age would immediately become a national problem. The same is true of pollution. Our advanced technology and wealth have made it possible to treat sewage and provide clean drinking water to the masses. As a result, poor sewage and water conditions that are accepted as facts of life in many countries would be totally unacceptable here.

Also, it takes a minimum level of affluence before environmental concern can be generated to the point where pollution is recognized as a pressing problem. When one is relaxing in an air-conditioned room and has a full stomach and all the modern conveniences that come with affluence, many things become problems that would be of no concern to those whose poverty status make basics such as food, clothing, and shelter the primary concerns. For example, many in the United States are concerned about the build-up of DDT in living organisms and see this as a serious problem. Unfortunately, this concern is a luxury that poor countries can't afford. In countries such as India, people are much less concerned about DDT in their systems than they are about dying from malaria or malnutrition, problems the use of DDT helps overcome.

The population controllers also have a point. People do pollute and the fewer of them we have, the nicer the environment will be for the rest of us. Unfortunately, trying to clean up the environment through population control is an indirect approach and isn't likely to be very effective from many environmentalists' point of view. Historically, the only effective means of controlling population growth have been extreme poverty, diseases, plagues, war, and high per capita wealth. Only the most enthusiastic depopulator would recommend the first four of these to protect the environment. That leaves high per capita wealth as a check on population growth. However, this will seem equivalent to running on a treadmill to those who see affluence as a major cause of pollution.

Even if population growth could be stopped or reversed in a way acceptable to all, it wouldn't, by itself, have much effect on pollution levels. Between 1946 and 1970, for example, population in the U.S. increased approximately 45 percent, while pollution levels rose from 200 to 2000 percent during the same period.[2] Even if we had experienced zero population growth since 1946, we would still have experienced substantial increases in pollution. It is doubtful that programs encouraging zero population growth will do much to alleviate our environmental problems. Vasectomies are great for preventing babies, but they don't do much to prevent pollution.

All the commonly identified causes of environmental decay are important to our comprehension of the pollution problem. But they do not either singly or collectively provide us with any real understanding of the fundamental cause. An important step toward understanding is taken by recognizing that many of our important environmental resources are not owned and controlled by individuals as transferable private property.

4. "FREE" GOODS CAN BE VERY COSTLY

As should already be clear from reading the first three chapters, there are important advantages realized when resources are privately owned and can be bought and sold in the market place. The use of privately owned resources requires paying (or forgoing) a price that reflects the value of the resource to others. This price not only informs each user of the value of the resource in alternative uses, but also guarantees that this information will be taken fully into consideration. No one will have a motivation to increase his or her use of a resource unless it is worth at least as much to that individual as it is to others. Privately owned resources will not be excessively used.

Those environmental resources such as our waterways and airsheds that, among other things, necessarily serve as repositories for pollutants are, by their physical characteristics, not easily parcelled out to individuals as privately owned and controlled property. Because these resources are not privately owned, their use is not governed by market exchange and prices. All of us make use of the commonly owned environmental resources for dumping our wastes, and we do so in the absence of information on the value of these resources to others. And even if somehow we could know this value without market prices, we would have little motivation to take it into consideration.

Consider, for example, your decision to drive your car to work or school. This requires the use of resources that are valued by others, such as gasoline, oil, and the labor required for automotive upkeep. But because these resources are privately owned and easily exchanged, you give full consideration to their value to others in the prices you pay. This is not the case with the air into which you vent your exhaust as you drive your car. The value others place on the clean air you foul is not made known to you, because the atmosphere—not being under the control of private owners—is not allocated among competing uses by market exchange. There is no price on the use of clean air that informs you of its value to others. And even if somehow you did know this value, in the absence of a price that you have to pay, there is little motivation to take it into consideration. The benefits that are generated by your polluting activities accrue entirely to you. The costs that result from your polluting activities are imposed almost entirely on others. Not surprisingly, you will put greater weight on the benefits from your polluting than you will on its costs.

The capacity of the commonly owned environment to serve as a waste-sink is seen by each of us as a free good. We are motivated to continue dumping our crud into the environment as long as the value of doing so remains positive, regardless of the value that others have to forgo as a consequence. The use of "free" goods can be very costly. From the perspective of the efficient allocation of our resources, our environmental resources are overused as waste-sinks relative to their use for providing environmental quality. Pollution is excessive.

This suggests that a solution to excessive pollution may be found by somehow establishing private property rights in the use of the environment as a waste-sink. Before discussing this possibility, however, it is important to recognize that, despite similarities between most privately owned goods and environmental quality, important differences remain. Because of these differences we cannot expect to find any perfect solutions to our environmental problems.

5. POLLUTION CONTROL AND PUBLIC CONTROVERSY

In many respects a clean environment is no different from any other desirable commodity. In a world of scarcity, we can increase our consumption of clean environment only by giving up something else. The problem that we face is choosing the combination of goods that does most to enhance human well-being. Few people would enjoy a perfectly clean environment if they were cold, hungry, and generally destitute. On the other hand, an individual choking to death in smog is hardly to be envied no matter how great his or her material wealth. Only by considering the additional cost as well as the additional benefit of increased consumption of all goods, including clean air and water, can decisions on the desirable combination of goods to consume be made properly.

Despite the similarity between a clean environment and most other desirable things, there is an important difference. For example, consider the difference between food and a clean environment. If an individual happens to be a gourmet, the benefit received from food will be quite high, and that person will probably purchase large amounts of high-quality food. This expression of preference does nothing to interfere with those of a neighbor whose preferences may be quite different. The neighbor may get as much satisfaction out of a McDonald's Big Mac as from filet mignon en croute with duxelles of wild mushrooms and might be appalled at having to spend as much on food as the gourmet does. Imagine the conflict if both of these individuals were required to consume the same foods. Fortunately for both of them, food, as well as most other goods, does not have to be consumed at a uniform quality by everyone in a geographical area. Food is a private good. This is not true of environmental quality, which has the characteristics of a public good. Everyone in a given geographical area will have to consume, and pay for, approximately the same level of environmental quality, and this can cause problems.

It is practically impossible to get widespread agreement on what the appropriate level of pollution should be. People with different preferences and situations are simply going to have different ideas about the costs and benefits of pollution abatement. For example, consider a community that contains a college and an oil refinery that emits large quantities of nauseating and potentially noxious fumes into the atmosphere. Who do you think is most likely to participate in a protest favoring stringent pollution controls on the refinery: the college students or the townspeople? It is a safe bet that the answer is the college students. Why is this? One may think that college students are more aware of and sensitive to the environmental quality of the community. Maybe. But the long-term residents of the community, those who plan on staying there and raising their children there, are certainly concerned about the air quality in their community. Indeed, they may well be more concerned about local pollution than the college students who, after all, will live in the community only until they graduate or flunk out. The difference between the townspeople and the students is probably not found primarily in a difference in the desire for a clean environment. The difference is probably best explained by the fact that the cost of cleaning up the environment will fall almost entirely on the townspeople. It is their jobs, incomes, and retirement plans that will be jeopardized by strict pollution control requirements on the refinery. The students will not have to pay this cost, since their job prospects and current income will be quite independent of the profitability of the local refinery. Not surprisingly, it is the students who will be eager to clean up the refinery. They will get many of the benefits and pay none of the cost. The townspeople will be a little less enthusiastic about environmental purity since they will be the ones paying for it.

The point of this discussion is not to decide which group is right or wrong. Both the students and the townspeople are quite rational, given the situation they face. The purpose is to emphasize that controversy is sure to arise when a community of people have to share a common, or public, good. Conflicts are inevitable because different people have different preferences and face different costs. This explains much of the controversy that revolves around environmental issues. If everyone could pay for and consume a preferred level of environmental quality, independent of the level paid for and consumed by others, controversy over environmental protection would disappear. There is no way to avoid completely this type of controversy when, as will always be the case, public goods are being provided in a community. It should be recognized, however, that one way that people somewhat spontaneously moderate controversy of this type is by sorting themselves out in relatively homogeneous groupings. Communities that contain people with similar backgrounds, preferences, and circumstances are more likely to avoid socially divisive controversies than are communities containing more diverse populations.

6. POLLUTION RIGHTS

Before suggesting an approach for solving the problem of excessive pollution, it will be useful to discuss just what that ideal solution would accomplish. First, and most obviously, we want pollution reduced to the efficient level, the level that maximizes the value of all of our resources. This means continuing to reduce pollution one more unit only as long as the value of the improved environmental quality is greater than the value that is sacrificed.

A second objective is to reduce pollution as cheaply as possible. There are two separate considerations here. If pollution is to be reduced as cheaply as possible, it is obvious that each pollution source has to abate at minimum cost. There are many ways to cut back on pollution, but in general there will be only one least-cost way. But even if all polluters are abating as cheaply as possible, it does not necessarily mean that pollution overall is being reduced at least cost. The pattern of pollution abatement over all sources is of great importance here. Since some polluters will be more efficient at pollution reduction than others, the least-cost abatement pattern will require some polluters to clean up more than others. In general, the least-cost pattern of abatement will find the cost of reducing pollution by one more unit the same for all polluters. If this condition is not satisfied, the cost of achieving a given amount of overall abatement can be reduced by having the low-cost abater reduce pollution by an additional unit and the high-cost abater reduce pollution by one unit less. This type of adjustment will continue to reduce abatement cost, without increasing pollution, until reducing pollution the additional unit costs everyone the same.

A third objective of a pollution-control policy is to establish incentives that will motivate advances in pollution abatement technology. Over the long run this is probably an even more important objective than the first two. For example, the cost of controlling pollution can be significantly reduced over time, even if the second objective is not fully realized, if consistent advances are made in the technology of pollution control.

It should be clear that these three objectives, 1) achieving the efficient level of pollution, 2) achieving pollution reduction at least cost, and 3) motivating advances in abatement technology, will never be fully realized. This is particularly true of the first objective. By not being able to own and control identifiable and separate portions of the atmosphere, for example, no one is in a position to require that a price be paid in exchange for fouling his, and only his, clean air. Without such exchanges and prices, we have no way of knowing the value people place on clean air. And without this information there is no way of determining the effecient level of air pollution. Likewise, private ownership of identifiable and separate portions of water in our lakes, rivers, and oceans is not possible, and thus there is no accurate way of determining the efficient level of water pollution. In the absence of market exchange, we have to rely on the political process to determine the efficient level of pollution. In a democratic political order, there is the presumption that the information provided by voting and lobbying will keep the political process responsive to the preferences of the citizens. To the extent that this presumption is justified, there is hope that political decision makers will arrive at a level of pollution that is not too far removed from the efficient level. Some of the problems with the political process that we discussed in Chapter 4 can, unfortunately, occur here, as will be discussed in the next section. But despite this, it is the politically determined level of pollution that we will have to live with.

Given that the target level of pollution is determined politically, we need to focus on the second and third objectives of a pollution-control policy. Economists see an opportunity to realize these objectives reasonably well by having the government create and enforce a system of property rights in the use of the environment as a waste-sink. Without going into a detailed discussion of implementation problems, the idea is simply to have the government issue transferable pollution rights that give the holder the right to discharge, say, one unit of pollution each week. The total number of rights issued would allow only that level of pollution determined as appropriate by the political process.* It is obvious that the scheme, assuming adequate enforcement, would serve to limit pollution to the politically accepted level. Also, each

---

*Many interesting problems come to mind when considering such a pollution rights policy. One is how to distribute the rights: have the government auction them off to the highest bidders, or simply give them away? If they are given away, how should these valuable rights be distributed among competing interests eager to receive them? After the rights are in the hands of the public, there remain problems of enforcement, making sure that people do not pollute without owning the legally required rights. Without minimizing these problems, it should be pointed out that they are no more, and may be less, troublesome than those encountered with the current approach to environmental protection that attempts to control pollution through direct government control and regulation.

polluter—having to reduce pollution to the level allowed by the number of rights held—will be motivated to do so at the minimum cost. But the crucial advantage in the pollution-rights approach comes from the fact that the rights are private property and can be sold.

Because the pollution rights are transferable, a market will develop for them and the resulting exchanges will determine a pollution-right price. This cost of discharging another unit of pollution per week is now equal to the price of a pollution right—the value others place on the ability to increase their pollution by one unit per week. In other words, people will be motivated to increase their use of the environment as a waste-sink only if the additional pollution benefits them at least as much as it would benefit others. A pattern of polluting activities results that maximizes the value that is realized from the allowable level of pollution. Another way of stating this is that the reduction in pollution necessary to realize the acceptable level is achieved with the least-cost (minimum sacrifice in valuable alternatives) pattern of abatement.

It is worth emphasizing that this least-cost pattern of abatement did not require any information on the part of the Environmental Protection Agency (EPA). The EPA does not need to know the cheapest abatement strategy for each and every polluter. Faced with a positive price for pollution rights, each polluter has every motivation to discover the cheapest way to reduce pollution and to utilize it. Neither does the EPA need to know anything about the differences in abatement costs among polluters. Each polluter will be motivated to reduce pollution as long as the cost of reducing one more unit is less than the price of pollution rights. With all polluters facing the same market price for these rights, this results in the cost of abating one more unit of pollution being the same for all polluters. This is another way of stating the requirement for the least-cost abatement pattern. The information and incentives generated by private ownership and market exchange automatically lead to the desirable pattern of pollution abatement.

The pollution-rights approach will also create an incentive for polluters to develop improved abatement technologies. Our economic history is full of examples of technological development that has allowed more output to be produced with less land and labor. Conspicuously absent have been technological improvements designed to conserve on the use of the environment as a waste-sink. Market prices on land and labor have always provided a strong incentive to conserve these resources. The absence of prices for the use of our atmosphere and waterways, however, made it privately unprofitable to worry about conserving their use. Marketable pollution rights would remedy this neglect.

There is another possible advantage to the pollution-rights approach that is worth discussing but which is not as significant an advantage as it may at first seem. So far the discussion has proceeded as if the only reason for purchasing a pollution right is to support a polluting activity. But pollution rights could also be purchased for the purpose of keeping them out of the hands of polluters, thereby reducing pollution. For example, groups interested in protecting the natural environment, such as the Sierra Club, Friends of the Earth, the National Rifle Association, and the Audubon Society, would have an opportunity to put some of their funds to direct use in reducing pollution by purchasing and hoarding pollution rights. If everyone who valued clean air could be depended upon to contribute toward the purchase of pollution rights for this purpose, then the price of these rights would reflect more than just their value in polluting activities; it would also reflect their value in providing a cleaner environment. In this case, if more pollution rights were issued than was consistent with the efficient level of pollution, the excess would be purchased and hoarded. The pollution rights approach would result in the efficient level of pollution as well as in the least-cost pattern of abatement.

Unfortunately, there is little reason to expect people, regardless of the concern they may express about the environment, to buy pollution rights to prevent pollution. Buying a pollution right to reduce air pollution, for example, reduces air pollution for everyone in the area, not just for the person who makes the purchase. So the total value of the reduced pollution is much greater than that realized by the one individual who pays for the reduction. Consequently, the value of keeping rights out of the hands of polluters could easily be greater than their market price and no one individual would be willing to buy one for that purpose.

Of course, individuals could band together for the collective purpose of contributing toward the purchase of pollution rights. But recruiting people into such a cooperative effort would not be easy. Each person would realize that, unless others joined the effort in large numbers, an individual contribution would do little good and would cost more than it was personally worth. On the other hand, these individuals also realize that, if others contribute in large numbers, they will be able to benefit as free riders from the clean air that others purchase. Either way the individual sees a personal advantage in not contributing to the common cause.

This is not meant to imply that the desire to reduce pollution will motivate no purchases of pollution rights. Environmental organizations exist that have to some degree overcome the free rider problem, and such groups would likely purchase and hoard some pollution rights. But it would be naive to believe that such purchases would come close to reflecting the full social value of clean air if the government issued pollution rights in excess of that number needed to support the efficient level of pollution. The best we can hope for is that the number of pollution rights issued will allow something close to the efficient level of pollution when they are purchased only for the purpose of polluting. But even without pollution reduction purchases motivating the efficient level of pollution, the minimum abatement cost feature of the pollution rights approach should still make it a very attractive means for controlling pollution.* This is particularly true given the alternative of having the government directly regulate and control pollution sources.

Briefly stated, the direct regulation and control approach has the government determine an acceptable level of pollution and then attempt to achieve this level by requiring individual polluters to reduce their discharges by specified amounts and/or by mandating the use of particular abatement technologies. In determining the acceptable overall level of pollution, this approach is on an equal footing with the pollution rights approach. In both cases, the acceptable level is determined through the political process. But direct regulation and control of pollution sources cannot be expected to achieve the required abatement as cheaply as will a market in pollution rights. Not knowing the least-cost abatement approach for each pollution source, the government agency charged with pollution control will generally require a uniform approach across each class of polluters, despite the fact that the most appropriate approach will vary from source to source. Neither will the government have the information necessary to determine the least-cost abatement pattern. In the absence of market exchange this information is effectively unknowable.

Despite the fact that environmental policy in the U.S. has, almost exclusively, taken the direct regulation and control approach, recently there has been a slight movement in the direction of more flexibility and reliance on market incentives. For example, the EPA has recently moved toward what has become known as the bubble approach. Rather than specifying the amount of pollution allowed from each pollution source within a plant or industrial complex, a hypothetical bubble is placed over the complex and it is the overall level of pollution generated within this bubble that the EPA controls. This gives the polluter the needed flexibility to adjust the pollution from each source in such

---

*An alternative to the pollution rights approach that also finds much favor among economists is pollution taxation. With this approach polluters can pollute all they want, but they are required to pay a specified amount for each unit of emission—with the charge, or tax, being the same for all polluters. Of course, different charges would be applied to different types of pollutants. The tax approach would have many of the same advantages as pollution rights in terms of motivating least-cost abatement and advances in abatement technologies. However, it could take much trial and error before the authorities know how high the taxes needed to be to motivate the desired pollution reduction.

a way that the costs of pollution control are minimized subject to the overall restriction on emissions.

From the bubble concept has come the possibility of buying and selling pollution offsets. Assume that a firm wants to move into an area that is already as polluted as allowed by EPA standards. Under the offset policy, the firm can set up operation by purchasing pollution offsets from an existing polluter in the area. This allows a firm that believes its new polluting activity will generate more value than existing polluting activities to transfer pollution from existing bubbles to a new bubble. This type of exchange, much like an exchange in pollution rights, allows the greatest value to be generated with a given amount of pollution. It also encourages polluters to come up with cheaper ways of reducing pollution, since the firm that reduces pollution is able to sell the pollution credit to others. Pollution reduction can be profitable.

Although the pollution market is still in its infancy, and many legal considerations are yet to be resolved, some offset exchanges have taken place. The Times Mirror Company completed a $120 million expansion of its paper plant in the Portland, Oregon, area after purchasing the right to discharge an additional 150 tons of hydrocarbons annually from other polluters. In Pennsylvania, Volkswagen Corporation was able to begin operations after arranging for pollution reductions from Jones & Laughlin Steel Company and the state transportation department.[3]

7. POLITICAL POLLUTION

Despite the advantages of pollution rights discussed in the last section and the cautious beginnings with pollution offset exchanges, the political response to our environmental concerns has been almost entirely to embrace the direct regulation and control approach. There are reasons for the political popularity of directly regulating pollution sources that have nothing to do with environmental concerns. In some cases, environmental concerns are simply a convenient vehicle for promoting hidden agendas that can actually result in a reduction in environmental quality. Before turning to a particular example, it will be helpful to recall from Chapter 4 the advantages special interests have over general interests in the political process. Interestingly, this deficiency in the political process is closely analogous to the problem that explains excessive pollution in private-market settings.

Government programs, expenditures, and protections often convey benefits that focus largely on particular industries or occupational groups. Agricultural price supports, restrictions on how much acreage can be devoted to tobacco production, and the purchase of expensive and largely inoperative military tanks from Chrysler Corporation are but a few of a large number of examples. Benefiting groups will have a strong motivation to become involved politically for the purpose of protecting and, if possible, expanding their particular programs. These groups will each be organized to one degree or another because of their common occupational interests and will often find it relatively easy to confront and influence key political decision makers. Of course, these special-interest programs will impose costs on the general public in the form of higher taxes and prices. But organizing the general public for the purpose of generating political opposition to these programs will face the same problems encountered by an environmental group attempting to get all those suffering from pollution to contribute toward the purchase of pollution rights. If others are successful in controlling a special-interest program, your taxes will be lowered whether or not you contributed to the effort. So when a program is being considered that benefits the few at the expense of the many, our political representatives can expect to hear from the few but not from the many. The resulting bias in political activity is not hard to predict.

We suffer from excessive pollution because the private benefits each of us receives from polluting activities are paid for, in large part, by a defenseless public. We suffer from excessive government involvement in a whole host of activities because the private benefits each of us receives from the government programs we favor are also paid for, in large measure, by a defenseless public. Of course, each of us also suffers from the pollution and pays for the government programs of others. Most of us would be willing to reduce our pollution and the programs we favor if everyone else would do the same. Unfortunately, this does not happen, because the political process is flawed for the same reason that the market for a clean environment is flawed: in the absence of private property and exchange, people are not able to communicate their preferences to each other in such a way as to ensure honesty and reciprocity.

The power that government has assumed in order to impose direct regulation and control over polluting activities has not been ignored by special interests intent on realizing private advantages completely unrelated to environmental concerns. An important case in point is the Clean Air Act, as amended in 1977.[4] The original Clean Air Act of 1970 was passed in response to widespread concern over a serious environmental problem. While we may quibble over whether or not this act was the best policy response to our air pollution problems, the evidence strongly indicates that it did have a favorable impact on air quality.[5] But it also had other effects.

The 1970 act imposed much tighter pollution controls in those areas that were heavily polluted—primarily the heavily industrialized

East—than in those areas that were relatively unpolluted—the sparsely populated West. This gave the West a significant advantage over the East in competition for industry, jobs, and tax revenues. The 1970 act also imposed tight standards on the amount of sulphur dioxide that new or newly modified electric power plants could discharge. How these emission standards were to be met, however, was not specified by the 1970 act. Electric power plants had two alternatives: 1) burn high-sulphur coal and remove the sulphur by installing expensive stack scrubbers, or 2) burn low-sulphur coal, in which case the standards could be met without scrubbers. Unfortunately for the Eastern coal industry and the United Mine Workers (which represents most miners in the East but has had little success in organizing western mines), the low-sulphur coal is found in the West. Rather than take a chance on the expensive and relatively untried scrubbers, many utilities, some as far east as West Virginia, found importing coal from Wyoming and Montana an attractive option.

The beneficiaries of the 1970 Clean Air Act were the general public, who enjoyed cleaner air and, as consumers of electricity, benefited from the flexibility that utilities had in meeting the Clean Air Act standards as cheaply as possible. But the general interests of the unorganized public are much more difficult to communicate through the political process than the focused and organized interests of the United Mine Workers and established eastern coal producers. A blatant example of the dominance of special over general interests in the political process came when Senator Howard Metzenbaum of Ohio successively engineered through Congress the "local coal amendment," as one of the 1977 amendments to the Clean Air Act. This amendment makes it illegal to import western coal into Ohio or Illinois if high-sulphur coal mining jobs are threatened in these states. In order to shelter fewer than 10,000 people from competition, consumers of electricity had to spend millions of extra dollars and breath dirtier air.

The major provisions of the 1977 amendments to the Clean Air Act were less transparently motivated by special-interest concerns, but were no less effective at protecting eastern interests against competition from the West. Environmentalists (many of whom wanted to halt development in the West), coal producers, and eastern industrialists found common cause in lobbying for the passage of the 1977 amendments to the Clean Air Act. As one result of the amendments, the Environmental Protection Agency was given formal authority to pursue a "prevention of significant deterioration" (PSD) policy. The PSD policy greatly added to the cost of acquiring the political permission necessary to shift industrial operations out of the East and into the West. Despite the fact that the environmental costs of increased pollution in the sparsely populated and largely pollution-free areas of the

West are significantly less than the environmental benefits to be derived from reducing pollution in the congested and heavily polluted areas of the East, the policy of PSD is designed to prevent such pollution transfers from taking place.

The 1977 amendments also imposed a "best available control technology" (BACT) requirement on all new sources of potentially significant pollution, regardless of whether they were located in clean or dirty areas. This provision forces all new coal-fueled power plants to use scrubbers regardless of the sulphur content of the coal they burn. Not being able to satisfy the pollution-control authorities by substituting western coal for the expensive scrubber technology, utilities in the East have little reason to purchase the more expensive western coal (western coal has a lower BTU equivalent than eastern coal and tends to be more expensive per BTU, particularly in the East).

Unfortunately, the price the public pays for the political privileges of the eastern coal interests is not just higher utility bills. In many cases the price is more pollution. For example, sulphur emissions from burning eastern coal with the scrubber technology are often greater than sulphur emissions when western coal is burned without a scrubber. Some observers argue that the overall effect of the scrubber requirement has been to increase the sulfate air pollution in the eastern half of the United States. Interestingly, this may also be true in the western states, even though low-sulphur western coal continues to be burned. It so happens that the scrubber technology requires some minimum level of sulphur in the coal that is being burned. Since the sulphur content of much Western coal is less than this minimum amount, sulphur often has to be *added* to the coal before it is burned. Also, a byproduct of using the scrubber technology is a "sludge" that is generally disposed of in land fills. This sludge is not biodegradable and is not firm enough to support buildings, so its disposal effectively removes productive land from use. It has been estimated that over the thirty-year productive life of an 1800-megawatt electric generating plant, approximately 1400 acres of land will be required for sludge disposal if the plant uses stack scrubbers. Finally, the scrubbing technology requires water in large quantities. The result is increased chemical and thermal water pollution that presents serious problems even when water is abundant. The problem is, of course, worse in the arid West.

Concern over environmental quality is, in the above case, a convenient rationale for the exercise of political power designed to favor the organized interests of the few at the expense of the unorganized interests of the many. This political pollution takes the form of higher prices, less efficient allocation of our resources between different sectors of the country, and more, rather than less, environmental pollution.

8. WHAT ABOUT SOCIALISM?

Some people feel that proposals such as pollution rights are feeble attempts to patch up a lousy system. Wouldn't it be easier to control pollution and prevent environmental decay if the government owned all means of production? It could be argued that in a socialistic society the ultimate decision maker, the state, will bear all the costs as well as receive all the benefits of pollution and will therefore be motivated to prevent excessive pollution. Unfortunately, as we have seen, the political decision-making process tends to favor narrowly focused interests over those concerns, such as pollution, that have a more general impact. The actual experience in socialistic countries strongly indicates that state ownership is no advantage in fighting pollution. The example of the Soviet Union is an informative one.

The Central Planners in Russia determine the level of output they expect in the different industries, along with the inputs they feel are necessary to achieve this output. The resulting plans filter down to individual plant managers, who are motivated by bonuses to meet or exceed their output quota while staying within their allotted inputs. But there has been little effort to consider the value of environmental inputs used in the productive process. As a result, the individual plant managers have no incentive to conserve on their use of the environment. In fact, the incentives have worked in the opposite direction. Anytime a manager is able to substitute environmental inputs, which aren't being monitored, for inputs that are, he will find it to his advantage to do so. Individuals seeking advancement in Russia soon learn that the most important consideration is how much their plant or region has increased production; whether or not the environment has deteriorated is of little importance. There is plenty of evidence that pollution control has received little emphasis in Russia. Even when pollution-control funds are available, plant managers are reluctant to use them, since production and their bonuses would suffer. Pravda, the official Soviet newspaper, has carried stories of many instances of industry failing to complete installation of planned pollution-abatement equipment.[6]

What we have just discussed doesn't indicate that the Soviet Union is any worse than the U.S. in terms of pollution. But it certainly doesn't give us any reason to believe that they or any other industrialized socialist country have been any more effective in dealing with pollution than we have. In fact, there are reasons to believe that certain institutional aspects of socialistic economies make it more difficult for them to tackle environmental problems effectively. Like our Army Corps of Engineers, Bureau of Land Management, and other federal agencies, the bureaucracy of socialist countries generates strong pressures to construct large public projects. In many cases, the act of building the project seems more important than its intended function. But in socialist countries the bureaucracy is a larger, more powerful force in the economy than it is in predominantly capitalistic countries. And with little or no private ownership of property under socialism, private citizens can do little to resist public work decisions by the state.*

This no doubt explains why beautiful Black Sea beaches in the Georgian Republic of Russia have been damaged as a result of the removal of large quantities of sand and pebbles by government contractors. Despite the passage of resolutions that seek to halt this removal, year after year the state continues to use this convenient source of construction material for their projects. Individuals are not permitted to own beach property privately, so no group other than the state has the power to decide how the beaches should be used, and the state has decided that they should be used for construction material.

Other examples of environmental disruption in the Soviet Union are readily available. In the early 1960s, formal plans were developed to build a large dam on the River Ili. The Ili is the source of 75 percent of the water for Lake Balkhash, the biggest lake in the republic of Kazakhstan. Strong justifications were made for the project. It was claimed that the dam would permit one million additional acres of land to be irrigated and brought into cultivation and that water transportation would be greatly improved. Only after the dam was well under way, over the protest of those living along the lake, was it brought out that the Minister of Power and some engineers in the republic of Kazakhstan had deliberately biased evidence to justify the dam. The original justification said nothing about the 750,000 to 1.5 million acres of productive land that would quickly be turned into a desert by the dam. By reducing the flow of the Ili, the dam would also increase the salt content of the lake and destroy the water supply of at least one town. Because of this belated evidence, it was decided not to fill the reservoir in five years as originally intended. Many specialists recommended taking as long as thirteen years. The formal agreement was to wait eight to ten years to fill the reservoir, but to the dismay of many, one year after the completion of the dam, the reservoir was one-quarter full.[7]

As Poland, another socialist country, has recently attracted worldwide attention, it has become painfully clear that the Polish environment is being sacrificed in the effort to maintain Poland's feeble econ-

---

*This shouldn't be taken to mean that the state can't override private interest in countries such as the U.S. It obviously can and does. But there can be little doubt that private pressure can be brought to bear more effectively on government decisions in a capitalist economy than in a socialist one.

omy. Acid rain of such corrosiveness has been falling on the Polish city of Cracow that most of the gold roof on the 16th-century Sigismund Chapel of Walwel Cathedral has dissolved.[8] The Gothic architecture is also being heavily damaged by the acid rain as carved figures are corroding away and stone and marble faces are discoloring and, in some cases, crumbling. The Polish Ecological Club (which did not surface until the brief period of freedom that began with the creation of Solidarity and has since been suppressed) urged that much of Cracow's Gothic architecture be removed from the outside and stored in museums. Nearby agriculture fields have been poisoned with deposits of cadmium, lead, zinc, and iron from the Lenin steel works. The traditional crops of sugar, beets, and green vegetables had to be abandoned. Salad greens, for example, contained lead concentrations of 42 ppm, which is 21 times greater than the maximum concentration consistent with safe human consumption.

There are surely fewer reasons to be optimistic that the environment will be more protected in socialist countries than in capitalist countries. A major factor here is the ideological bias that socialist countries have against private ownership. With the prevailing view of socialism that important resources belong to everyone, it would be awkward for any socialist country to create private property rights in the use of the environment as a waste-sink, as is required by the pollution-rights approach. But in the absence of such a property-rights approach, people are in effect allowed "free" use of the environment for discharging their wastes. Letting polluters pollute "freely" will result in the same problem of excessive pollution, whether they are capitalist polluters or socialist polluters, whether they are polluting for a profit or a bonus for exceeding their quota.

Neither socialism nor capitalism has a particularly good record to date for environmental protection. Any system that hopes to come to grips with environmental problems in a serious way will have to recognize that the assimilative capacity of the environment is a scarce good like all other resources. Because of this fact, it is essential that some form of social accountability be required of those using this capacity. There is no more effective arrangement for promoting social accountability than private property. Unfortunately, this is an arrangement that socialist countries can be expected to resist.

DISCUSSION QUESTIONS

1. Clean, clear air is obviously preferable to smog. Yet millions of people choose to live in Los Angeles, where smog alerts are common

occurrences, rather than Woonsocket, South Dakota, where there is no such thing as smog. What does this tell you about trade-offs people are willing to make? How is a decision to live in L.A. rather than Woonsocket similar to a decision on whether or not to smoke cigarettes? Assuming your income would be the same in Woonsocket as in L.A., where would you choose to live?

2. Would the desirable level of pollution increase or decrease if:

   (a) pollution abatement technology greatly improved?
   (b) outdoor activities declined in popularity with more people preferring to drink beer and shoot pool?
   (c) medical advances overcame some of the health problems associated with dirty air?
   (d) we were permanently cut off from foreign oil supplies?

3. Do you think a pollution-rights policy would have been worthwhile in the West during the frontier period? Why or why not?

4. Ideally, there would have to be different pollution rights for different pollutants. Also, you would want to have different numbers of allowed pollution rights in different locations, allowing more in areas where pollution does little harm than in areas where pollution is very harmful. This means restricting the ability of a polluter from buying a right in one area and using it in another area. Furthermore, in the same area it will generally be desirable to limit the use of existing pollution rights during some periods when pollution is more harmful, such as during temperature inversions.

   All of these considerations present problems in implementing a pollution-rights scheme. Explain how these problems also exist with (1) a policy of direct regulation and control, (2) a policy of pollution taxation.

5. If instead of making an environmental group such as the Sierra Club buy pollution rights, the government simply gave them a large number, would this lower the cost to the Sierra Club of reducing pollution by holding rights off the market? Why would you expect the Sierra Club to hold more rights off the market if they received them at no charge than if they had to pay, even though their cost was the same in either case?

6. If you define environmental quality broadly to include the quality of work environments, protections against disease, and in general, the safety, convenience, and comfort of our everyday environment, then clearly we benefit from much higher environmental quality

than ever before. Do you believe it is appropriate to define environmental quality this broadly? Why or why not?

7. In what way is the controversy over environmental issues similar to the controversy over national defense or to the controversy over public education?

chapter 8

Conserving Our Resources

1. CONSERVATION AND DIFFICULT CHOICES

Ask a roomful of people to raise their hands if they are in favor of
conservation, and most hands can be expected to go up. The importance
of conservation is something we can expect almost everyone to agree
on. If you're opposed to conservation, you're likely to be considered a
very irresponsible individual. After all, the conservation of our natural
resources has to be of utmost importance, considering the necessity of
natural resources for everything we do. The importance of our fossil
fuels, metallic ores, minerals, forests, wilderness areas, and wild life
hardly needs to be emphasized.

Unfortunately, if we really decide to get serious and come to grips
with specific problems, much of the agreement over conservation will
vanish. Conservation means entirely different things to different people. For example, what do you think of the following statement?

The object of our forest policy is not to preserve the forest because it is
beautiful . . . or because it is refuge for the wild creatures of the wilderness . . .
but . . . the making of prosperous homes . . . Every other consideration comes
as secondary.

It's safe to say that the statement would be considered shocking and irresponsible by many conservationists. It would be labeled a despicable attempt by some land developer to justify the rape of our forests for a quick profit. But this statement was not made by a greedy land developer. It was made by Gifford Pinchot, the man generally recognized as the father of the conservation movement in the United States, in a speech to the Society of American Foresters in 1903.

To Pinchot, and to many other conservationists both past and present, conservation has meant the scientific management of our natural resources. The sole purpose of scientific management is to allow man to extract the largest possible yield from these resources in order to increase our supply of roads, hospitals, foods, homes, airplanes, energy, and schools. To these conservationists, the premise that man has every right to exploit natural resources to the fullest has never been questioned. Conservation and development go hand in hand.

This attitude is not shared by all those who consider themselves conservationists; many feel that true conservation requires that nature be preserved in its natural state. To these people, development is anathema, doing irreparable harm to our legacy of wildlife and wilderness areas. It isn't surprising that there have been serious conflicts among those who consider themselves conservationists.

Conservationists of both development and preservation persuasions, as well as those who take compromise positions, would largely agree that our natural resources should be used for the maximum benefit of man. The conflicts arise from the fact that decisions regarding natural resource use, like all other decisions, require that tradeoffs and sacrifices be made. Different individuals and groups have different evaluations of the benefits and costs associated with natural resource use. For example, most people will agree that conserving our water resources and the fertility of our soil is desirable. In many areas the best way to do this is to dam rivers and create reservoirs. In this way, water can be kept from eroding our land and rushing to the sea unused during periods of high flow; it can be made available for irrigation and drinking during periods of low flow. Unfortunately, the choice is not one of simply choosing to conserve our water and land. Dams can be constructed only at the expense of destroying white water rivers and natural valleys and canyons. With different opinions about the relative value of conserving water for commercial use versus conserving beautiful rivers and valleys, we can expect the construction of dams to be supported by some and vigorously opposed by others.

Examples of this type of controversy are easy to find. In the first decade of this century, a dam was proposed across the beautiful Hetch Hetchy Valley in Yosemite National Park in order to increase the supply of water to San Francisco. A bitter controversy followed, with John Muir, the founder of the Sierra Club, and others vigorously opposing the project. The project was eventually approved and the dam was built. San Francisco got cheaper water, but a magnificent valley was lost.

Currently another bitter debate is raging over the use of federal funds for the enhancement of national parks. Secretary of the Interior James Watt has proposed spending more funds on physical improvements of existing park areas—bridge and road repairs, building renovations, and so on. This has been opposed by some wilderness enthusiasts who advocate channeling these funds towards the acquisition of new public lands. The question of improvement of existing lands versus purchase of new lands is not one which can be resolved by a simple "conservation–anticonservation" argument. Both policies are a form of conservation, but each has a different group of beneficiaries. Park visitors desiring to cruise through beautiful scenery in safety and comfort would favor Watt's policy, whereas those preferring to rough it in isolated splendor would rather have additional wilderness areas.

Sometimes the debate over resource use is put in terms of a choice between exploitation today or preservation for the benefit of future generations. Some conservationists would have us retard economic growth so that we consume less of our limited resources, leaving more for future generations. Every barrel of oil consumed today is one less barrel left for tomorrow. Others argue that economic growth through the exploitation of our resources actually benefits future generations, by contributing to the construction of capital resources—plants, machinery and equipment—which then produce higher outputs of goods and services in the future. By preserving some resources in their natural state, we will leave a smaller amount of productive capital for future use.

These examples not only illustrate the types of conflicts among conservationists but also serve to point out a very important fact: choices have to be made between the conservation of some resources and the expenditure of others, and these choices affect future occupants of our planet who can have no say in our decisions. It's not very useful to label some individuals and groups as conservationists and accuse others as being against conservation. The important issue isn't a matter of simply being for or against conservation. It is a matter of deciding how best to respond to the hard choices between conserving some resources and expending others. These choices have to be made in our world of scarcity.

2. RENEWABLE AND NONRENEWABLE RESOURCES

Not only does conservation mean different things to different people, but many people feel that it also means different things for different resources. This comes from the fact that natural resources have different regenerative capacities. Those that can replenish themselves are referred to as *renewable* resources, whereas those that cannot be replaced after they are used are termed *nonrenewable*.

Extensive exploitation of many renewable resources is consistent with their conservation even when conservation is taken to mean indefinite preservation. In fact, additional harvesting of renewable resources can sometimes increase their quality and regenerative capacity, as has been demonstrated with forests and animal populations. This obviously isn't the case for nonrenewable resources. Exploitation here will eventually lead to exhaustion—with no possibility of replacing that resource. Because of this, many people have recommended that nonrenewable resources never be used when there are renewable substitutes. It has also been recommended that we stop the practice of taking just the best and easiest-to-reach deposits of our nonrenewable resources, moving to new sites as soon as old ones become difficult to exploit. For example, when less than half the oil is pumped from an oil pool, the pool is usually abandoned, even though it is still possible to capture a great deal more. These recommendations are made with good intentions and the hope of ensuring that our nonrenewable resources will last as long as possible. But following them would be inadvisable. Passing up plentiful deposits of nonrenewable coal in order to burn scarce supplies of wood certainly doesn't make any sense. Also, long before all the oil was pumped from an oil pool, the energy required to capture an additional barrel would far exceed its energy content.

Recycling is often recommended as a way to expand greatly the effective supply of many of our nonrenewable resources, if not actually making them renewable. Some materials can be usefully recycled almost indefinitely. Unfortunately, this can be a very energy-intensive process, requiring large quantities of other resources. This is another example of the trade-offs between conserving one resource and expending another. Therefore, recycling is not always desirable.

There is also a question as to whether some natural resources should be considered renewable or nonrenewable. One can ask, for example, whether or not the Hetch Hetchy Valley is irreparable. Certainly, it can never be restored exactly the way it was at the turn of the century. But it wouldn't be impossible to drain it, remove most of the accumulated silt, and restore it to a very beautiful valley. So while it wouldn't be very accurate to claim that Hetch Hetchy is completely renewable, it would also be an exaggeration to say that it is totally nonrenewable. But the important question here is whether the benefits that have resulted from the use of the Hetch Hetchy as a reservoir have exceeded the value of this valley in its best alternative use. This is the question that should be asked any time the use of a resource is contemplated, regardless of how it is classified.

3. TOMORROW IS FOREVER, BUT TODAY IS MORE IMPORTANT

The importance of considering the cost of resource use cannot be over-emphasized. There is no way to judge whether allocating natural resources to a particular use makes sense, unless the cost is considered. As we well know by now, the cost of devoting resources to one use is the value that is being forfeited by not using them in their highest valued alternative use. Only when the cost is as low as possible are they being used in the activity the creates the largest benefit.

So we see that deciding on the proper use of our natural resources requires that many alternative uses be compared—not only those currently available but alternatives that may appear in the future. The petroleum that we use to power automobiles is not only unavailable for alternative uses today; it is also unavailable for future use. We not only want to avoid allocating a resource to one use when it has a higher value in an alternative current use, but we also want to make sure that the resource does not have a higher valued future use.

How do you compare a future benefit with a current one? One hundred dollars worth of purchasing power to be received next year isn't worth as much as $100 worth of purchasing power today. If you had a choice between $100 today or a year from now, you would have little trouble deciding which to take. What we are doing when we choose the $100 now is discounting the future. Although most would agree that the future is important, discounting the future is a sensible thing to do. For one thing, there is no such thing as a guaranteed future benefit—we live in a world of uncertainty. Also, most of us are, by nature, impatient. It's just more fun to get nice things now than it is to get them later. Discounting the future also applies to receiving undesirable things. The further into the future we can postpone an undesirable occurrence, the better. Death is generally considered to be undesirable, but its inevitability doesn't normally concern us very much as long as we feel it is still far off.

This is not to say that people are unwilling to forgo current benefits in return for something in the future. But they will not do so unless they receive a premium. This explains why no one will lend you $100 today unless you promise to pay back more than $100 later. This additional payment is the interest that has to be paid when money is borrowed.

What does all this have to do with resource use? Quite a lot. When a decision has to be made between using a resource today or saving it for later, we need to be able to compare the benefits. If this comparison is to be made realistically, the future benefit has to be discounted. For example, assume that the rate of discount on the future is 5 percent per year, and the benefit from current usage is worth $100. The future benefit after one year will have to be worth at least $105, if saving the resource is worthwhile.

Many people feel that if resource use decisions are left up to private interests, the profit motive will prevail, and the quick-buck operators will ravage our natural resources with no thought given to our future needs. If by *quick-buck operator* we mean someone who prefers a buck today to a buck tomorrow, then we all qualify as quick-buck operators. But what about the charge that private owners of natural resources will make decisions that ignore our future needs because of their bias towards current profits?

Consider how the owner of a forest, for example, might be expected to harvest the trees and sell them for lumber. The owner could cut them all down at once and sell them off. But would that be smart? Of course the forest owner prefers to make money as soon as possible. But if he or she is like most business owners, that individual is more than willing to postpone a current benefit from owned resources if these resources can be directed into activities that will yield a high return. If he or she can get 10 percent on those resources in alternative investments, the owner certainly will not accept less than 10 percent on an investment in the forest. To do so would be undesirable. Resources should be directed into those activities where they will generate the greatest return and wealth. Certainly this is the best way to provide for the future.

Getting back to the owner's forest—at any given time, some trees in the forest, the younger ones, will be growing faster than 10 percent per year. The owner won't harvest these trees, since they are increasing in value faster than alternative investments that could be made. But when the trees mature and their growth drops to 10 percent or less, it then becomes profitable to cut them and market the lumber. It would be shortsighted to do otherwise. This releases resources (land, water, etc.) that can be used to start a young stand of trees that will grow at a much faster rate. In an effort to make as large a profit as possible, the private owner of a forest will manage resources in such a way that they will do the most to increase future wealth. There's no need to worry about the supply of lumber for the future when the forests are owned by individuals and firms seeking as large a profit as possible. The lumber will be there; profits depend on it.

But we don't want all of our older trees cut down for lumber. People enjoy established trees and forests. They provide us with beautiful places for hiking and camping. Do private owners of wilderness areas ignore these desires? Of course not. If people really do desire wilderness experiences, it will be profitable to provide for such experiences. There has recently been a big increase in the number of people who are interested in camping, hiking, and just getting out in the forests and by the streams. And profit seekers have responded. The number of privately owned camping grounds in the U.S. has increased substantially in the last decade. Companies have bought up large areas of wilderness land in order to maintain it as wilderness, selling memberships that provide interested individuals opportunities to fish, hunt, camp, and explore in places that really allow you to enjoy nature. But the best way to appreciate the advantages of private ownership as a means of preserving our natural resources is to consider what happens when these resources are not privately owned.

4. EVERYONE'S PROPERTY IS NO ONE'S PROPERTY

Consider for a moment a stand of trees that doesn't belong to anyone in particular but is available for everyone's use. Each individual with access to these trees will have a desirable pattern of use in mind. Each will recognize the desirability of letting the young, fast-growing trees remain for future use and replacing those trees that are cut down with new ones. But no one owns these trees, and no individual will benefit by leaving the smaller, easier-to-cut trees or by planting new ones. The tree that a conscientious individual saves or plants will be grabbed by someone else. The best policy for each person to follow is to get his while the getting is good. It's obvious that under these circumstances, rapid use will result, with little thought given to future needs. This type of situation is well described by the following observation: "Given two thirsty, if not greedy boys, two straws, and one glass of lemonade, . . . it becomes a sucking contest in which the one that sucks the least is the biggest sucker!"[1]

The stand of trees discussed in the above paragraph is an example of a *common property resource,* in which no one has ownership rights, but many have free access. Unfortunately, the over-exploitation of valuable common property resources is not confined to hypothetical examples. More than two-thirds of the earth's surface is unowned. Most of the oceans and the valuable resources in them belong to no one. These resources are allocated strictly on a first-come, first-served basis. The problems that arise from the common property nature of these resources are not hard to predict. Icelandic gunboats have fired on British fishing vessels. The complaint was that foreign fishing activities were seriously depleting the number of Icelandic cod and other commercial fish in what Iceland considers its territorial waters. For similar reasons, Ecuador and Peru have regularly seized U.S. tuna boats over the last decade.

Marine mammals, such as whales, seals, and polar bears, are being threatened with extinction as a result of excessive exploitation. Technological developments, such as faster ships, explosive harpoons, radar and sonar, along with the knowledge that the whale you save for later will be killed by someone else, have resulted in near extinction of the blue whale. It has been estimated that less than 5 percent of the original population of 200,000 are left.[2]

Whales and other marine mammals are not the only valuable wildlife species threatened with extinction because they don't belong to anyone. Experts estimate that the wildlife in Africa is only a tenth of what it was just 50 years ago. Poachers kill hundreds of thousands of African animals every year. Elephants are killed for their tusks, leopards for their skins, and countless wildebeest are slaughtered only for their tails, which can be used as fly whisks. Many species are in danger of extinction, including several species of the spotted cats.[3]

If you're not convinced that lack of private ownership is the primary reason these animals are being depleted so rapidly, ask yourself if cows, pigs, chickens, or turkeys are in any danger of extinction. Of course they aren't. The individual who postpones their slaughter until they are mature and goes to the trouble of breeding them is the same individual who receives the benefit. If property rights were established for endangered animals, their survival would be assured.

Similar reasoning applies to the preserves on which our wildlife depends for survival. Political battles have been raging for decades over the use of government-owned lands, and this conflict has escalated in recent years with the increased demand for mineral resources that may be contained in these lands. Mining and energy companies argue that national security and the rising cost of natural resources make imperative the exploitation of our domestic mineral and energy resources. Wilderness enthusiasts have followed a counterstrategy of persuading the government to declare ever greater expanses of land as untouchable open space. The problem with the political solution is that neither party to the conflict has any incentive for considering the opportunity cost of a "favorable" political outcome.

To see this most clearly, consider an example of a privately owned wildlife preserve.[4] The Audubon Society's Rainey Wildlife Sanctuary, consisting of 26,800 acres of marshland in Louisiana, is a haven for diverse species of beast and fowl. The sanctuary is operated for the convenience and enjoyment of the wildlife, excluding the not-so-rare homo sapiens, who are encouraged to frequent other establishments. The one exception to this discriminatory practice is the coming and going of employees of three oil and gas companies, which have secured from the Audubon Society rights to drill and extract natural gas and oil from the Rainey preserve. The Society's motivation in leasing drilling rights on the sanctuary is clear: at the cost of minimal disruption of the local ecology, the Audubon Society gains revenues with which it can acquire other lands.

Private ownership of the preserve motivates the Society to consider the commercial value of the oil and gas reserves in their land management decision. Naturally, as wildlife preservation is their primary objective, the Society carefully oversees the activities of the oil companies so as to minimize the ecological impact. However, it is clear that their objectives of wildlife preservation would not be furthered by banning the drilling operations from the sanctuary. By sacrificing the pristine environment of a small part of the sanctuary, they are able to purchase much larger tracts of wilderness to further their goals. The greater is the price of oil and gas, the stronger is the incentive for the Society to lease drilling rights on additional sites. In this way the Audubon Society unconsciously balances the public's desire for wilderness with society's demand for energy.

Compare this situation with the squabble over a comparable piece of government-owned land. If an oil company applies to the government for permission to drill, the request will be fought tooth and nail by wilderness groups, none of which would have any financial incentive to do otherwise. No group would be motivated to weigh the ecological costs of exploitation against the benefits of energy consumption. Were public wilderness areas to be turned over to wilderness groups, an incentive would immediately be created for the balancing of these costs and benefits. Ironically, mining and energy companies would encounter a more accommodating environment in which to do business if these lands were owned by the same wilderness groups that are presently unbending in their opposition to the private "rape" of public lands.

The extension of property rights may not always be possible, of course. For example, some animal species do not reproduce in captivity. While this problem may be solved if a firm owns a large "ranch" on which animals roam freely, it is not so easily solved in the case of the blue whale, which travels several thousand miles a year during its mating cycle. The principle that depletion of resources results from lack of ownership rights does, however, suggest some broad directions for resource management policy. Many, for example, favor the principle of common ownership of the oceans by all mankind. This kind of pie-in-the-sky proposal is a move in the opposite direction from what is needed. The United States continues to insist on a limitation of territorial boundaries to twelve miles out to sea, permitting our fishermen to exploit the oceans with reckless abandon. From the viewpoint of long-run resource management, it would be wiser to encourage countries like Ecuador and Peru to take over management of the 200 miles of territorial waters they are so eager to claim. It would be well worth the extra nickel per can of tuna we might pay today if fishing were controlled to avoid depletion tomorrow. The remedy is not more common property. Proper resource management demands further extensions of well-defined ownership rights.

5. YOU PAY—I BENEFIT

As we well know, when resources are conserved, certain benefits are received and certain costs are incurred. When a conservation project is being considered, it is always interesting to ask, who receives the benefits and who suffers the costs? This is the surest way of determining who will be for the project and who will be against it.

Saving the wild animals of Africa is a case in point. Obviously, many people benefit from a large stock of wild African animals: hunters who want big game; fashion plates who like coats of cheetah fur; tourists who want to watch from an air-conditioned bus as a lioness chases down a wildebeest on the Serengeti Plain; and many others, mostly from the non-African countries. But maintaining large numbers of these animals also involves a cost. Vast amounts of land and wilderness have to be left undeveloped to accommodate them. And this land is needed for the development of agriculture and cities by rapidly growing African nations. What most Africans want is an expanding economy with increasing per capita income. They want a small part of what we have already. But we are telling Africans that they have an obligation to the rest of the world to perpetuate large numbers of wild animals. This is predictable, since we reap the benefit and they bear the cost. If Africans have such an obligation, don't we owe it to the rest of the world to return Illinois and Indiana to the buffalo, where millions roamed just 200 years ago?

A more important example of conflicting interests, arising from resource policy, is that of the present generation benefiting at the expense of future generations. Are current benefits from resource exploitation being realized at the expense of generations yet unborn who will inherit a planet stripped of the resources necessary for the good life? What is the prospect for continued economic growth in the face of growing resource scarcities? The earth obviously contains only a limited supply of resources. Many of the most important of these resources are nonrenewable. Once consumed, they are gone forever. Until 1970 our economy was growing at a rate that doubled the output of goods and services approximately every 14 years, with resources being devoured in ever-increasing amounts. Many people are convinced that this cannot continue much longer. They feel that resource exhaustion will soon precipitate not just a halt in economic growth but a collapse in industrial production and an end to society as we know it. This prediction is hard to ignore. How we respond to resource scarcity—and how effective that response is—are issues of vital importance.

6. THE PROPHETS OF DOOM

Fears about the adequacy of our natural resources are not new. Thomas Malthus, an English minister (1766–1834), receives credit for being the first to draw wide public attention to the potential of natural resource scarcity to impair population and economic growth. Malthus based his dismal predictions on the dilemma of limited food supply for a rapidly growing population. Without social measures to check this growth, he foresaw population increasing until a further expansion could not be supported. Then the standard of living would have a natural tendency to fall until people had just enough to maintain life.[5] Malthus never explicitly considered the problem of resource depletion, but as a result of his writings, many became concerned about our ability to support a growing population and expanding economy with a limited resource base.

In 1865 the English economist, William Jevons (1835–1882), published *The Coal Question,* which renewed some of the concerns that Malthus had generated 50 years before.[6] Jevons raised doubts about the feasibility of continued industrial growth because of the fixed supply of coal. The growing industrial economy in Jevon's day required larger and larger amounts of energy, of which coal was the primary source. Jevons believed that if coal consumption continued to increase at the same rate, coal supplies would soon be exhausted.

The conservation movement that flourished in the United States from approximately 1890 to 1920 was, in part, concerned with the limits of our natural resources and the consequences of their depletion. During this period, the first attempts were made to estimate how large the resource supply was. Once these estimates were made, the next step was obvious. From estimates on the remaining stock and information on rates of utilization, many predictions were made, and most of them were frightening. For example, in 1910 Gifford Pinchot stated that at the current rate of consumption, timber would be gone in less than 30 years, and anthracite coal in 50 years.[7] If a 1944 publication had been correct, 21 out of 41 resources considered would now be completely gone. These included manganese, zinc, lead, tin, and nickel.[8]

It would be easy to cite other examples of past predictions that have caused public concern about the adequacy of our national resources to provide for the needs of the future. It is apparent that these dismal predictions have not yet been realized, even though many are overdue.

But just because we have been able to avoid the consequences of resource exhaustion in the past doesn't guarantee that we will be able to do so in the future. Many people don't think we will. Recently, a team of researchers from the Massachusetts Institute of Technology (MIT) published predictions based on a computer model that warned of global disaster within the next 125 years.[9] The likely cause of this predicted disaster is the exhaustion of our resources. Other factors, such as pollution and food shortages, according to the model, can precipitate a major industrial and population collapse before resources are exhausted. But even if these other problems are avoided, resource exhaustion will result in collapse before the year 2100.

This is a frightening story and one that has created a great deal of discussion and concern. This concern has been enlarged by dramatic statements in the press projecting how many years we will be able to continue our present rates of resource consumption before various resources will be exhausted. At present rates of consumption, known reserves of lead, copper, aluminum, zinc, and sulphur will all be exhausted within 45 years.[10] The energy crisis has convinced people in a most painful way that a vital nonrenewable resource is becoming increasingly scarce. Fortunately, a correct understanding of the meaning of known or proven reserves dispels a good deal of this concern. Known reserves are those that geologists have actually identified; exploration has taken place and a quantity of a given resource has been found. For a mining company, known reserves are analagous to the inventory in a store, in the sense that the relation between reserves and current rates of extraction tells the firm whether or not it should seek new deposits. Exploration and discovery of mineral resources is an expensive proposition, and companies are interested in grubbing around in the dirt only if additional discoveries are necessary to sustain desired rates of extraction. No one is intensively searching for phosphorous or coal these days, since we already have a supply of known reserves that will last hundreds of years. On the other hand, the high price of oil and gas and the relatively small ratio of reserves to consumption rates have an army of wildcatters combing the countryside for undiscovered pools of these fossil fuels.

Considering known reserves from the business point of view, it is not too difficult to realize that it is a dubious concept for measuring true resource scarcity. Proven reserves of most resources tend to stay at approximately some multiple of current rates of consumption, just as a store holds an inventory roughly equal to some multiple of sales. These ratios (reserves divided by consumption rates) are often not large, suggesting to the naive an extreme degree of resource scarcity. Mankind has been extracting and using lead, for example, since at least as far back as Roman times, and now we have only 10 years of lead reserves left! You can see how easy it is to be alarmist when basing an argument on proven reserves.

True, you might say, in the past discoveries have always happened to come along to replenish levels of proven reserves, but what is to guarantee this will continue to happen? Other than proven reserves what measures do we have for resource availability? The U.S. Geological Survey computes the concept of "ultimately recoverable reserves," which is one hundredth of one percent of the amount of each resource estimated to be contained in the top kilometer of the earth's surface. You will be happy to know that we have enough ultimately recoverable lead to last 162 years at present rates of consumption and aluminum to supply our current requirements for 68,000 years. But so what? These figures tell us little, if anything, about resource scarcity from an economic point of view.

One lesson from earlier chapters is that scarcity is reflected in price and that this is the best indicator of resource availability. According to this criterion, the scarcity of our most important mineral resources, *including fossil fuels,* has declined dramatically over the long span of our industrialization. When measured against the cost of labor, for example, coal was four-and-one-half times as expensive in 1900 as in 1970, iron six times as costly, copper eight times as expensive, and crude oil more than ten times as expensive in 1900 as in 1970.[11] Using relative prices as a measure of scarcity, our resource base is actually growing.

7. THE GROWING RESOURCE BASE

What are we talking about when we say our resource base is growing? Clearly it is absurd to claim that the physical quantity of resources buried in the earth is greater now than it was 100 years ago. However, resource scarcity cannot be defined meaningfully in terms of what is buried in the earth. The relevant stock of resources can be discussed only in terms of the technical and economic feasibility of recovering and using it. Once this is realized, it is easier to understand how our resource base can expand through time to keep up with rapidly increasing consumption.

Because of technological advances, resources that had limited value at one time have subsequently become very valuable. In 1940 Vermont granite was considered useful for little more than construction and tombstones. Today it is seen as a potentially important source of fuel. Each pound of Vermont granite contains uranium, with the energy equivalence of 150 pounds of coal. Nitrogen can now be extracted directly from the atmosphere and used in the production of chemical fertilizers that significantly improve the productivity of our farm land. Enormous taconite supplies were once considered useless, even though they contained up to 70 percent iron, because the iron was held there inseparably. Now, however, iron can be extracted cheaply, and taconite is considered a significant source of iron. Sand is a common resource that few people paid any attention to until the advent of the silicon chip. Now silicon chips have revolutionized society, leading to new lifestyles and techniques that economize on scarce resources. Home computers, for example, permit programmers to work at home, thereby conserving the gasoline they would otherwise use in commuting. Industrial robots work with greater accuracy than human workers and so save on raw materials wasted in defective products. And there are countless more subtle ways that silicon is replacing other scarce resources.

Technical advance has made it easier to discover and recover valuable resource deposits. The days of the old prospector with the reluctant burro are gone. Techniques now exist for locating nickel and iron deposits by measuring variations in magnetic fields. Important mineral deposits have been located by analyzing the minerals in local vegetation. Copper deposits were discovered in Africa as a result of photographs taken from satellites. Drilling techniques have advanced rapidly. In the early 1960s, drilling in much more than 100 feet of water was practically impossible. This is no longer the case, and drilling in much deeper water is now being considered. There is every reason to believe that these technical advances will continue.

Another crucially important aspect of technological development is its ability to increase the efficiency with which resources are used. As an example, average crop production per acre on U.S. farms has grown by 50 percent since 1960, and output per unit of hour of farm work has tripled over this same period. This has resulted from improvements in fertilizers, pesticides, and seeds. Almost seven pounds of coal was required to generate a kilowatt-hour of electricity in 1900. In the 1960s, less than nine-tenths of a pound was required. Over the past 50 years, the output that can be produced from a given amount of inputs—capital, labor, and natural resources—has increased 2 percent per year. This means that every 35 years technology has allowed twice as much output to be obtained from a given quantity of resources. This increase in technical efficiency has the effect of increasing our resource base, even if no new discoveries are made.

Accidental discoveries and unanticipated spin-offs have obviously accounted for some of the technological advances that have expanded our resource base. But many of these advances were the direct result of responses to anticipated scarcities. With the approaching exhaustion of the high-quality Mesabi iron ores came increased research efforts by the steel companies to exploit taconites and low-grade ores. Companies are currently spending millions of dollars on research into deep sea exploration, motivated by the prospects of cheaper sources of valuable resources. Oil companies have invested heavily in the development of improved techniques for the discovery and recovery of crude oil. The 2 percent per year growth in output that a given quantity of resources can produce is largely the result of firms constantly seeking less-expensive production techniques.

Resource scarcities motivate technological advances that expand our usable stocks. This has been the situation in the past, and there is every reason to believe it will continue to hold true in the foreseeable future. Any prediction that assumes a fixed stock of resources is certain to be overly pessimistic. The MIT researchers who wrote *The Limits to Growth* claim to have taken technological progress into consideration by increasing their original estimate of the current resource base by a factor of 8. Global collapse is still their prediction, and they feel that using a factor of 8 is "more optimistic than realistic." Actually, it is more pessimistic than realistic. Even without any new resource discoveries, the yearly percent of increase in technical efficiency has the effect of doubling resources in 35 years, and increasing them by a factor of 16 in 140 years. Thinking of our resource base as fixed, therefore, is simply not a realistic way to view the real world.

8. RESPONDING TO SCARCITIES

In a market economy, approaching resource scarcities will trigger signals in the form of increasing prices, and they do more than simply warn of the resource scarcities. Increasing prices provide the motivation for actions that will mitigate the effects of these scarcities. These actions fall into two categories: those that actually expand our usable resource base, and those that conserve on the use of resources. Obviously, these responses are important, and ignoring them ignores the most important ways that the harmful effects of resource scarcities are avoided. Unfortunately, the MIT model, which predicts resource exhaustion and global collapse by the year 2100, did not include resource prices.

The most obvious way that higher resource prices lead to an expansion of the usable resource base is through increased exploration. As the price goes up, exploration efforts become more profitable and will be increased. The result is additional resource discoveries. But higher resource prices will expand our relevant resource base in ways not related to new discoveries. Large amounts of important resources are presently ignored, even though they could be recovered and used. Why?

Because it is not economically feasible to exploit them. Other available resources are cheaper to utilize because of such considerations as proximity to population centers and difficulty of extraction. But if the price of a resource increases, previously ignored deposits will become profitable to recover. What is considered the usable resource base can be very sensitive to changes in price. For example, it was estimated that at coal prices in 1951, our useful coal resources were approximately 30 billion tons. But at prices 50 percent higher, useful coal resources would have been approximately 600 billion tons.[12] Even without any additional technological advance, only a modest increase in the price of some of our resources would make it feasible to exploit many of the metals and minerals in the oceans. This would result in an enormous expansion in the usable resource base.

Users of resources can be exceptionally creative in their response to higher prices. This normally means substituting more plentiful resources, those whose prices haven't risen, for the resource that is now more costly. Substitution possibilities are enormous. Natural gas heating can be substituted for electrical heating. Better insulation, storm windows, and warmer clothes are all substitutes for any type of heating fuel. Cinderblock construction is a substitute for wood construction. Smaller cars and slower driving can be substituted for gasoline. Better insulated and thicker electrical transmission wires are a good substitute for electrical production. Chemical fertilizer is a substitute for land, and recycling is a substitute for mining. These substitutions have actually been made in response to changing prices, and the list could be expanded almost indefinitely. As the relative prices change in response to scarcities, we can rely on the self-interest of resource users to make those substitutions that will conserve the resources that are most scarce.

An interesting example of this type of response is the reaction to the increasing scarcity of wood in the U.S. When the United States was first settled, wood was abundant. In fact, it was overly plentiful. In many places trees were a nuisance that had to be cleared off before land could be used. With labor being scarce and wood so plentiful, it isn't surprising that little labor was expended to conserve wood, but much wood was expended to conserve labor. Huge fireplaces were built so that large logs could be burned. This wasted a lot of wood but saved a lot of cutting and chopping. Houses were built with logs or thickly cut planks, again substituting abundant wood for scarce labor. Even roads were built of wood. In 1850 wood accounted for 90 percent of all fuel-based energy in the U.S.

With an expanding population encroaching on what was once wooded land, wood ceased to be so abundant relative to labor and other resources. The price of wood began to increase, almost quadrupling be-

tween 1870 and 1915.[13] As this happened, wood was used more conser-
vatively. Instead of huge firplaces, wood was burned in pot-bellied
stoves. This conserved wood but required much more labor to prepare
the logs for burning. However, with the higher prices for wood, substituting labor for wood now made sense. More care was taken to get the
most usable wood from a log; planks were cut narrower and with thin-
ner saws. Stone, block, metal, and other materials were substituted for
wood in the construction of homes. Wood was used less and less as a
fuel. By 1915 wood accounted for less than 10 percent of the fuel-based
energy in the U.S., quite a drop from the 90 percent level 65 years
earlier.

As a resource becomes scarcer and its price increases, we can be sure
that a great deal of effort will be made to recycle it. There is no need
for public-spirited pleas to convince people of the advantages of recycling resources that are really scarce. We can rely on self-interest to do
the job. Nobody has to be told of the advantages of recycling gold and
silver. The assay office of the federal mint in New York has been able
to meet its operating cost by recovering gold, platinum, and other
scarce metals from the wash water of employees and the gases that are
generated when these metals are melted. The fact that so little effort
is made to recycle most of our resources is evidence that they aren't
expected to be very scarce in the foreseeable future.

Some of our environmental problems are the result of the relative
abundance and cheapness of some natural resources. If natural resources were less plentiful, more old newspapers and magazines would
be saved, fewer beer cans and bottles would be carelessly discarded, and
the automobiles that are abandoned by the thousands each year would
be sold to recycling centers instead of being left along our streets and
roads. Many of our pollution problems would be reduced if our natural
resources became increasingly scarce. But it does not appear that acute
resource scarcities will be the solution to our pollution problems. There
is little evidence to indicate serious resource shortages in the foreseeable future.

9. ENERGY CRISIS OR POLICY CRISIS?

Many will object to the statement that there is little evidence that
resource scarcities will be a serious problem in the near future. What
about the dramatic oil and gas price increases we have experienced in
recent years? What about the gasoline shortages manifested during
1979? During that same year, the federal government enacted a multi-
billion dollar program to foster the development of synthetic fuels,
despite the unresolved environmental implications of such develop-

ment. Surely this is evidence that there is something wrong with the rosy picture of declining resource scarcity presented earlier in this chapter.

It is worth recognizing at the outset that various interest groups have used the perceived "energy problem" to further their own interests. The energy problem during the 1950s was one of overabundance of cheap foreign supplies of crude oil—or at least this was the problem from the point of view of some segments of the petroleum industry. Domestic producers convinced the government to establish quotas on the importation of crude oil, for reasons of national security, of course. These quotas severely restricted the amount of oil that could be imported and substantially increased the price of petroleum products. It has been estimated that the oil import quotas were costing the American consumer up to $7 billion per year during the fifties and sixties.

The national security argument in support of oil-import quotas does not really hold much water. Reducing the supply of foreign oil coming into this country caused us to draw down our own petroleum reserves, so we would have less available during a national emergency. In addition, the restriction in supplies discouraged the development of refining capacity, so that when foreign oil did flow more freely during the sixties, there was insufficient capacity to meet the demand for refined products.

The government also has a long history of controlling energy prices. Since 1954 the Federal Power Commission (FPC) has had the authority to regulate the price of natural gas flowing through interstate pipelines. Throughout the 1960s the commission's policy has been to hold the line on price increases, and in this it was quite successful. Prices per thousand cubic foot rose only from 18.2 cents in 1961 to 19.8 cents in 1969. In 1970 consumers were paying about 20 percent less per unit of energy for natural gas than for oil.[14] By holding down prices, the FPC was discouraging producers from exploration and drilling activities which would have added to reserves. During the early 1970s, the inventory of known gas reserves declined as new discoveries diminished, while demand continued to grow. Many observers have interpreted the decline in known gas reserves as an indication that we are running out of gas, and this impression was heightened when natural gas shortages appeared during the severe winter of 1977.

Natural gas prices have started to increase dramatically as the country moves toward the eventual decontrol of prices scheduled for 1985. These price increases have homeowners plugging holes and throwing up storm windows and have caused increased drilling and exploration. Known reserves worldwide have now doubled over the level of 1970 and are sufficient to last 50 years at present rates of consumption. Clearly there was no real shortage of gas, only a deficiency of incentives for producers to find it and for consumers to conserve it.

Throughout the 1970s the federal government has controlled the price of petroleum products in a way that moved the country away from its stated objectives. Economy-wide wage and price controls, which had been imposed in 1971, were removed in 1973 from all products with the exception of oil. With gas at the pump selling at 30 cents a gallon, consumers were tanking up their gas-guzzling behemoths with reckless abandon. Gasoline consumption was rising at 4 percent per year, just as it had throughout the sixties. Meanwhile, domestic production had peaked in 1970 with the depletion of "easy" oil, so the increased demand had to be met by foreign supplies. At the time of the 1974 oil embargo, we were importing oil equal to 30 percent of total consumption.

The embargo convinced people of our vulnerabilty to the will of the oil-producing countries and led to the political goal of reduced dependence on foreign oil. The goal was apparently supposed to be realized through means other than price incentives, for Congress's approach to the problem in 1976 was to extend price controls on oil until 1979 and to order the Energy Research and Development Administration to roll back the price of domestic oil. The consumers obviously got the message since they bought a record number of automobiles from the big-car divisions of U.S. manufacturers during the next 12 months, while compacts were left unsold.

These were the golden years of OPEC. U.S. consumption of gasoline soared above pre-embargo levels. Much of this increased demand was met by foreign supplies, as imports grew to 50 percent of consumption by mid-1979. In part this increased foreign dependence was achieved through a maze of controls and regulations, one part of which was the entitlements program.

The objective of regulation of the petroleum market has been to hold the U.S. price below the world price while providing adequate supplies of oil. A simple ceiling on U.S. prices would obviously not do the job, since oil would be diverted to foreign markets to be sold abroad at the higher world price. The solution was to subsidize the importation of foreign oil and tax domestic production. In essence, the system worked like this. The regulatory authorities set the price at which domestic producers could sell oil to refiners.* In early 1978 the average price of domestic crude was set at $9.50 per barrel. For the right to purchase this cheap oil, refiners had to purchase "entitlements" costing about

---

*This is a great simplification. Domestic oil was classified as "old" or "new" according to the age of the well, and different prices were set for each category.

$2.50 per barrel, so that the effective price to the refiner was $12. At the same time, the refiner could purchase foreign oil at the world price of $14.50, but to make it worthwhile, for every barrel of foreign crude imported, the refiner *received* an entitlement worth $2.50. The net price was again $12.

The net result of this scheme was that the price to the refiners, and hence the price relevant to consumers, was held below the world market price. Consumers facing bargain prices for oil had little incentive to conserve, so total U.S. consumption was higher than it would otherwise have been. In addition, the price to domestic producers was held below its equilibrium level, so there was less incentive to expand production from domestic sources. Diminished levels of domestic output were compensated by increased imports of foreign oil, made less expensive by the entitlement that came with each barrel. It is no wonder that our dependence on foreign sources grew, and overall consumption levels expanded to historic highs.

Energy policy in the 1970s was riddled with inconsistencies. We were encouraging total consumption and importation of foreign oil as described above, while the stated objective of every administration to hold office during the decade was to reduce our dependence on foreign suppliers. In 1977 the price of natural gas from old wells was held at 52 cents per thousand cubic feet, while gas was selling on intrastate markets at $2, and we were importing from Canada at $2.12. Natural gas found at depths of 15,000 feet or more below the earth's surface was freed from price controls. There exists less incentive to explore and extract gas at lesser depths, so we are again consuming an energy source that is more costly to produce than some feasible alternatives.

In May, 1979 we began a phased deregulation of oil prices, and in January of 1981 controls were lifted from the petroleum market. In the early part of 1981, gasoline prices spurted, but soon there were reports of a worldwide oil glut, and prices of both crude oil and refined products retreated slightly. U.S. oil consumption declined by 2.2 percent in 1981, and imports have fallen to 30 percent of total consumption. In the petroleum market the so-called crisis is over.

10. EXPLOITATION AND GROWTH

So maybe the energy crisis was only a short-term phenomenom, and we will be able to supply our resource needs into the foreseeable future. But if we can, isn't it only because we are exploiting the developing countries in the world? The U.S., with only 5 percent of the world's population, consumes many times that percentage of the world's resources. Nearly all of the U.S. consumption of tin, manganese, chrome, and nickel is imported from other countries. A large percentage of the copper, oil, iron ore, lead, and zinc that the U.S. consumes is supplied by others. Many see this as conclusive evidence that we are taking advantage of the emerging countries of the world by exploiting their rich raw materials to supply our resource needs.

When people accuse the United States, as well as other economically developed countries, of exploiting the developing countries, what do they mean? Are the resources being taken against the will of these countries or taken without just payment? Does the purchase of resources from these developing countries retard their development? Admittedly, confronting questions like this is more difficult than repeating catchy slogans about exploitation of the third world. But they are questions that deserve some thoughtful consideration.

What prompts most trade is the opportunity for two parties to make a mutually advantageous exchange. If one individual is skilled at producing food and another individual more efficient at making clothes, a natural trading situation exists. Both will be better off to concentrate on the activity that they do best—trading for the other item—instead of attempting to produce both items. The terms of the exchange will have to leave both individuals at least as well off as they would be without exchange, since either of them can refuse to trade. This is true whether we are talking about individuals or countries.

The industrially advanced nations of the world definitely have an advantage in producing finished manufacturing goods. But to realize this advantage, they need much larger quantities of raw materials and resources than they can provide themselves. As a result, they are willing to make attractive offers to the countries that will supply these resources. And offers have to be as attractive as those made by other countries for the same resources. The developing countries have an advantage in providing raw materials. Since their industrial capacity isn't fully developed, they find that they can get more finished goods by trading raw materials for them than if they produced these finished goods themselves. This type of trade provides developing countries with a way of speeding up their own development. It is much easier for the developing countries to obtain the products of advanced technologies and industrial capacity by exchanging raw materials for these things than by attempting to produce them internally.

However, when particular groups or companies appear to reap huge gains from international business in natural resources, the gains to the little guy are easily overlooked. In 1974 Indonesians demonstrated against Japanese exploitation of their natural resource wealth. Later that year, when a weakening economy forced Japan to curtail timber imports, Indonesian sales to Japan tumbled 40 percent. Timber prices in Indonesia dropped 60 percent, and numerous local companies went out of business, causing extensive unemployment in timber-producing areas. Suddenly the people of Indonesia were crying for more "exploitation" by Japanese business.[15]

It can be argued that it does a country little good to develop a modern industrial base if it does so at the expense of its natural resources. It's true that a country that pursues economic development through trade will develop at the expense of some of its resources. But what country has ever developed without expending some of its resources? The United States was a net exporter of raw material and resources until the 1920s.

But using existing resources doesn't necessarily result in a smaller usable resource base. As we have seen, with technological advances we have historically had a rapid expansion of our relevant resource base. And technological advance can be achieved only by using resources. To paraphrase an old saying about money, it takes resources to make resources. Presently, the developed countries are most capable of using resources to make technological advances. By currently exchanging raw materials for finished products, developing countries are doing more than taking the most rapid road to their own development. They are directing resources into those areas where they have the greatest chance of effecting technological breakthroughs that could expand the world's usable resource base.

Developing countries are plagued by many problems not touched on in the brief comments above. Many times international trade doesn't help the people in developing countries nearly as much as it could. It's not unusual to find few of the benefits filtering down to the masses. The advantages of trade can easily be used to finance extravagant living for a politically privileged few, with little being done to develop the country. Licensing arrangements between third-world governments and multinational corporations sometimes lead to a protected monopoly position, which again reduces the masses' share of the gains from trade. Trade barriers imposed by industrialized countries inhibit the growth of manufacturing industries in third-world nations.

But the fact that developing countries are not benefiting from trade as much as they could is not a valid argument against international exchange. This exchange serves to direct the world's resources toward the most efficient uses. By using the world's resources in the most efficient way, we can best take care of current needs and at the same time expand our resource base to take care of future needs as well.

DISCUSSION QUESTIONS

1. A popular accusation is that Americans have been wasting energy for years. How does such an accusation compare with claims that

the early pioneers wasted lumber? For years people allowed large amounts of heat to dissipate from their poorly insulated homes. Were they wasting energy or saving insulation?

2. Do you see a common cause for both excess exploitation of some of our natural resources and the pollution of our air and water?

3. Many people believe that since we have only a limited amount of oil in the ground that can technically be recovered, we will eventually exhaust it completely. Are there reasons to believe that this will never happen? What is the difference between technically recoverable oil and economically recoverable oil?

4. Do you think we would be better or worse off today if our forefathers had used lumber sparingly, consumed a great deal less coal and oil, mined less iron ore, and made much greater efforts to recycle nonrenewable resources?

5. Many have supported gas rationing because otherwise market prices would increase, which would hurt the poor. If you were debating an individual who took this position, how would you respond?

6. Full deregulation of natural gas prices will occur in 1985. In 1986 would you expect gas prices to be higher than, lower than or the same as if there had never been price controls? Why?

7. Everyone claims to be in favor of conservation. Yet most people have a negative view of speculators, despite the fact that speculators take resources out of current consumption in order to increase their availabilty in the future. Why this dislike of those who actually promote conservation?

chapter 9

Markets and Mythology

1. OPPORTUNITY COST REVISITED

Some might object to the discussion of the market system in previous chapters, contending that certain important features of modern-day capitalism have been ignored. In this chapter we propose to examine several common objections to the performance of the market system by employing the concept of opportunity cost implicitly and explicitly in our analysis. This important concept is also used to analyze several interesting social issues not directly related to criticisms of the market economy.

The pervasiveness of advertising and fashion changes, the inefficiencies of product distribution through numerous middlemen, the harmful effects of speculation, and the wastefulness of unemployment are often cited as objections to the capitalist system. People often fail to recognize that important functions are performed by each of these institutions. Criticisms of each of these processes should include consideration of the costs of eliminating them. Also, the market system has invaded some areas deemed inappropriate by some, and a timely example of this imperialism of the marketplace is the replacement of military conscription with an all-volunteer force. Here again, a careful accounting of costs reveals important insights into the conscription-volunteer debate. Finally, some difficult issues in identifying costs are tackled in a discussion of the 55-mile-per-hour speed limit. A careful analysis of all of these issues, employing the concept of opportunity cost, will lead to conclusions quite contrary to those implied by the conventional wisdom.

2. ADVERTISING AND THE MANIPULATION OF CONSUMERS

One of the pillars of support for the market system is the notion of consumer sovereignty. The consumer, through dollar "votes," determines what shall be produced, and therefore production must respond to individual preferences.

A contrary view, disseminated primarily by John Kenneth Galbraith, is that firms in modern society have "means for managing what the consumer buys," and that this condition "sends to the museum of irrelevant ideas the notion of an equilibrium in consumer outlays which reflects the maximum of consumer satisfaction."[1] Since consumer sovereignty does not exist according to this view, there is no reason to expect that the prevailing pattern of production provides a maximum of well-being to the individuals in society. The myth of scarcity has prompted us to be overly concerned with efficiency while neglecting the quality of life. According to Galbraith, we would have long since reached the nirvana where the supply of industrial products would "become routine in the manner of water from a waterworks in a year of adequate rainfall" had not advertising convinced people of the importance of ever-increasing production.[2]

Some social critics take a position even stronger than Galbraith's. According to Charles Reich, "Corporations decide what they want to produce, and they convince people that they want it, thus fashioning their own market."[3] Many critics of society find the orgy of consumption, in which many choose to indulge, quite repugnant. Advertising is found to be the likely villain that causes the masses to act in such a barbaric fashion and prevents them from rising above the baser materialistic pleasures.

If we consumers really are manipulated by the producers, as this view implies, much of our analysis of the market system is suspect. The premise of consumer sovereignty, the problem of scarcity, and the importance of efficient production are fundamental to economic reasoning. However, there is no evidence to support such strong contentions about the effects of advertising. Existing studies of the impact of advertising on consumer behavior indicate that advertising can have some effect on persuading people to choose among products that are substitutes for one another, in particular in shifting consumers between competing brands. Contrary to Galbraith's reasoning, one cannot infer from such effects that advertising distorts the whole pattern of consumer preferences. To say that a process that induces people to purchase Froot Loops rather than Cheerios undermines the whole principle of consumer sovereignty is a fairly gross extrapolation of the known effects of advertising. Such views also divert attention from the important role that advertising does play in supplying information about products and prices.

Before turning to the evidence of the effects of advertising on consumer behavior, it is useful to examine some of the implications of the Galbraithian position on advertising. Let us examine first the assertion that expenditure patterns, as influenced by advertising, no longer represent a maximum of consumer satisfaction. This claim must be based on the contention that only the fulfillment of natural wants, uninfluenced by advertising, can provide real satisfaction. Other wants—those contrived by advertisements—are artificial, and their fulfillment should not be considered a worthy objective for the economic system. For this to make any sense, there must actually exist the distinguishable categories of contrived and natural wants. But with the possible exception of mother's milk, can any of our demands be considered truly innate? Certainly the desires for food, shelter, and water might be considered in some sense more basic than our demand for, say, aesthetic things. But even for the basics of life, there exists a tremendous variability in consumption patterns because of environmental influences. One need only reflect upon the variety of ways in which people satisfy their basic needs for calories and nutrients to see that this is the case.

Our preferences are shaped by our total environment, one part of which is advertising, and it is therefore not meaningful to speak of one preference as inferior or less natural than another. Is an appreciation for Mozart, for example, which is by most accounts an acquired taste, considered to be of less importance than our more natural cravings? People who have been molded by their environment into an appreciation for Mozart will tell you otherwise. And just as one person's environment produces an appreciation for Mozart and fine wines, another will be led to football and Schlitz beer. Does the fact that advertising may have entered into the second person's decision to go with Schlitz make those tastes inferior to any other environmentally influenced preference? Since there is no means for distinguishing between natural and important tastes versus unnatural and inferior ones, there is no rationale for the view that the fulfillment of preferences that have been influenced by advertising provides any less satisfaction than the fulfillment of others not so affected.

Even if it were agreed that advertising has deleterious effects, what kind of policies might we enact to deal with the problem? Most people would suggest that firms should be restricted to providing advertisements of a purely informative nature, and that in particular they should be restrained from persuading people by the use of deceptive advertising. Unfortunately, it is not always easy to distinguish between deceptive promotional practices and purely honest ones. The case of the Federal Trade Commission (FTC) ruling against the Red Fox Overall Company illustrates the problem. The Red Fox firm had been providing satisfied customers with cotton overalls for almost 30 years when the FTC ruled that the use of the Red Fox brand name was deceptive. For, as the FTC correctly asserted, there was not a single fox fur to be found in the overalls produced by this firm. Such labeling was considered deceptive by the FTC. But to the many customers who had purchased overalls over the years, the Red Fox brand name provided useful information about product reliability.

Perhaps this overzealousness followed from the FTC campaign against deceptive advertising by manufacturers of synthetic furs. Advertisements for furlike synthetic materials are forbidden to include any mention of the word *fur*. Were it not for the fact that pictures can easily convey the message that the materials offered for sale possess some of the qualities of animal fur, it would not be possible to infer such important information from an ad for synthetic fur products. Clearly the suppression of the word *fur* eliminates a great deal of the informative content of the advertisement.

When the FTC moved to ban cigarette advertisements from radio and television, the question of distinguishing between informational and promotional content was not really involved. Such action is generally placed under the category of censorship. While one might consider cigarette smoking a dangerous and filthy habit, it should be recognized that an extension of this principle could bring an end to the advertising of such dangerous products as automobiles, skis, airline travel, and cholesterol-laden dairy products.

While nobody is in favor of deceptive or harmful advertising, we should be reluctant to accept measures that tend to restrict the flow of information about consumer products. A more reasonable approach would be to hold firms liable for false claims about products. Damaged parties could appeal through the courts for compensation for expenses incurred in the consumption of some good that did not perform according to the firm's contention.

Finally, who should pass judgment on what is to be produced if not the individual consumers in society? If advertising has so distorted our preferences that our consumption demands no longer reflect our most important wants, who then is sufficiently free of the persuasive powers of advertising to pass judgment on the true importance of various products? It is a small step from the claim that individuals are incapable of managing their personal consumption to the assertion that they are not capable of governing themselves.

Many critics of advertising would have us believe that it has transformed us from contented, simple people into raving consumers who rush lemminglike from product to product in response to a barrage of obnoxious commercials. Fortunately, there is evidence that advertising has not had such effect. Advertising can create wants only in the sense that a desire for a product cannot exist until people are informed of its existence. Abstracting from this purely informational role, there is no evidence that the general pattern of consumption is any different from what it would be if advertising did not take place. On the contrary, countries with differing patterns of advertising display a similar composition of consumption expenditures, and even in countries like the Soviet Union where advertising is severely restricted, the demand for consumer products looks very similar to that in capitalist countries of comparable wealth.

If the Galbraithian view of advertising is correct, why is it that firms find it necessary to spend considerable sums on research of consumer preferences and the marketability of their products? Why is it that between one-third and one-half of all new products are withdrawn within one year as failures? Certainly the power to manage demand, if it really existed, could be employed to avoid such costly market failures.

Finally, if advertising is in fact effective in controlling consumer preferences, we would expect the brands that are most heavily advertised to demonstrate greatest success in maintaining a large share of the market. There is, however, no evidence that this is true. How can the Galbraithian position be reconciled with the fact that the market share of three heavily advertised detergents—Rinso, Super Suds, and Oxydol—fell from 48 percent in 1948 to a mere 5 percent five years later; or that Camel, Lucky Strike, and Chesterfield accounted for 42 percent of cigarette sales in 1956 but only 18 percent in 1966? That these figures are not exceptions is demonstrated by a more comprehensive study of the relation between advertising and market shares. Lester Telser examined the change in market share of the four leading brands in 28 food product lines (which are not heavily advertised) and in 15 toiletries and cosmetic products (which are heavily advertised). He found the market shares of the leading brands in the food products industries were more stable than those of the leading toiletries and cosmetic firms.[4] Apparently, advertising heavily does not sufficiently manipulate consumers to guarantee a persistently strong market share for any particular product.

Since market shares appear to be the least stable in heavily advertised product lines, it is apparent that advertising enables new brands to break into existing markets. In this sense, advertising serves the important function of providing information on the availability of new products.

We do not wish to claim that advertising has no faults or even that it is the ideal means for spreading information. The success of *Consumer Reports* attests to a strong reluctance to rely on advertising as the most accurate and complete source of information. It is also the case that much advertising is wasteful and redundant and provides little of informative value to consumers. This is most often the case in competitive advertising between long-standing brands of the same product. But if the alternative to advertising is censorship, there is little doubt that the inefficiencies of repetitive and uninformative advertising impose a cost that is small, relative to one imposed by governmental control of promotional activities.

It is difficult to tolerate an industry that destroys your favorite scenery with billboards or interrupts your TV and radio entertainment with annoying jingles. Perhaps this displeasure with advertising is converted into a fear of its impact on society. No evidence has been presented by the critics of advertising to demonstrate its purported effectiveness in creating consumer wants. Certainly firms find it profitable to advertise—sometimes out of self-defense against competitors, sometimes to publicize a new product. But there is no evidence that advertising has had any significant impact on the overall pattern or level of consumption that prevails in our economy.

3. ELIMINATING THE MIDDLEMAN

According to the sales pitch of many retail stores, the unfortunate middleman in our economy has been eliminated more times than the "bad guys" in John Wayne movies. Everyone wants to eliminate the middleman so that you, the consumer, can save a bundle.

Retail merchants are not the only ones promoting the elimination of the middleman. Some critics of the capitalist system point to the billions of dollars spent on sales and distribution of merchandise as economic waste. A majority of food buyers have placed the blame of rising food prices squarely on the shoulders of the middleman. There is implicit in all these positions the presumption that the middleman does not perform a useful service, and hence products can be offered more cheaply if he is circumvented. There is an all too common tendency to assume that the distribution of goods and the provision of information about them can be achieved without cost. Unfortunately, this is not the case, and billions of dollars worth of valuable resources must be spent on activities associated with the middleman.

Take, for example, a typical food product. A bushel of wheat has to pass through many hands between the farmer and the individual household. First of all, most farmers sell their wheat to a grain dealer or turn it over to a farmers' cooperative. Farmers are specialists in growing food products, and they would rather not deal heavily in the problems of managing a huge sales operation. Thus they sell their wheat to groups who specialize in the trading of grain. These firms are experts in the mechanics of marketing grain. They keep in touch with market conditions, at home and abroad, and maintain close contact with buyers and sellers.

The unprocessed wheat, since it is fairly unappealing to consumers in that form, is sold by the grain dealers to millers or other food processors. It is this group that is pointed out for special condemnation in the battle against high food prices. Some have pointed out, quite correctly, that the percentage of the household's food expenditures that goes to the food processor has increased substantially in the last several years. But people are buying greater amounts of processing with their food. Frozen dinners, canned sauces, precooked meats, prepared desserts, and so on are accounting for larger and larger shares of household food purchases. Processors are not extracting more revenue for their services; they are simply providing more of those services in accordance with consumer preferences.

After processing, the food product moves on to the wholesaler, who specializes in the distribution of goods to smaller retailing units. The miller, who produces flour, does not want to bother selling individual bags of flour to the several thousand food retailers in the area. The miller is a specialist in processing wheat, not in distributing it to retail outlets. The wholesaler relieves the miller of this burden by purchasing flour in huge quantities, and then reselling in smaller quantities to individual merchants.

Wholesalers don't want to bother with marketing the product to individual consumers. They specialize in the distribution of large quantities to individual retailers. Their expertise is not in display and promotion of the product. This task is left up to the retailer, who is an expert in marketing techniques and local consumers' wants.

It is no wonder, then, that by the time the final product reaches the consumer, the price greatly exceeds the basic cost of production. But this does not mean that consumers are not receiving a dollar's worth of goods and services for each dollar in expenditures. While it is true that they are not receiving one dollar's worth of food product, they are realizing one dollar's worth of food plus processing and distributional services. The only way to eliminate the middlemen is to eliminate the services they provide.

Now, of course, some large retailing concerns also have their own wholesale operations and sometimes even their own processing units. But this does not mean that the middleman is eliminated. In such cases we simply have two or more middleman operations carried out by one enterprise. Since all processing, wholesaling, and retailing operations are still carried out, there are no savings to be passed on to the consumer. It does not matter if Safeway Stores has its own wholesaling operation or purchases through some other firm. Some firm is providing distributional services, and the consumer will have to pay for it.

It is possible, of course, that certain savings can be realized in the area of product distribution if a single firm has control over a large-scale operation. Wholesaling and retailing activities, for example, may be more efficiently performed if they are provided jointly by a single firm with extensive marketing activities. While some savings may then be available, this is a result of greater efficiency in performing middleman services, not a result of eliminating them.

In the case of discount stores, prices are actually reduced by the elimination of some middleman's service, usually at the retail level. Consumers pay lower prices and also receive less retail service in the form of information and shopping convenience. Many find this worthwhile, but the fact that higher-priced stores can coexist with discount houses indicates that many consumers are willing to pay for greater shopping convenience and assistance than is provided by discount houses. Discount stores really have eliminated middlemen, but they have also eliminated the services that they provide.

4. SPECULATORS: THE MESSENGERS OF BAD TIDINGS

During the agricultural price surge in 1973, the complaint was sometimes heard that speculators were benefiting from, and even causing, the price increases. While consumers were paying significantly higher prices, farmers were not receiving much of the gain, because they had long since sold their produce to speculators. Alas, the wily speculator had swindled the farmers out of their rightful reward, and the higher consumer prices were merely fattening the purses of those who never touched a plow.

Why do we put up with this profiteering nonsense? Speculators are condoned because they perform a useful service for society. They act to assure an orderly allocation of a commodity over time. Were speculative markets to be outlawed, some other means would have to be found for storing goods when they were in excess and releasing them when quantities were scarce.

If grains are harvested once a year, for example, it would not be desirable to have all the grain consumed within three months of the harvest. We want to save enough so that our level of grain consumption will be fairly even over the entire twelve-month period. Conceivably this could be accomplished by individual farmers, who would release their harvest only gradually or by individual households, who could purchase their entire year's demand at the time of harvest. But the farmer wants to make money from efficient farming techniques and does not want profits to be erased by a shift in market conditions over the year. The consumer does not want to store produce in bulk, particularly if there is the danger of spoilage. So a third party is found who is willing to bear the risk of price changes and undertake storage responsibilities in the hope of making a nice profit along the way. This third party, the speculator, purchases grain when it is abundant and its price is low in the hope that its price will rise sometime in the near future. The individual farmer is, of course, also free to speculate, but most often he or she would prefer to have someone else bear the risk involved.

Organized speculative markets permit individuals to make contracts today that specify the terms of sale for some time in the future. This enables some persons to avoid certain kinds of risks, while permitting others to accept these risks in the hope of making a speculative profit. A wheat farmer may have to decide in May how much grain to grow for harvesting and marketing in September. Most farmers would like to be able to make this decision without facing the uncertainty of price changes in the intervening months. They therefore arrange in May to deliver a certain quantity of wheat in September at a price that is set by contract. When they do so, they forgo the opportunity of making windfall profits if September prices are high because of a bad harvest in other parts of the country, but more importantly they insure themselves against a financial loss if the bottom falls out of the grain market. Since they are eager to have this insurance, they should not complain then if the price of wheat rises between May and September, leaving the speculator with a huge profit which would have been their own. To complain about the speculator's profit at this point is like arguing that last year's life insurance premiums were worthless because you did not die during that period.

On the other side of the market, we also have mill operators, who would like to contract now for future deliveries of wheat without the risk of price increases over the next several months. Speculators will be forthcoming, and they are willing to provide just such a contract at a certain price.

Exactly what prices are established on such *futures* contracts depends on people's expectations. For example, if blight is expected to ruin a large part of next September's corn crop, September corn prices will tend to be high. Farmers promising September delivery of corn will be guaranteed a high price, and feed grain processors contracting to buy in September will need to agree to purchase at high prices. If the crop turns out to be successful after all, September prices will be lower than expected, but the farmer is protected against any loss as a result. The speculator who purchased the futures contract is the big loser. The feed or grain processor, of course, missed out on a windfall profit but had no way of knowing in advance which way prices would go. He or she is stuck with the high-priced contract but has no justification for complaint since the contract was willingly assumed to avoid losses from a price rise.

So we have seen first of all that speculation permits people to insure themselves against losses due to unpredictable changes in market conditions. This analysis also enables us to see how speculative markets provide for an even distribution of the product over time. Suppose again that in May there are expectations of a crop failure in September. Prices on contracts for delivery in September are bid up. Seeing this, firms engaged in the storage of grain hold more grain off the current market in order to sell it at the higher price in September. With grain withheld from today's market, the current price begins to rise. Consumers cut back on their current consumption of this product because of the higher prices. This is a reasonable and desirable occurrence, for rational planning would call for lower consumption levels today in order to save sufficient amounts for the future when grain harvests are expected to be poor.

Notice that this comes about purely as the result of individual speculators trying to make a profit. No government agency has to step in and order food to be saved for the future. Rationing occurs in an orderly way, through changes in prices on current markets and futures contracts.

The importance of speculative markets can perhaps best be appreciated by examining conditions in their absence. In 1959, for example, the futures market in onions was abolished. Fluctuations in onion prices since 1959 have been considerably more erratic than they were before 1959 when the market existed.

In Spain, during the Civil War, people became annoyed at the speculators who always bought up the crops at harvest time, only to sell them later at much higher prices. This not only gave speculators a healthy profit each year, but also caused the prices at harvest time to be much higher than they otherwise would be. People drove these profiteers out of town, and, as expected, prices at harvest time were very low. Everyone rejoiced and consumed food lavishly, often using products wastefully as animal feed, since they were so cheap. But with no speculative activity, there was no inducement to save for the future. Grains ran out long before the next harvest, and severe hunger resulted.

India has had frequent problems with regional droughts and consequent crop disasters. When speculation was outlawed, there was no mechanism to even out consumption over time or to attract additional food from other nondrought regions. When speculation was permitted and even encouraged, futures markets did develop and food consumption was spread evenly over time and place. The difference between disastrous and more mild incidents derives not entirely from the severity of the climatic conditions but at least partially from the existence or absence of speculative markets.

There is a temptation, it is said, to punish the bearer of bad tidings rather than blaming the true source of the difficulties. The speculator is like the messenger with bad news; he or she does not cause crop failure, but merely responds to it, bidding up prices and thereby providing the information that food is becoming scarce and that measures to conserve should be taken. In the same way that killing the messenger makes people worse off by eliminating their source of information, so does the removal of the speculator prevent the communication of information about future scarcities. Speculators perform an important service in an economy, and it is necessary to provide the opportunity for profit if this service is to be provided under a market system.

5. UNEMPLOYMENT CAUSED BY TOO MANY JOBS

When asked why we have unemployment, most people will respond that there are not enough jobs. It is widely believed that unemployment is the result of people looking for work and not being able to find it. With the slightest reflection, however, it is easily seen that this cannot possibly be true. After all, this is a world of scarcity that we live in, and the obvious implication of scarcity is that we all want more goods and services—goods and services that can only be produced by having people work. There is quite literally an unlimited amount of work to be done. We would all like to have more people working for us, producing more of the things we would like to have. For example, each of you would surely be willing to hire every student on your campus to wait on you, run errands for you, and so on, if only the wage that you had to pay was low enough.

Of course, it is silly to consider a wage so low that you would be willing to hire everyone on your campus. Because of scarcity and the fact that there is an unlimited number of jobs to be done, it would not be a good idea to have the entire student body working for you. The important object is not simply finding jobs for people (that is no problem), but finding those jobs in which the value of the workers' contribution is as high as possible. And because there are so many jobs to be done, it is not always easy for people to find those jobs that are best suited to their skills and training. When entering the labor force for the first time or returning to the labor force after having dropped out for a time, it would make no sense to take the first job that came along. With the large number of possible jobs available (at a sufficiently low wage), it does make sense for people to remain unemployed long enough to search out and find an acceptable one. In other words, much of what is seen as unemployment exists because of the large number of jobs that have to be considered before deciding on the one that is most acceptable.

The unemployment that comes from searching for the best job is often referred to by economists as *frictional unemployment.* A better name would be *fictional unemployment,* since searching for one's best employment opportunity is a very productive activity. Anytime there is a shift in consumer preferences or an improvement in technology, some workers will find their effort in existing jobs less valuable than it would be in alternative employment. It is obviously desirable in this situation for workers to shift out of less-valuable employment and into a more valuable one. In the real world, where there is no such thing as complete information, searching out the more valuable employment is the same as producing very valuable knowledge. While people are unemployed, they can be producing knowledge about where their best opportunities exist.

It follows that a certain amount of what we think of as unemployment is desirable. While zero unemployment may sound like an ideal situation, it would, in fact, indicate very poor economic performance. Not allowing any unemployment is the same as not allowing workers to respond appropriately to the changing demands of consumers and the improved opportunities that result from technological advances. The only policy that could genuinely guarantee zero unemployment would be a policy of complete economic stagnation.

Indeed, the economic progress that we have made since the day of our grandparents and the increased wealth we enjoy is the direct consequence of destroying jobs. Increased agricultural productivity destroyed millions of jobs on the farm; The advent of the automobile eliminated many blacksmith jobs; Advances in telephone technology eliminated the jobs of many telephone operators;* Pac Man has eaten up the jobs of many pinball machine manufacturers, and so on. One way to look at this process is to see technological progress as destroying jobs. And it does destroy particular jobs. But it is more useful to see technological progress as releasing valuable resources (primarily labor) from less-productive effort so that they can be put to more productive use elsewhere. Every time one job is destroyed by technological progress, other, more productive, jobs become available.

One often hears the question: will the trend toward increased automation result in a trend of increasing unemployment? The best answer to this question is: *unfortunately,* no. Only if we overcome scarcity will it be true that reducing the amount of labor required to produce desirable things will cause a long-term increase in unemployment. Unfortunately, there seems to be little hope of overcoming scarcity. No matter how productive we become, we will still find ourselves wanting more than is available, and human effort in one form or another is still required to produce what we want. Only in the absence of scarcity would there be massive and permanent unemployment. Without scarcity, for example, economists would be unemployed, since our job is to study and explain the effects of scarcity. But that would be fine with the authors of this book. Who would want to be working in a world without scarcity? We would want to get on with the full-time job of consuming. But unfortunately scarcity abounds, and increased automation will not increase long-run unemployment.

Of course, automation will increase temporary unemployment as people shift to more productive jobs. This temporary unemployment can be disruptive to peoples' lives, and this is a cost that should not be dismissed. As any economist can tell you, everything has a cost—and economic progress is no exception. We suspect, however, that most people would agree that economic progress has been worth this cost if they realistically compared current standards of living with that which prevailed, say, 100 years ago. Yet it may be appropriate to reduce this cost to the unemployed by providing unemployment compensation and other forms of assistance. One has to recognize, however, that by reducing the personal cost to the unemployed of searching for work, job searches will last longer than otherwise. This has the effect of increasing the measured rate of unemployment. Also, the fact that many households now have more than one member employed reduces the cost

---

*If we still had to handle telephone calls the way we did at the beginning of the 20th century, over half the U.S. population would have to be employed as operators to handle the current volume of calls.

when one becomes unemployed. For example, almost half of those families in which one or more members were unemployed in 1980 had an income of at least $20,000.[5] Even so, most of the unemployed are not without jobs for long periods of time. In early 1982, a period of high unemployment, the median duration of unemployment was $8\frac{1}{2}$ weeks, and almost 40 percent of the unemployed were re-employed within 4 weeks.[6]

But, again, we want to point out that unemployment can be very long and disruptive for those looking for a new job. And although some unemployment is indicative of a healthy economy, excessive unemployment is not. Unemployment can become excessive, for example, when those who are looking for new jobs have expectations that do not conform to actual economic conditions. A discussion of this problem is more appropriate for a book dealing with macroeconomic topics and will not be pursued here, except to say that serious attempts to reduce inflation will generally lead to excessive unemployment for a time.[7]

The problem of unemployment is simply another consequence of the more general problem of scarcity. In the absence of scarcity, unemployment would not be a problem because there would be no demand for people to work. But given that we have an abundance of scarcity, unemployment will be a problem because there are too many jobs to be done.

6. FASHION, FREEDOM, AND AFFLUENCE

Fashions in clothing seem to be constantly changing. The authors certainly cannot keep up. Our lapels are narrow when they should be wide, our ties are wide when they should be narrow, and our 100 percent polyester leisure suits are still in the closet waiting for a comeback. Women have it just as bad, maybe worse. Pantsuits are out and designer jeans are in (assuming you have the right imprimatur across your behind). Skirts are still going up and down, although they haven't become as short as they did in the late 1960s. And now what appears to be a short skirt may turn out, upon closer inspection, to be a *skort*—loose shorts that look like a skirt. As of this writing, skorts are "moving up" in the fashion world. It seems that women's hats are in again, and knickers are attempting a comeback. But by the time this book goes into print, who knows what people will be wearing?

It was not always so. Fashions have always been subject to change, but it was more modestly paced in the past. George Washington was able to stay with his powdered wigs, ruffled shirts, and breeches a lot longer than your authors were able to stay with their leisure suits. Also, the women during George's day were able to fashionably subject themselves to corsets and bustles for many years. Why is it that clothing fashions are changing more rapidly now than in previous times? Some people will immediately argue that rapid fashion change is but another example of the wasteful influence of Madison Avenue advertising. Since we have already argued that advertising is not able to dictate public tastes to the extent many people believe, we do not want to give Madison Avenue too much credit here, although it certainly deserves some. But if you do not like rapid fashion changes in clothing, the real culprits are freedom and affluence. Let us explain why.

It has to be recognized first that clothing is valued for more than its ability to provide comfort and cover our nakedness. Many of our outfits do very little of either. For many people, clothing is a way of making a statement about their lifestyle, their wealth, or importance. People who are financially successful, for example, will often want to advertise this fact, and one way of doing so is through expensive clothes that distinguish them from the masses. Historically, not having to engage in dirty physical work was an unmistakable sign of wealth and high social standing. So clothing could attest to one's wealth by being expensive and by being ill-suited for any but the most leisurely and sanitized activities. The woman who wore a suffocating corset, a protruding bustle, and shoes that looked like stilts, was obviously not a woman who was burdened with physical labor.

Of course, many people who are not particularly successful, wealthy, or of high social standing like to appear to be, at least on occasion. One way of doing this is by dressing like socially prominent style setters. Where do we find these style setters? They used to be found among royalty, military heroes, or the successful in business. Today they come from even more varied backgrounds and accomplishments and can be found in *People* magazine. They are almost always people who are envied by many because of some fascinating attribute or accomplishment. They are also people who generally enjoy being distinguishable from the common crowd. For this very reason, style setters will seldom stay with the style they started once it becomes popular among the masses. The success of a clothing fashion can sow the seeds of its own destruction, as the style setters move on to different fashions about the time their creations are selling well at K-Mart.

Having their distinguishing fashions copied by commoners can be most inconvenient to the social elites. They would like to be able to advertise their standing without having to adjust their wardrobes constantly. This was not much of a problem in feudal societies where the peons knew their place, and even if they did try to get uppity, they didn't have the money to pull it off. However, just in case a man of low birth attempted to dress the role of a wealthy gentleman in 14th-century England, it was declared against the law. King Edward III decreed:

All esquires and every gentleman under the estate of knighthood, and not possessed of lands and tenements to the yearly amount of 200 marks, shall use in their dress such cloth as does not exceed the value of 4 marks and a half the whole cloth; they shall not wear any cloth of gold, or silk, or of silver, nor any sort of embroidered garment, nor any ring, buckle, nouche, riband nor girdle; nor any ornaments of precious stones, nor furs of any kind; their wives and children shall be subject to the same regulation.[8]

A century later in England, which was before men's trousers, the style in men's coats found them so short that the man of fashion who bent over, rather than stooped down, exposed his buttocks. Again, the socially elevated wanted to protect their fashion against the imitation of the culturally crude. So an English law, passed in 1475, proclaimed:

Nobody below the rank of Lord, Esquire, or Gentleman may wear a coat, cape, or smock so short that when he stands erect it fails to cover his private parts and buttocks, in which case he pays a fine of 20 shillings.[9]

The poverty of the masses and laws of this type served, during historic times, to protect the affluent against mass imitation and kept the rate at which fashions changed relatively slow. Fashions in clothing still changed, of course, but largely as a result of competition for status among the restricted few at the top of the social ladder. It took removal of legal restriction on dress, increased wealth, and the real possibility of upward mobility before rapid changes in fashions began to occur. Today, no matter how famous or rich you happen to be, it is impossible to protect your wardrobe against the mimicry of the many. As the wedding of Prince Charles and Lady Diana approached, careful precautions were taken to make sure that the design of Lady Di's wedding dress was kept secret. But before the royal couple had exchanged vows, thousands of wedding dresses that looked identical to Lady Di's were being produced around the world for less-exalted brides.

Because of the freedom and affluence made possible by free-market economics, the average person quickly knows what the style setters are wearing and has the freedom and affluence to acquire fashions that, if not identical, are close imitations. This is the reason clothing fashions change rapidly. It is a problem that those living in the Soviet Union, Poland, Communist China, and Cuba are not burdened with. There are very few leisure suits hanging in their closets. But in our opinion, leisure suits and rapid fashion changes are a small price to pay for the freedom and affluence that we are so fortunate to have.

7. A RETURN TO THE DRAFT?

Throughout most of the post-World War II era, the United States has relied on conscription to fill the ranks of our armed forces. The perceived need for a large standing army, even during times of peace, required that a large percentage of eligible young males be recruited into the military. Tensions arising during the Viet Nam War and the inequities of the system of selective conscription, with deferments and exemptions, undermined political support for the draft and paved the way for the present system of voluntary military service.

Since 1973 the branches of the military have relied on economic incentives to meet their personnel needs. Over the past ten years the all-volunteer armed force has come under attack from a number of military leaders, members of Congress, journalists, and academics. The criticisms range from the claim that the AVF is too expensive to the contention that the services are unable to attract the quantity or quality of soldiers necessary to maintain an effective fighting force. With blacks accounting for approximately 22 percent of enlisted personnel, many question the equity of our present system of recruitment. Some are now arguing for a return to the draft; others recommend an alternative system of incentives involving preferential treatment for veterans in public service jobs and educational subsidies.[10] With the nation already registering youths for a possible conscription and proceeding to prosecute nonregistrants, it is important that we look carefully at these issues.

In 1978 the General Accounting Office determined that the all-volunteer force cost U.S. taxpayers an extra $3 billion per year over the manpower costs under the draft. However, that the all-volunteer force is more costly than a system with conscription is an illusion. Personnel costs are not less under a draft; they are simply shifted on to one particular group, namely the draftees. If the military were to attempt to reduce personnel costs by cutting pay and relying on the draft to fill the ranks, this would simply shift a portion of the cost from the taxpayers to the draftees. The cost of a young person's service in the military, remember, is the value of those opportunities forgone. Generally, the opportunity sacrificed here is a civilian job, with a value equal to the salary and nonmonetary compensation one could expect to receive. With military pay reduced below that which individuals could receive in civilian jobs, and assuming some preference for civilian over military lifestyles, the draftees would suffer a cost equal to the amount that they would have to be paid to join voluntarily.

Suppose, for example, that military salaries were reduced $3000 below the levels necessary to maintain a full-strength, all-volunteer force, and that any deficiencies in recruitment were made up through conscription. For every person drafted to serve, the taxpayers save $3000, but the individual draftee suffers a cost in terms of income forgone and aversion to military duty valued at $3000. Personnel costs to society as a whole are no different in either case. The only difference is in who pays the cost—the taxpayers as a whole or the men who are unfortunate enough to be drafted.

The question of equity is seldom addressed in these terms. The issue of equity under the AVF has to do with representativeness: to what extent are we relying on disadvantaged youths in society—blacks and those from lower socioeconomic classes—to carry the burden of defending our country. Only 14 percent of this country's population is black, but more than 20 percent of all enlisted personnel and over 30 percent of Army enlisted personnel are black. In addition, the services are recruiting a disproportionate number of youths without high school diplomas and persons from low-income families.[11]

No one should be surprised at these figures. When recruitment is based on economic incentives, those facing less favorable civilian employment opportunities will be most strongly attracted by recruitment into a military service that does not discriminate by race and pays equal wages to each rank, regardless of educational attainment. Nor is it clear if such data should be viewed with alarm or even concern. Not only are blacks disproportionately represented in the enlisted ranks, but with significantly higher re-enlistment rates than whites, blacks under the AVF have more than doubled their percentage in the officer corps as compared with the pre-Viet Nam period.[12] Military service, particularly in the officer ranks, has proven to be a valuable training ground for civilian employment, with service veterans earning significantly more than nonveterans of comparable backgrounds.[13] Would a more "selective" service be to the advantage of youths who presently view military recruitment more favorably than civilian opportunities?

Those who answer yes argue that today's volunteers are recruited under a system of economic conscription. They serve because the civilian sector has failed to provide a viable alternative. Consequently, the least advantaged in our society face the preeminent risk of becoming casualties in our next war. When risk of injury or death is involved, the burden should be shared more evenly across society. However, such reasoning is certainly not applied to civilian occupations which are not only risky but also contribute significantly to our national security. How often has conscription been suggested for city police forces? What about a coercive arrangement to guarantee that the middle- and upper-class whites are fairly represented on sea-based oil rigs or in the coal mines? The answer is that not only would such a system lead to an inefficient use of valuable labor resources, but also workers who incur risks receive, on the average, compensating wage payments. Such workers accept these high-risk jobs, just as some individuals join the Army, because they see such opportunities as more favorable than existing alternatives.

To put this issue into clearer perspective, suppose we decided to remedy these perceived "inequities" by returning to the draft. As long as military pay remained comparable to civilian pay, the services would continue to receive applications for enlistment from various socioeconomic groups roughly in the same proportions as they do now. Of course, the military could accept fewer black or lower-class volunteers, but it is doubtful that such conscious discrimination is what the critics of the AVF are recommending. Alternatively, the government could let military pay fall below civilian pay so that there would be a shortfall of volunteers. Now in this situation the volunteers are not only carrying the burden of defending our country, they are serving at substandard wages. Furthermore, a disproportionate number of these volunteers would still come from the lower socioeconomic classes, and even though this may be evened out somewhat by the more representative group of draftees, we would still have an unrepresentative enlisted force.

The issues of cost and equity are minor in the eyes of those who contend that we are not meeting our personnel goals under the AVF. One frequently encounters articles in the press grousing about the failure of the AVF to recruit the quantity and quality of personnel we need for an effective fighting force. While effectiveness is impossible to measure until we are actually confronted with military involvement, we can at least evaluate the objective characteristics of the present force relative to those under the draft and consider the trends in these characteristics over the ten-year period of all-volunteer recruitment.

The first point is concerned with absolute numbers. Contrary to widespread misconceptions, the all-volunteer force has been largely successful in meeting the goals for active duty personnel. In every year since its inception, active-duty strength has been within one and one-half percent of congressionally authorized ceilings.[14] Recruitment has been adequate in spite of the fact that military pay has not matched the growth in civilian pay. Between 1975 and 1979 military pay declined by about 10 percent relative to earnings in the private sector.[15] The very strong recruitment of 1980 and 1981 was due to a surge in rates of military pay that more than kept pace with civilian earnings.

Critics argue that the services have been able to fill their quotas only by reducing educational and mental test score standards. There can be little doubt that by permitting military pay to fall behind civilian wages, we have not attracted recruits of the highest educational levels and mental abilities, and it is no surprise that the quality of recruits improved in the early eighties with the increase in military pay. In any case, the evidence does not support the claim of lower standards under the AVF. In 1979, 88 percent of all enlisted active duty personnel had a high school diploma, compared with 81 percent in 1972—the year of the last draft calls—and only 75 percent in 1964, just prior to the draft calls for Viet Nam.[16] As a high school diploma has been observed to be a good predictor of success in the military and a strong indication of the qualities the services desire, these are encouraging facts indeed.

However, population changes will make it more difficult to meet the goals of numbers and quality of personnel in the future. The number of 18–20-year-old males will decline by 18 percent between now and the late 1980s. While this could make recruiting more difficult in the future, the demographics are not as unfavorable as these figures might suggest. First of all, today's military is recruiting women in much greater numbers than before (11 percent of total planned strength for 1983), and this opens up a pool of potential recruits far exceeding the decline in male youths. Second, the size of the active force required under the AVF is lower (2 million versus roughly 2.5 million maintained prior to Viet Nam) than under the draft due to greater employment of civilians by the military and higher re-enlistment rates. Finally, the reduction in the youth population will still leave us with a larger pool to draw from than we had in any year prior to 1967.[17] If we maintain current numbers of 18–20-year-old males on active duty, the military will be drawing a smaller fraction of this population than in any pre-AVF year.

As a final indictment of the AVF, critics are quick to cite reports of poor attitude, lack of discipline, and pampering of recruits. A typical subjective analysis of the attitudes in the ranks is given by this quote by the late Representative William Steiger of Wisconsin:

I would like to share with you the findings of a study I have made regarding the state of the Army . . . . Volunteers repeatedly said that recruiters had misled them as to the job opportunities and assignments. Dependents stated that medical care was difficult to obtain and, when given, was delivered in a callous and impersonal manner. Experienced commanders stated that discipline had never been worse; that rates of court-martials, article 15s, and absences were at alltime highs. Units were often unable to train due to the absence of key personnel. Senior enlisted men complained that the quality of troops had declined significantly and that the growing number of individuals in mental group IV had made training and discipline nearly impossible . . . .[18]

After detailing numerous additional grievances, Representative Steiger pointed out that his tour had taken place in 1971, at the height of the draft. As these are precisely the complaints that one hears about today's Army, it is useful to place such criticisms in the perspective of other recent experiences. The Army has always experienced a certain amount of grousing, disciplinary problems, and negative attitudes. There is certainly no reason to expect the AVF to be immune to these.

Some feel uncomfortable with imperialism of the marketplace—the intrusion of economic incentives into areas previously reserved for government directives and resource allocation by coercion. Few institutions more coercive and arbitrary than military conscription can be imagined, and yet critics of the AVF would advocate some return to this system for meeting our military personnel goals. A review of the evidence shows that the use of economic inducements can satisfy our objectives in terms of numbers and quality, and if we wish to raise standards or strengths, an increase in relative pay will suffice. A draft would be neither less costly (when correctly considered in terms of opportunity cost) nor more equitable, remembering our experience with draft deferments and low pay during the 1960s. A system of economic incentives remains the least capricious and most efficient means for dealing with this problem of resource allocation.

8. DEATH ON THE HIGHWAYS

Late in 1973 the Arab members of the Organization of Petroleum Exporting Countries (OPEC) imposed an embargo of oil shipments to the U.S. and other nations supporting Israel in the war against Egypt and Syria. In an effort to reduce petroleum consumption, states were urged to limit highway speeds to a maximum of 55 miles per hour, and a national speed limit was enforced through threat of highway fund cut-offs. While the actual savings of gasoline fell short of expectations, there was a dramatic reduction in highway fatalities following the adoption of the 55-mph speed limit. As a result, continued support for maintenance of the speed limit has come from arguments for saving lives rather than saving gas.

It is the unhappy task of economic analysis to point out that any benefit, such as the saving of lives, comes at some cost, and as usual we might ask if the gains from this policy exceed the costs. However, many contend that human life is priceless, and there is no basis for objectively placing a value, in terms of dollars or other measures, on the saving of lives. This raises some interesting issues. Certainly, if you are asked if you would accept a large nontransferable gift on the condition of immediate and certain death, there is no amount you would accept for such a prospect. In this sense, your life is priceless. However, in the real world, life-and-death decisions are not this simple. Generally, people face choices between alternatives that may affect their life expectancy with some (possibly unknown) probability, and people do in fact make decisions that imply some trade-off between the risk of a reduced life span and the denial of some pleasure-giving or income-producing activity. Smokers sacrifice years of probable life expectancy for the joys of a regular dose of nicotine. Some motorists neglect the upkeep of safety equipment on their automobiles, trading off risk of death or injury for a little extra cash in the pocket. Surveys indicate that fewer than 20 percent of all motorists regularly use seatbelts, suggesting that a little extra time and comfort is worth a considerable increase in the risk of a traffic fatality.

Society as a whole, represented through governmental decisions, also is faced with decisions which will alter life expectancies. A decision to support research on nuclear power represents some implicit valuation of risk versus reduced energy supplies. Expenditures on public-health projects increase life expectancies while diverting resources from other valued alternatives. The improvement of health standards through the regulation of air quality imposes costs on consumers in the form of higher costs of production and hence higher prices for consumption goods. Since valuation of risk of death or injury is implicit in many such collective as well as private decisions, it is senseless to argue that the value of human life should be placed above economic considerations. Through individual actions, each member of society indicates the value he or she places on increases in life expectancy, and collective decisions should reflect this valuation as well. The optimal level of risk is not zero, just as the optimal level of pollution is not zero (see Chapter 7). As the riskiness of any project or activity is reduced, it becomes increasingly costly to gain further reductions in risk. Eventually, the reductions in risk become so expensive that members of society would prefer channeling valuable resources away from safety toward other desirable objectives. This point will be reached long before risks are reduced to zero.

This logic applies with equal force to the imposition of a maximum speed limit. The evidence is fairly clear that by lowering the speed limit on open highways to 55 mph, average speeds and variability of speeds have been reduced, and traffic fatalities have dropped substantially. Total traffic deaths peaked in 1973 at 54,000 and dropped to 45,000 the following year. Traffic fatalities per 100 million vehicle miles fell from 4.12 in 1973 to an average of 3.25 throughout the late seventies.[19] Average speeds have fallen by more than four miles per hour since the adoption of the speed limit, and this has accounted for much of the reduction in traffic fatalities. It is reasonable to suppose that further reductions in average speeds, through enforcement of an even lower maximum speed limit, would lower fatalities even more. In fact, we could reduce traffic fatalities to zero simply by forcing all motorists to drive at speeds so slow that there would be no harm upon impact.

Clearly no one is advocating a maximum speed limit of two miles per hour, and yet this is the sort of policy that would be necessary to eliminate the risk of speed-related traffic fatalities. The obvious reason that members of society do not prefer such a policy is that, despite lip-service to the sanctity of human life, we do not wish to incur the costs of a zero-risk speed limit. The primary cost of low speed limits is the waste of time spent on the highways, and individuals reveal the high value they place on this time by voting with their accelerator pedal. The fact that the *average* highway speeds across the U.S. have exceeded 55 miles per hour in every year since the enactment of the national speed limit indicates the intensity of individual feelings towards wasting time on the highways.

This reasoning should not be interpreted as an argument for abolition of highway speed limits. It is recognized that there exist serious external costs that speeders impose on others, and therefore the choice of highway speeds should not be left up to individual motorists. However, the establishment of the national speed limit was not made through a consistent weighing of costs and benefits. In fact, the valuation of reduced probability of death or injury is anathema to most policymakers, although many policy decisions must implicitly involve such calculations.

Some analysis of the 55-mile-per-hour speed limit indicates that the value of reduction in the risk of traffic fatalities is exceeded by the cost of the additional time expended on the highways. Consider first the costs in additional time. By reducing average speeds, the 55-mile-per-hour speed limit has increased the amount of time people spend on the highways. When total mileage is divided by average speeds before and after the imposition of the speed limit, we find that each year people spend a total of 425,400 additional person years on the highways as a result of the national speed limit.[20] If people value their time at the average earnings for private nonfarm workers ($15,500 annually), this total loss of time would be equivalent to $6.6 billion.

Consider now the savings of lives due to the speed limit. The fatality rate (per million vehicle miles) had been trending downward throughout the 1950s and 1960s. In 1974, there was a sharp drop in fatalities not accountable by this trend, and much of this drop may be attributed to the speed limit. Controlling for changes in other variables that could affect fatality rates, the speed limit has been estimated to save 7466 lives per year.[21] Allowing for average life expectancies, this amounts to a total savings of 316,600 years of life expectancy.[22] Therefore, 425,400 extra person-years are spent on the highways in order to save only 316,600 years of life expectancy.

One might argue that this is a false comparison. I might, for example, be willing to spend two extra hours on the highway, listening to my 60-watt Kenwood tape drive through four Alpine high-performance speakers and enjoying the scenery, in order to increase my life expectancy by only one hour. In other words, time spent driving may not be a total loss; death presumably is. Therefore, we need a more sophisticated evaluation of life expectancy. Studies of wage premiums that must be paid to workers who face above-average risk of death or injury may be indicative of the monetary value persons place on changes in life expectancy. By considering how much extra income individuals must be paid to incur a slightly greater risk of death, empirical studies have estimated the valuation of one life expectancy to be $390,000.[23] The saving of 7466 lives due to the speed limit is therefore valued at a total of $2.9 billion. Again this falls short of the value of time lost previously calculated at $6.6 billion. In fact, even if individuals value their time at only half of the average wage, the speed limit is still not cost effective. The value of lives saved still is less than the value of time wasted on the highways.

Economists cannot say that the value of a human life is $390,000, but they can interpret those individual actions that imply a personal valuation of life expectancy. The willingness of individuals to place their lives on the line for extra income or to avoid the inconvenience of buckling-up suggests an individual valuation of life expectancy that can, in turn, be quantified. When such analysis is applied to the question of the 55-mile-per-hour speed limit, it appears that the law is preventing people from making the kind of time-risk trade-off they would prefer. Individual valuations of the increase in life expectancy are apparently not as great as the additional time expended to reduce the risk of death.

DISCUSSION QUESTIONS

1. If advertising is not effective in manipulating consumer preferences, why do firms engage in costly advertising?

2. One implication that Galbraith draws from his analysis of advertising is that large-scale commercial advertising has led us to excessive consumption of private goods and underconsumption of public goods. Even accepting his contention that advertising can alter consumption patterns, what is omitted from his analysis that would lead us to the opposite conclusion?

3. In terms of the use of manpower in civilian and military service, is there any difference between an all-volunteer system and one in which there is conscription with the possibility of a draftee hiring someone to serve in his place? Explain.

4. According to economic theory how would attitudes toward risky driving change with (a) income or (b) age?

5. There exists a well-organized market in foreign exchange (currencies of the various countries of the world). Drawing from the discussion of speculation in commodity markets, what service do you think is provided by the speculators in the foreign exchange markets?

6. Speculation will tend to stabilize prices over time, as long as speculators purchase commodities when they are abundant and sell them when they are scarce. Explain why this is so. What assurance do we have that speculators actually do behave in this way? What happens to the speculators who do not act so as to stabilize prices over time?

chapter 10

Discrimination

1. SOURCES OF GRIEVANCE

In the Constitution of the United States, prior to the Fourteenth Amendment, Negroes were counted as three-fifths of a man in the determination of a state's representation in Congress. In economic terms, even today blacks are counted as three-fifths, for this is their median income relative to that of whites. Women in this society fare no better.

Racial and sexual discrimination are complex issues, calling for analysis by social scientists from all fields. While as economists we are not likely to do justice to a discussion of underlying sociological and psychological aspects of prejudice, we can analyze the implications of discriminatory behavior for the economic status of disadvantaged groups. We examine in this chapter the extent of sexual and racial discrimination and try to determine the reasons for persistence of income differentials between groups in a market society.

Those fond of speaking out about what is "good about America" will often point to the tremendous rise in prosperity that has benefited all groups in society. Median incomes for all groups—men and women, black or white—have risen substantially for many years. And yet our cities have erupted in racial strife. Women have demanded equal rights. What is good about America doesn't seem good enough to those who must continually look up from the bottom of the economic ladder.

While economic progress has been achieved by all groups, considerable income disparities between groups persist. Absolute income gains have been realized by the disadvantaged groups in society, but relative positions have changed very little. On the average, blacks have received less education than whites, an education that is frequently of inferior quality. Racial prejudice bars the door to some occupations for many of our black citizens. Partly as a result of these particular disadvantages, median black income today is approximately equal to 60 percent of that of whites. Median female income is only 40 percent of the male median. Some of this difference is due to the fact that women occupy a disproportionate share of part-time and temporary positions. However, even for women working full-time, full-year, median income is still only 60 percent of the male median. The persistence of inequality, in spite of some absolute income gains, is discouraging to the disadvantaged groups in society. Let us consider the data in more detail.

2. THE DISADVANTAGED MAJORITY

Women earn substantially less than men, and unfortunately there is no evidence that their relative position is improving.[1] Since 1960, female (full-time, full-year) median income as a percentage of the male median has actually fallen slightly, from 60.7 percent to 60.0 percent in 1976.

Part of this income difference can be accounted for by the fact that women tend to dominate low-wage occupations. However, even within each occupation, women earn less than men. Female managers and administrators earn 60.8 percent as much as their male counterparts. In clerical work and sales, where women are heavily represented, their relative median incomes are 67.0 and 52.0 percent, respectively.

Just what is it that accounts for male-female income differentials? A large part of the difference can be accounted for by "institutional discrimination"—the attitudes and institutions of our society, which cause women to adopt roles that are not conducive to career advancement. Child-rearing, in particular, discourages many women from acquiring the formal education and continuous work experience that are essential in preparation for a career. But there is an additional discrepancy in income that cannot be accounted for by differences in training, education, or work experience. This residual income differential is pure economic discrimination against women for no other reason than that they are females.

The greatest problem confronting women is their record of participation in the labor force. Only about 38 percent of women worked full-time, full-year in 1979, as compared with 71 percent of men. Child-rearing responsibilities cause many women to take on temporary or part-time jobs or to leave the labor force altogether. Consequently, women often do not receive the advancement and on-the-job training that accompanies long and continuous experience at work. Employers also recognize that women are more likely to leave their jobs because of pregnancy or a husband's transfer to another city. Thirty-eight percent of women jobholders leave their jobs within three years, compared with 29 percent of males. Firms are consequently less interested in hiring women, particularly for an occupation that involves some investment in training.

From the employer's perspective, a certain amount of discrimination by firms against women can be viewed only as rational behavior toward profit maximization. A high probability of turnover for females makes a firm willing to hire and train women only if they can do so while paying a lower wage. It is, however, unfortunate that young women with solid career aspirations will continue to be judged by the labor participation record of their predecessors. A firm has little means for determining whether a 21-year-old college graduate will stay with the job or become a labor force dropout.

With career aspirations conflicting with other goals, women are slightly less interested than men in higher education. While approximately the same percentage of men and women finish high school, only 13.5 percent of females complete four or more years of college compared with 20.8 percent of males. Furthermore, the fields in which women most often obtain degrees—English, languages, and the arts—provide fewer employment opportunities than such male-dominated fields as business and engineering. Our whole process of socialization from the time of birth contributes to the attitudes that cause women to select themselves out of educational programs with the greatest career opportunities.

In summary, differences in occupation, continuity of job experience, and educational attainment or training may account for the observed income differentials between men and women. Such factors may objectively measure productivity differences between the sexes, so that earnings discrepancies would be the natural consequence of profit-maximizing employment decisions by business firms. However, studies of male-female earnings that control for these factors indicate that considerable inequality would persist even if these productivity differences were eliminated. One comprehensive study by Mary Corcoran and Greg Duncan found that only 2 percent of wage differences between men and women was accounted for by differences in formal education, 11 percent was due to job training, and 28 percent was attributed to other work history.[2] Thus more than 50 percent of the wage difference could not be explained by these objective factors. Randall Brown, Marilyn Moon, and Barbara Zoloth found a similar unexplainable wage difference when looking within specific occupations.[3] The implication of these findings is that elimination of occupational, training, or job tenure differences will go, at the most, only halfway to equalizing male and female earnings. Roughly speaking, we might hope to increase relative female earnings from 60 percent to 80 percent of male earnings by eliminating productivity differences, but the 20 percent gap would persist. We could define this remaining gap to be the amount of pure wage discrimination facing women, solely because they are women.

3. THE COST OF BEING BLACK

Discrimination against blacks can likewise be broken down into productivity and wage-discrimination components. Naturally, the factors underlying racial discrimination are different from those influencing sexual discrimination. Educational deficiencies and regional differences, for example, play a much greater role in the economic condition of blacks.

For most of the early postwar period, black median family income as a percentage of the white median held fairly steady at 52 percent. The decade of the sixties, however, was a period of relatively strong progress for American blacks, and by the end of the decade noticeable signs of improvement were being observed. Civil rights legislation in the early sixties forced open doors to economic advancement that previously had been closed. Occupations and opportunities for education that previously had excluded all but a small number of blacks now accepted large black representation. The sixties were also a period of strong rising prosperity for all groups in society. A booming economy, climaxed by the tight labor markets of the Vietnam War period, was of particular benefit to the minority groups, who are so often the last to be hired. Low unemployment rates and rising personal incomes moved the black median income up to 63 percent of that of whites by the end of the decade, but over the decade of the seventies, despite programs of affirmative action, black median family income has been stuck at about 60 percent of the white median.

This income gap may be accounted for by a number of factors. One

reason for the relatively low incomes of blacks is that a disproportionate number of blacks have lived in the South. Average incomes in
the South tend to be lower than those in any other region, and this
disadvantage is compounded by the fact that the relative income position of blacks in the South is the lowest of any region. Substantial
migrations out of the South have improved Negro incomes in the past,
but the reduction in the number of southern blacks left to migrate
reduces the prospect for further significant improvement from this
source.

The differing age distribution between the races is a surprisingly
important source of earnings differences. Individual earnings generally reach a peak in the 45- to 55-year-age bracket. Consequently, a
population subgroup that is disproportionately young will exhibit relatively low average earnings. The median age of blacks in the U.S. is 22
years, compared with the white median of 30 years.[4] Clearly, the average black worker is at a lower position on the lifetime earnings curve
than is the average white, and this alone may account for some differences in median incomes between the races. This factor is augmented
by the evolution in attitudes and treatment toward minorities in recent
decades. Blacks who are currently in the prime of their earning years
(45–55-year-olds) were educated and channeled into jobs when educational policies toward blacks and occupational discrimination left
them at very low relative starting positions. Consequently, blacks over
45 earn only 60 percent of what whites of a comparable age earn, while
younger blacks (aged 18–24, for example) starting out in a more favorable racial climate, have earnings that are 83 percent of those of the
general population.[5] If we can assume this younger cohort will maintain its relative position as it moves through the age distribution, this
will result in a considerable equalization in measured black-white
earnings.

Educational differences also account for some of the differential. In
1960 the median number of school years completed by blacks was 2.4
years less than the median for whites. While this gap was virtually
eliminated by 1975, differences in the quality of educational resources
do remain. Encouraging is the fact that the wage gap between white
and black workers diminishes at higher levels of educational attainment, and again this is especially true for those most recently
entering the labor force. Blacks receiving a college degree within the
past five years do not differ significantly in their earnings from their
white counterparts.[6]

Although the evidence for younger blacks and especially those with
higher education is encouraging, overall substantial differences in
earnings between blacks and whites do persist. Corcoran and Duncan
again found that about half of the wage gap could be explained by

differences in age, region, education, training, and work history. The 50 percent of the wage gap not accountable by these factors represents pure wage discrimination—the cost of being black.

4. ECONOMIC DISCRIMINATION

Where income differentials are caused by differences in age, education, occupation, or region of employment, the problem is not difficult to understand. Workers are paid according to their productivity, and productivity is affected by these factors. When individuals of equal productivity, however, receive unequal wages, the analysis is somewhat more complicated. Since a substantial portion of black-white and female-male income differentials are not derived from objective differences in productivity, it is important to understand the economic implications of this pure economic discrimination.

It is an unfortunate fact of life in our society that many individuals have "tastes" for discrimination. Some would put it more bluntly by saying that these people are bigots or sexists. In general, people wishing to exercise these tastes will have to pay a premium to do so. If men and women make equally good dentists, but people prefer to have their dental work done by men, they will have to pay a premium to exercise this preference. If all the sexists in town patronize the male dentists, they will need to bid competitively against one another for these services; the fees of male dentists will be bid up appropriately. The few who recognize that they can receive dental care of equal quality from women will find little competition for the services of female dentists and, hence, can get away with a lower dental bill. Likewise, an employer who insists on white Anglo-Saxons as employees is cutting himself off from part of the available work force. If he artificially restricts the supply of workers he is interested in hiring, he will have to pay higher wages than if he allowed all to compete equally for employment. Firms that hire blacks and whites of equal skill will have a much greater pool of workers from which to draw. Since blacks are cut off from certain employment opportunities, they must compete for the limited number of positions open to them by offering to work at relatively low wages. Firms equally willing to employ blacks as well as whites thus find they can hire blacks at a wage lower than the discriminating firm must pay for its lily-white labor force.

So employers and customers who wish to exercise their prejudices must generally do so at some cost. By restricting the range of people with whom they wish to do business, they are not availing themselves of every opportunity to reduce costs and therefore must pay for exercising their prejudices.

Other groups in society stand to gain from discrimination. In restricting the availability of employment opportunities to certain groups, the effective competition among workers for some jobs is naturally less than it otherwise would be. Discrimination reduces the effective supply of workers to particular industries and thus increases the incomes of white males employed in these industries. The implications are developed more fully in the last section of this chapter. The groups most seriously affected by discrimination are obviously the groups against which discriminatory practices are directed. This is so well understood that we often fail to recognize that consumers and employers practicing discrimination impose a cost upon themselves as well.

The phenomena of employer and customer discrimination can be viewed in another manner. Since such parties are willing to pay a premium to exercise their prejudices, they would be willing to forgo practicing discrimination only if they were adequately compensated by lower costs. A lot of sexists would quite willingly abandon prejudices if a female dentist could save them 50 percent on their dental bills. But if disadvantaged groups are prevented from competing by offering services at a lower cost, those who prefer to discriminate will have no incentive not to do so. A prejudiced employer might hire blacks if he could get them for wages 10 percent lower than white workers demand, but if both groups can be hired only at the same wage, he will choose the whites.

None of this analysis is meant in any way to condone the practice of discrimination. We are interested only in examining the impact of such practices on all parties involved. To summarize, we have found that discrimination imposes costs upon the group practicing discrimination as well as those against whom discrimination is directed. In addition, consumers or employers with tastes for discrimination will forgo practicing discrimination only if they are compensated by lower costs. Let us consider a few specific applications and extensions of this analysis.

Equal pay for equal work is an objective few of us would disagree with in principle. As an immediate policy prescription, however, it is likely to have unfavorable effects if imposed in the face of existing prejudices. Equal-pay legislation generally requires employers to pay an equal wage to all workers of comparable abilities engaged in similar work regardless of race, creed, or sex. Employers who prefer to hire white males will, however, employ females or blacks only if they can get them for a lower wage. Legally prevented from doing so, they will simply opt to employ white males exclusively. If this is the effect of equal pay laws, then women and minorities will be isolated from many employment opportunities that offer chances for skill development and advancement. We have already seen, for example, how one particular kind of equal pay law, the minimum wage law, has reduced employment opportunities for black teenagers. This implies that as a means for achieving income equality, equal-pay legislation is likely to have adverse effects. While equal pay for equal work may be a desirable goal for society, if we attempt to achieve this state through direct legislation, it will most probably have the unfavorable side effect of restricting the availability of employment opportunities for women and minorities. This consideration has led to the recommendation and adoption of quotas in hiring, requiring the employment of various groups in proportion to their representation in the local population. Such practices are a form of reverse discrimination against, for example, white males, and they are currently the subject of much academic and legal debate.

More importantly, since enforcement of such policies must focus on obvious identifiable outcomes of the hiring process—average wages and numbers of minorities hired—employers can still practice discrimination through less obvious means. A major component of worker compensation is on-the-job training; this component amounts to as much as 40 percent of total compensation to young workers, although it does not show up on any paychecks. Edward Lazear has found that with the decline in wage differentials for young workers, there is a compensating increase in the difference in on-the-job training provided to young white and black workers.[7] The implication of this finding is that earnings differences will grow as these workers mature, when the differing levels of training become reflected in differences in productivity and hence wages.

Our analysis has focused on the problem of job discrimination, which arises from the prejudices of the employer directly. There also exist many instances of discrimination in which the employer has no prejudicial feelings himself but merely acts in a manner consistent with the preferences of his customers and majority employees. The owner of Orville's Grill may be just as happy selling hamburgers to blacks as he is serving whites, but if a lot of bigoted whites do not want to eat there, Orville is surely going to refuse service to blacks. Similarly, firms may find that integrated working conditions impose extra costs on them because prejudiced white workers will work in an integrated shop only if they are compensated by an abnormally high salary. Again, the firm will find it profitable to maintain segregated working conditions. Forced integration, then, imposes additional costs upon the firms, who in these cases were not the source of prejudicial attitudes. In fact, there is some evidence that customer discrimination may be a greater source of the problem than is discrimination by firms.

Consider, for example, discriminatory practices against women. Women may receive relatively low pay either because employers are sexists or because consumers are sexists and will deal with female workers only if they are charged lower prices. Which effect is more important can be determined by comparing relative incomes of self-employed and other-employed women. A self-employed woman by definition cannot have a sexist employer, so any economic discrimination that she experiences must be the result of customer discrimination. We would expect that if women are disadvantaged economically because of sexist employers, the position of self-employed women should be superior to that of women employed by another person. But the data indicate exactly the opposite. Wages of self-employed women are equal to only 41 percent of those of males in comparable situations, while women who are not self-employed receive wages equal to 58 percent of those of their male counterparts.[8] Thus it appears that in the case of women, at least, customer discrimination is a more important force than is employer discrimination.

Employers, fellow workers, and consumers can each be responsible for discrimination against particular groups in our economy. Discrimination obviously imposes a cost on the individuals against whom discrimination is directed. At the same time, discriminating employers and consumers generally incur a cost for indulging in their prejudices. As we have seen, a direct implication of this is that those engaging in discrimination will forgo exercising their prejudices only if they are compensated financially, say by lower costs.

A direct consequence is that a reduction in competition tends to increase discrimination. Institutions that discourage low-cost disadvantaged workers from competing or practices that reduce competition among firms will increase the incidence of discrimination. In fact, a monopolistic position in any market is a fertile breeding ground for discriminatory practices. Where competition is weak or nonexistent, the risk of being under-priced by a low-cost competitor is negligible, and there is less incentive to reduce discriminatory practices. Several illustrations of this principle are offered in the next section.

5. COMPETITION VERSUS PROTECTION

Firms and labor organizations in a number of industries have been able to protect themselves from competition, often with the assistance of government regulations. In these instances there is less cost to engaging in discrimination than there would be if competition were active. Firms in a competitive industry that engage in discriminatory hiring practices will find their prices undercut by nondiscriminatory competitors. An active competition will force firms to abandon discriminatory practices in order to reduce costs to the minimum level. Firms whose profits are regulated, however, have little incentive to reduce costs, and employers in such firms may give vent to their prejudices without suffering economically. Similarly, most labor unions are forced by the fear of nonunion competition to engage in as comprehensive a membership policy as possible. Some, however, have been able to protect themselves from competition from nonunion workers, and they can consequently practice restrictive membership policies without fear of losing jobs to nonunion personnel.

Historically, there is evidence linking the more severe cases of discrimination to protected markets. Prior to federal regulation of the railroads, blacks in the South were represented in disproportionate numbers in this industry. The protection against competition afforded by the ICC permitted the railroads to engage in discriminatory employment practices, leading ultimately to the total exclusion of blacks from most railroad occupations.[9] Occupational licensing generally restricts competition among professionals, often through granting control over entry to those already in the profession. We have already seen examples of discriminatory licensing practices by examining and licensing boards (Chapter 6). The government itself is not subject to competitive pressures and may discriminate freely according to public sentiment at the time. The 1920s and 1930s were periods of general hostility toward blacks, and this was reflected in government hiring policies. The number of black postmasters was cut in half between 1910 and 1930, and the Navy ceased accepting blacks at this time—even though historically blacks had served in this branch in substantial numbers.[10] While public sentiment has shifted to the favor of minority groups, there is no guarantee that we will not return to a period of greater racial hostility.

The evidence from labor union membership also supports the monopoly-discrimination linkage. We would expect that unions that are able to protect themselves from nonunion competition have little incentive to open their doors to minority groups. This is the case for many craft unions whose members practice a trade that requires a certain degree of skill as well as a license, in many cases. Such labor organizations have a great deal of control over the supply of workers in the industry, for often they control the training and licensing program for the industry. Under these circumstances nonunion workers find it difficult if not impossible to practice the trade; therefore, the union faces little or no outside competition. Consequently, there is no incentive for the craft union to practice an open membership policy. Industrial unions, on the other hand, have considerably less control over the supply of workers in the industry. The skill requirements are generally quite low, and there are no licensing requirements for practicing the trade. Consequently, industrial unions face a continual threat of competition unless they engage in a comprehensive membership policy. An industrial union that restricts groups of workers from membership will find firms in the industry employing nonunion workers or using the outsiders as strikebreakers. The threat of nonunion competition forces industrial unions to maintain an open membership policy.

As expected, serious cases of restricting entry of racial minorities have been found in various craft unions. Theoretically, memberships in the various craft unions are open to any qualified individual, regardless of race. But in practice, admission into craft unions often involves passing examinations and serving in an apprenticeship program. Many times acceptance into an apprenticeship program requires a personal contact or even a relative within the union. Other times unnecessarily difficult examinations are used to limit enrollment in the program. In either case, blacks find it hard to qualify. In 1960 only 3.3 percent of all enrollees in apprenticeship programs, most of which are in the building trades, were black. In the South the percentage of black apprentices has actually declined over this century; from 1890 to 1960 the percentage of black apprentices in Alabama declined from 22 percent to 5.3 percent, in Georgia from 31.7 percent to 6 percent, and in Virginia from 19.3 percent to 4.4 percent.

Nor is the record in the North anything to be proud of. In 1961 the Commission on Civil Rights found only 7 out of 1667 apprentices in St. Louis craft unions were black, or less than one-half of 1 percent. In Detroit only 2 percent of all craft union apprentices were black.

This minute black representation is also characteristic of full union membership in many craft unions. New York Plumbers Local No. 1 had only six blacks out of 3000 members in 1963. All of them were holders of B cards, which entitled them to work at $3.25 per hour as opposed to the $5.15 per hour that A cardholders received. In Cleveland in the same year, only three out of 1400 members of the Brotherhood of Electrical Workers were black. In 1967 nationwide membership of plumbers' unions was only 0.2 percent black, and 0.6 percent of the members of electricians' unions were black.[11] While entry restrictions are supposedly designed to exclude unqualified workers, employers apparently find more qualified black workers than do the unions. The Human Rights Commission found that "whenever the employer had control over hiring, some nonwhites were employed. But in those trades where contractors traditionally relied on the locals for referrals, nonwhites were effectively excluded from construction trades employment."

Free entry into all professions is an important condition enabling disadvantaged groups to enter occupations that provide possibilities for high incomes. Laws and institutions, which protect the monopoly position of one group, do so at the expense of another. Too often this other group is one that can least afford it. Labor unions are certainly not the only labor organizations practicing discrimination while protected by monopoly position. Some professional organizations are guilty of the same.

Women, for example, comprise only 3.5 percent of dentists and less than 10 percent of physicians in this country. While there are no formal restrictions against women doctors, the huge educational demands and discouraging attitudes toward female medical students keep most women from seeking a career in medicine. Where a labor or professional organization has secured the power to regulate entry into its own field, the danger of abusive use of licensing power is particularly great. While virtually no organization today expects to get away with a black or female exclusion clause in its charter, many will design qualification requirements so that it is extremely difficult for members of these groups to obtain licenses. The licensing qualifications are supposedly imposed in the interest of protecting the public from inferior quality. The actual effects are an increase in the incomes of members of the protected profession and the exclusion of racial minorities and women.

Contrary to much popular belief, discrimination is not caused by the capitalist system. In fact, a competitive market system actually provides incentives for the abandonment of discriminatory practices. Employer discrimination, on the one hand, can be practiced only at some cost to the firm. Nondiscriminatory firms will tend to have lower costs, and they will eventually drive their high-cost discriminatory competitors out of business. Customer discrimination is likewise practiced at some cost to the consumer. As long as competition prevails in any trade, consumers will have the opportunity of purchasing more cheaply from those parties against which the majority is discriminating. To many, the opportunity to save a buck provides a rather strong inducement to abandon one's prejudices.

The essential condition for the market system to reduce discrimination is the existence of competition. Where monopolistic practices or legal restrictions prevent women or racial minorities from competing for employment opportunities, economic discrimination will persist. The most effective form of antidiscrimination policy is the destruction of legal and institutional barriers to competition by disadvantaged groups.

DISCUSSION QUESTIONS

1. The text attributes any difference in incomes—after controlling the effects of educational, occupational, and geographic differences—to pure race or sex discrimination. What other factors besides discrimination could account for some of this residual income difference for the groups discussed in the text?

2. One important disadvantaged group in our society not discussed in the text is the group of older people. What are some of the institutional arrangements that encourage discrimination against this group?

3. Between 1949 and 1959, it was observed that the median income of black males relative to whites declined in all four major regions of the country, while for the country as a whole the relative income position of the black men remained unchanged (about 52 percent of that of white males) over this same period. How can this apparent contradiction be resolved?

4. Pure economic discrimination has been measured by the income difference that remains after controlling for income differences due to education, age, occupation, and geographic region. In what sense is this figure a low estimate of the total effect of discrimination?

5. Explain how the income loss to minority groups and women is also a direct loss to society as a whole.

6. The text suggests that the only way to ensure equal pay for equal work with no employment loss for those discriminated against would be to institute a system of quotas. Discuss the ethical and economic aspects of a quota system from both sides of this issue.

chapter **11**

Insufficient Income: The Root of All Poverty

1. POVERTY AMID AFFLUENCE

Viewed in the aggregate, the U.S. economy has attained truly impressive levels of wealth. Because of the tremendous stock of industrial capital that previous generations have amassed, most of us have been freed from a concern with day-to-day subsistence that has plagued 99 percent of mankind throughout history. And yet a significant proportion of our population has not shared in this prosperity. Substandard housing, inadequate diets, and insufficient clothing remain a reality to millions of families in the United States today.

Why has the system failed these people? What is it that determines individual incomes in a market economy? We must obtain answers to these questions and others in order to understand the problem of poverty and to be able to recommend wise and compassionate policy measures to deal with the problem. It is also important to know which groups in our society are more likely to be poor. How effective are present efforts to deal with poverty, and what are some alternative measures for dealing with this problem? In the analysis of these questions, we will find that evidence from recent policy measures provides us with important clues about how and how not to construct an effective antipoverty policy.

2. RICH MAN, POOR MAN

In 1981 Robert Charpie, President of the Cabot Corporation, earned $3,300,000 in salary and bonuses. The average U.S. worker received $12,621 during the same year. While many jobs requiring difficult manual labor pay $10,000 or less, some individuals receive incomes of over 10 times that amount in interest and dividends. A member of the U.S. Congress receives $60,000 per year, while Magic Johnson will make that much playing basketball for 21 days.

Obviously, there is a great disparity in individual incomes, and there is no apparent explanation of these differences in terms of individual effort or virtue. These incomes are determined, as the radicals are fond of stating, when men sell themselves as commodities on the open market. In fact, men and women sell not only themselves, that is, their labor services, but also any other resource that can be used in production, and it is from the sale or hire of these resources that individual incomes are determined. People will receive incomes in accordance with their ownership of productive resources and the return which they can receive from those factors. In this cold and impersonal way, the price system metes out the rewards.

Unfortunately, people are not all equally endowed with human and physical resources, and consequently income disparities are very great. Why some resources are more productive than others and hence yield a greater return is not difficult to understand. But what explains why some individuals have been blessed with human or financial advantages, while others suffer impoverishment because they own no productive resources? This is a question that will continue to trouble philosophers and social scientists for all times.

While some do not like to admit that people may be privileged from birth in this society, there can be little doubt that this is the case. In spite of inheritance taxes, families are able to pass on huge fortunes from generation to generation. We all pay lip service to equal opportunity—particularly people with a $100,000 inheritance. Intergenerational transfers of wealth are not the only sources of inequality. While we might excuse our parents for not having accumulated a fortune for their loving offspring, why couldn't they at least have passed along some chromosomes to make us beautiful or talented? While it is recognized that environmental factors—in the broadest sense of the term—do play a role in determining human characteristics, inheritance was certainly important in developing Cheryl Tiegs's income-earning assets, or Magic Johnson's, for that matter. Equal opportunity ends, in reality, at the moment of conception.

In spite of this important influence of heredity, there is still considerable mobility among income groups from generation to generation. People are able to invest in themselves through education and acquisition of work experience, and this investment in "human capital" will increase income-earning opportunities. But then one is led back to the unanswered question of why it is that certain individuals are endowed with those characteristics—aggressiveness, persuasiveness, ingenuity, and the like—that enable them to improve their positions in society. While we may not have a very good understanding of how such income-generating characteristics are acquired, economists can explain why certain human resources are valuable and hence why some individuals receive higher incomes than others.

The most highly paid individuals—athletes, movie stars, corporate executives—are those who have command over a unique human resource that is valuable to society. The skill of Dave Winfield and the talent of Barbra Streisand are two unique human resources that provide handsome incomes for these two people. The authors of this book also have unique singing voices, but unfortunately there is little demand for their particular art form. Uniqueness is obviously not sufficient to provide a good income; the resource must also be capable of producing something of value to the consumers in society. There is considerable interest in watching Winfield play baseball or in listening to a Streisand record, an interest reflected in people's willingness to pay for these opportunities. Consequently, the New York Yankees and Columbia Records are willing to pay handsome salaries for the use of these services. Now if there were a host of athletes with the skills of Winfield, the Yankees could get away with offering significantly less for his services. If his abilities were not so unusual, competition would force his salary down to a level comparable to that in other professions.

It is the same interplay of relative scarcity and productive capability which determines the salaries that all of us receive for our labor services. In fact, the return on any factor of production depends on (a) its relative scarcity and (b) its usefulness in the production of something of value to society. For example, land that is naturally irrigated and furnished with topsoil will receive a higher rent than less fertile acreage. Unskilled workers are twice damned by the above rule; not only is the productivity of their labor service fairly low, but they also are confronted by the availability of a large number of competitors who can provide the same labor. Those in possession of highly productive, unique resources earn large incomes. The poor on the other hand, are those who have little or no nonhuman resources and whose own "human capital" does not yield a very large return. It will become apparent from the description of poverty groups that all categories of poor Americans are impoverished because they do not own an adequate quantity of productive resources.

3. WHO ARE THE POOR?

In 1962 Michael Harrington discovered poverty in America. In his book, *The Other America,* he made known to millions of Americans that there was a significant proportion—one-fourth by his count—of the population in this country still living in poverty. Since that time, the federal government has engaged in a considerable effort to eradicate this problem, and, incidentally, has spent a significant amount of anti-poverty funds to learn which families are poor and why.

Some people deny that poverty actually exists in the United States today. Certainly by comparison to underdeveloped countries where homeless masses suffer from malnutrition, the degree of poverty in the U.S. is minor. But a substantial number of families in America are hungry, ill-clothed, and inadequately housed. Humpty Dumpty tells us that when we use a word, we can choose it to mean anything we want. Let us be clear when we use the term *poverty* exactly what it means and what conditions it describes.

One approach to a definition of poverty is that of the misery-loves-company school. People feel poor only if their standard of living is low relative to that of their peers. When we are not referring to a situation in which people are being deprived of basic necessities, it is perhaps reasonable to suppose that families with $5000 incomes do not experience feelings of inferiority and shame if everyone else is in the same condition. Poverty then is a result of unequal incomes—not of some absolute level of deprivation. This implies that an equal increase in all incomes as the result of gradual economic growth will not eliminate poverty. Only an equalization of incomes will accomplish this. Adherents of this view contend that the poverty line distinguishing the poor from the nonpoor should be set relative to average incomes, rather than in terms of some absolute number of dollars. For example, it is often suggested that our goal should be to provide everyone with an income that is at least equal to 50 percent of the nation's median income.

The alternative view, and the one upon which poverty analysis and policies are based, is that poverty exists for those whose incomes are insufficient to provide them with an adequate existence. Adequacy is defined with reference to studies of consumption patterns by low-income individuals. It has been discovered that low-income families find it necessary to spend twice as much on nonfood items as they spend on food. Thus to determine that level of income necessary to provide an adequate existence, economists have estimated the cost of the Agriculture Department's economy food plan and multiplied this by three. In recent years this has implied a poverty line of $8410 for a family of four. This figure is adjusted yearly to allow for price increases. This figure will vary with the size of the family, location, and the year, but it does give us some absolute standard by which we can measure the extent of poverty and evaluate our progress. Using this definition, let us now turn to the question of who is likely to be poor and why.

In 1978, 24.5 million individuals—11.5 percent of the population—had incomes below the poverty line.[1] This was exactly the number classified as poor in 1969, indicating no progress in the fight against poverty over most of the decade of the seventies. This compares unfavorably with a drop in the number of poor from 39.5 million over the previous decade. Robust economic growth in the sixties had succeeded in lifting 15 million people out of poverty, but further gains have become increasingly difficult as the incidence of poverty has become more concentrated in groups whose incomes are relatively unresponsive to general prosperity.

In particular, poverty is disproportionately concentrated on blacks, aged individuals, and families headed by females. More than 27 percent of black families, 27 percent of unrelated persons over 65, and 50 percent of female-headed families were poor in 1978. For black families and female-headed families, there has been little change in poverty incidence since 1969, while the aged have experienced a substantial reduction in poverty status over the period. With the growth in social security benefits, the percentage of those 65 and older who are poor has been cut to about half of what it was in 1969.

The discouraging fact about these figures is that this relative constancy of poverty levels has been accompanied by a massive growth in public expenditures on social welfare programs. During the seventies, social welfare expenditures (excluding education) by governments at all levels more than tripled. Adjusting for increases in the cost of living, these expenditures were still 80 percent higher at the end of the decade than they were at the beginning.[2] Furthermore, these expenditures have succeeded in lifting some people out of poverty. In 1978 the number of people in poverty was 44 percent lower than it would have been in the absence of social security and other cash transfer programs.[3] So although social welfare expenditures have increased substantially over the decade and although these programs do reduce the incidence of poverty, official figures show little evidence of poverty reduction during the seventies.

There are two factors which can account for this apparent paradox. The first is that pretransfer incomes have become less equal. The share of wages and salaries going to the bottom 40 percent of wage earners has fallen from 10.7 percent in 1948 to 9.4 percent in 1977. Transfer payments have compensated for this decline in relative earnings, but at the same time transfer programs may actually have aggravated the problem of *earnings* inequality by reducing work incentives. As an example, the percentage of aged males in the work force fell from 46 percent in 1950 to 24 percent in 1972, a period which saw a fifty-fold increase in social security payments. The authors of one study who examined these figures concluded that "...much of the effect of the retirement programs has apparently been to replace the earnings of older workers with transfer payments without affecting their position in the income distribution."[4] We will return to the work-incentive features of other programs later in this chapter.

The second factor is that the official figures overstate the number of persons actually below the poverty line. The Social Security Administration counts as income only those transfers which are in the form of cash. "In-kind" transfers—food stamps, medicaid and medicare, housing subsidies—clearly improve the real income position of recipients, but these transfers are not included as income in counting the number of poor persons. Several studies that have analyzed the impact of transfers in-kind have determined that these programs have reduced the level of poverty substantially below that indicated by the official figures. Rather than 11.5 of the population, the number of poor persons is closer to 4 percent when the value of in-kind transfers is considered as part of their incomes.[5]

In summary, there are significant pockets of poverty in this country, although substantially smaller than indicated by the official figures. Our massive expenditures on redistribution programs do reduce the number of families who are poor, although much of the recent expansion in social welfare expenditures has not been reflected in a smaller number of those officially classified as poor. Before we analyze our antipoverty programs in more detail, we might first consider whether a purely market solution to the question of income distribution has ethical or economic support.

4. THE BURDEN AND BENEFITS OF INCOME INEQUALITY

"The Poor ye shall have always with you," says the Bible. To date, no society in man's history has proven the Bible wrong. In fact, an examination of historical data by the economist, Vilfredo Pareto, revealed a remarkable constancy in the distribution of incomes throughout history and across nations. The poorest fifth of the population always received approximately the same percentage of that nation's income. Some curious interaction of political and economic forces has prevented all societies in history from substantially reducing inequalities.

One wonders then if the government should engage in a conscious attempt to alter the distribution of incomes. As this is a question that philosophers and economists have debated for centuries, we cannot expect to come to any consensus on this issue. It is important at this time, however, to examine some of the arguments in favor of and against the reduction of income inequality.

Defenders of the existing degree of inequality will often claim that the rich are in an enviable position because of hard work and ingenuity. They have made the greatest contribution to society's output and therefore are entitled to the greatest reward. While there is an element of truth to this position, the argument ignores the importance of luck and inheritance in the determination of incomes. Insofar as people are paid according to the productivity of their resources, it is true that the largest incomes go to those who make the greatest contribution to output. But where is the element of sacrifice and effort from those who have inherited wealth? Some of the richest people in the United States are living off an income derived from their inheritance. While the private ownership of capital does serve a useful function in allocating resources among their competing uses, it is difficult to justify their incomes as a reward for this service. One can justify their incomes only as a reward to their parents, who worked to amass a fortune with the intention of passing some on to their heirs. One aspect of the reward to those who have worked to acquire a large estate, the argument runs, is the privilege of setting their heirs up with the advantage of an inheritance. In a debate on value judgments it is not possible to logically confirm or deny this position, of course, but it is clear that a society that permits families to pass on wealth to their heirs will have more inequality than one with confiscatory inheritance taxes.

The notion that "the laborer is worthy of his hire" also ignores the role that luck plays in determining people's incomes. An individual's income can change radically, through no fault of his or her own, as a result of shifts in consumer preferences and advances in technology. Farm incomes have suffered a long-term depression as the result of tremendous advances in technology, not because farmers today are less virtuous or diligent than those 50 years ago. In ignorance of its true redistributional effect, the public continues to support the farm subsidy program because of a general feeling that poor farmers are deserving of an income higher than that which the market has determined for them. School teachers who suddenly find themselves without a job or employed at lower wages because society has made a collective decision to shift expenditures away from education are the victims of bad luck. They are still well trained and presumably quite willing to work and probably don't beat their spouses, so one might say they are just as deserving of high incomes as they were before the shift in the population distribution or society's preferences. There are, of course, continual changes in tastes and technology such as these, and some people benefit and some will be adversely affected as the result of circumstances beyond their control. This does not, however, imply that society has an obligation to maintain the incomes of those who have suffered financially from such changes; as pointed out in Chapter 6, it is actually desirable from society's point of view to allow structural changes to have an impact on incentives. The point is that individual incomes are partially determined by factors beyond the worker's control. Hence, one cannot say that the most industrious and virtuous will necessarily receive the highest incomes. There is no reason to believe that the pattern of incomes determined by the market will be desirable by any ethical criterion.

So, depending on resource endowments, the distribution of incomes determined by the market may or may not be desirable. However, this "distributive" role of pricing in the market for productive resources is only one aspect of this market. In addition to determining individual incomes, the prices of productive resources provide information and incentives to which people will respond so that scarce resources will be employed in those lines of activity most useful to society. This is what economists call the "allocative role" of pricing productive factors. While one may dislike the particular distribution of incomes that the market has determined, it would be dangerous to play Robin Hood without due regard for the consequences that intervention into these markets may have on the allocation of scarce, productive resources. Although we have briefly considered the allocative role of prices and markets in Chapter 2, we want to return to this issue with a specific emphasis on the role of incentives in the pricing of productive factors.

The income that an occupation pays is obviously an important factor in the decision of what employment to accept or prepare for. If the salary paid to engineers falls significantly, fewer young people will enroll in engineering programs, and some existing engineers will move into other occupations. Likewise, there has been a huge migration from the farms over the last fifty years as the result of declining farm incomes. While these adjustments may be painful for the individuals involved, from society's point of view they are very desirable. Relatively low compensation to a particular occupational group simply means that their services are valued more highly somewhere else in the economy. Low incomes provide the incentives for people to shift to other lines of employment. Conversely, relatively high incomes in some professions indicate that society places the highest value on the use of labor in this line of activity. These high incomes provide the incentives for people to train for these higher-paying careers.

Income inequality is essential if scarce resources are to be used where they are most valuable. Without inequalities, talented individuals will not have the incentive to offer their labor services where they could make the greatest contribution. If a doctor were paid as little as a cab driver, who would be willing to undertake the years of training required to become a M.D.? How many corporate managers would be willing to work the long hours that they do if they were paid no more than, say, a bricklayer? Communists suggest that the "new man" will be motivated by the desire to serve society, not greed, and that therefore wage differentials will not be needed as incentives in the new society. But the creation of the "new man" does not solve the information problem; how is the dedicated Communist to know where his services would be most useful in the absence of market prices that convey this information? Societies wishing to solve this problem without income inequalities have found it necessary to rely on some form of coercion. While high incomes do provide an incentive for people to move into the correct line of work, so of course does a directive from the government. Abstracting from any ethical considerations about the personal freedom aspects of coercion versus market incentives, one may wish to refer to the arguments in Chapter 2 in weighing the relative advantages of the market versus the planning approach to the problem.

Granting the usefulness of income differentials in channeling our productive resources into their most efficient uses, one might still argue that the magnitude of the income differences reported earlier far exceed what is necessary to provide appropriate information and incentives. Severe inequality can impair the efficient use of labor, if, for example, individuals lack the means to invest adequately in health care or education necessary to be productive members of society. If socially undesirable behavior, such as crime, is related to poverty, equalization of incomes could improve the welfare of all members of society. Finally, to the extent that the equality of opportunity within the political process is not possible with unequal incomes, our ideals of political equity also require the goal of greater income equality.

The ethical arguments and some economic arguments do not support the free-market solution to income determination. On the other hand, permitting the market for productive resources to establish individual incomes does have desirable allocative effects. Some may say that income differentials are morally repugnant, but inequalities do serve the purpose of directing people into occupations most important to society. Thus, if one objects to the particular pattern of incomes that the market determines, *the attempt to rectify undesirable inequalities should involve a minimal distortion of the allocation of productive resources established by the market.* That is, policies should be designed so that they interfere as little as possible with the incentives determined by the markets for productive resources. While this is a tricky task, it will become apparent in the examination of alternative policy proposals and programs that some can accomplish this more effectively than others.

5. POVERTY PROGRAMS: THE BUREAUCRAT KNOWS BEST

During the great depression, the federal government initiated programs designed to alleviate the economic distress of the impoverished. Many of our antipoverty programs since that time have taken the services approach, in which the poor are offered a particular service—housing, job training, medical care, and so on—rather than direct income supplements. (The welfare program, a topic to be taken up in the next section, is, of course, an income-supplement program.)

The fundamental premise behind the services approach to poverty reduction is that the legislators and the program administrators know better than the poor families themselves what these people really need. Rather than giving each poor family $1500 worth of job training, housing, and food stamps, the government could simply provide each family with $1500 in cash. Many view this alternative with horror, expressing the fear that the poor will squander their money on liquor, a color TV, or a fancy car, while taking no care for providing for their children or investing in their own development. To some, the condition of poverty is proof enough of an inability or unwillingness to care for themselves or their offspring.

However, the evidence on voluntary expenditures by the poor does not substantiate this position.[6] In 1960, when food, medical care, and housing subsidies to the poor were miniscule or nonexistent, families with incomes below $3000 were devoting 72 percent of their consumption expenditures to these basics. Of the remaining 28 percent, more than one-fourth each went to clothing and transportaiton. Obviously, this does not leave much for the typical poor family to squander. Old demon rum and its cousins gobbled up a full 1 percent of the average poor family's consumption expenditures (amounting to all of $21 per year) versus 1.9 percent of the expenditures of those with incomes over $15,000. There is a subtle arrogance behind the notion that the poor are incapable of spending their money in a way that will improve their welfare.

Despite this evidence, services and in-kind transfer programs to aid the poor are massive. In 1979 the federal government spent $6.5 billion on food stamps, $12.2 billion on health care and medical programs, and $4.5 billion on public housing. In 1980, $8.9 billion was spent on job training and placement under the Comprehensive Employment and Training Act. The impact of the services approach to poverty reduction is examined in two case studies, worker training and public housing programs.

A. Worker Training

Nearly 50 percent of poor families are headed by a worker who is either not fully employed throughout the year or does work the full year but at a wage too low to lift the household out of poverty. By providing such individuals with appropriate skills, it should be possible to increase their employability and the wage that an employer would be willing to pay for their services. Government training programs could accomplish this if the only factor separating one from a well-paying job is an insufficient or incorrect set of skills. While this is certainly the case for some individuals, others may be unemployed or underemployed because of more general personality traits, such as irresponsibility, lack of ambition, and so on, or because of racial or sexual discrimination. Evidence from existing programs indicates that training does improve job situations slightly for those completing the programs, but that those most disadvantaged by discrimination or personality factors that reduce their employability benefit very little from these programs. We will examine the evidence from the Job Corps and the Manpower Development and Training Act (MDTA) programs, both now subsumed in the Comprehensive Employment and Training Act. (CETA).

The Job Corps presents a case study of one program that has attempted to deal aggressively with the most severe unemployment and low-wage problems. A part of the War on Poverty, this program called for the establishment of youth training camps, where young people would be taught general and specific skills that would help them secure employment and earn a decent wage. This was a bold program as it attempted, intentionally or not, to deal with some of the most unemployable youths available. High school dropouts, most with tragically low reading and arithmetic skills, were recruited into the program. Although enrollees were supposed to stay in the camps for two years, almost 90 percent left within one year. There was some attempt to correct these problems by more careful screening, but such a policy tends to exclude those who would benefit most if the program were successful. There were some slight gains in wages for those who completed the program, but at a considerable cost. Yearly expenditures per entrant were $8076 in 1967,[7] approximately double the cost of a year's education at Harvard.

Even the reputed gains of Job Corps training are questionable. One favorable analysis found trainees with six months' tenure in the program raised their hourly wage by 12 cents. However, a control group of youths accepted for training who chose not to enroll kept pace with this wage gain, and unemployment rates for graduates remained at a discouraging 30 percent or more. Seventy percent of trainees were not working in jobs related to their training, and the continued low wage and high unemployment rates kept most graduates below the poverty line.[8]

To some extent the failure of the Job Corps was a result of the fact that it attempted to reach the truly disadvantaged and unemployable youths. Other programs may have better records of success, but only because they do not deal with the really difficult cases. Possibly the Job Corps is indicative of the actual cost of a manpower program for the most disadvantaged groups in society.

A larger and apparently more successful training program was established by the MDTA. Participants were trained in either an institutional setting or on the job, with the federal government compensating the private employer for training costs. On-the-job trainees showed remarkable wage gains, particularly those who came from the more disadvantaged groups in society. Disadvantaged workers were earning an average of $1400 more in annual income after on-the-job training than before—an average gain of over 50 percent. Such before and after comparisons can be misleading, however, as nonenrolled persons comparable to participants may have realized similar gains. In fact, a subsequent study which analyzed the wage gains of a control group—individuals matched to participants by age, sex, race, and earnings histories—found MDTA trainees did not gain relative to their control group counterparts. Summarizing the evidence from a large volume of studies on the MDTA, Professor Henry Levin concludes: "it appears that the disadvantaged are likely to experience some increase in earnings from MDTA participation, but the increases may be quite small and inadequate to remove them from poverty status."[9]

B. Low-Income Housing

The federal public housing program was initiated by the Housing Act of 1937. Designed partly as an aid to recovery from the great depression, the Act also had the purpose of providing low-cost housing for the poor. Under this law, the federal government provides financial aid to local housing authorities, who contract with private developers for the construction of new low-cost housing. The local authorities own and operate the buildings, selecting among qualified applicants for tenants, and renting the dwellings at a cost no greater than the cost of maintenance and operating expenses. The federal subsidy covers the interest and principle payments on the housing loans.

The public housing program is an inefficient means of assisting low income families in meeting their housing needs. The first inefficiency crops up at the construction phase, where it has been estimated the government spends 20 percent more per dwelling than private companies would for units of the same rental value.[10] Second, there is a distortion in the spending patterns of public housing tenants, created by the fact that the program provides a specific dwelling (at subsidized rental payments) rather than an unrestricted cash transfer. Constrained to accept the housing provided if they do not wish to forgo the subsidy, families consume a quantity and quality of housing services that does not necessarily match their own preferences. We might argue that this coercion is necessary to make sure the poor budget a sufficiently large share of their expenditures for housing, but the evidence suggests that with an unrestricted cash transfer of value equal to the rent subsidy, these families would actually consume more housing than under the present arrangement.[11]

Finally, although the program is large, it accommodates only a small fraction of poor families. In 1972 only 5 percent of families with incomes below $5000 were living in public housing.[12] Consequently, there is a long waiting list of applicants for these units, and the authorities find it useful to screen out undesirable tenants: women with illegitimate children, people convicted of a crime, partners of common-law marriage, those suffering from mental or physical illness, and those who have difficulty holding down a job. The collection of this information naturally involves an invasion of the applicant's privacy. Nor does the program really eliminate the environment of poverty; the impoverished continue to live among their own kind, and horror stories of the demoralizing life in the public housing projects abound.

One asks, if the government insists that better housing should be provided for the poor, why then does it not simply provide rental vouchers that poor families could use in supplementing the rental payments on a dwelling of their choice? In fact, over the past eight years the Rand Corporation has been administering an experiment with rental vouchers involving more than 1300 families. These families have received rent supplements, averaging somewhat more than $100 per month, to be used to help make rental payments. The families are free to choose rental units from any of the participating landlords, rather than being restricted to live in public housing. Initial fears that the subsidies would be dissipated in higher rents have not been realized; rents and property values have not increased significantly. The money allocated to the voucher program is efficiently spent, as 85 percent of all program expenditures have gone to rent payments, compared with only 57 percent under public housing.

There is no need for the government to be directly involved in the provision of housing units itself; private builders can respond adequately to the desires of the households. Private housing construction has led to a gradual but consistent improvement in housing quality and quantity. From 1950 to 1960, the total number of homes classified as standard increased from 29.1 million to 47.4 million. While in 1940 only 51 percent of all housing was standard, in 1960 this figure was 81 percent,[8] and in 1973, 93 percent.

The public housing program and job training programs administered under the CETA are apparently not the most effective uses of anti-poverty funds. Yet such a services approach to fighting poverty will continue to have significant political support over the direct cash transfer alternatives. This political advantage stems from the existence of some nonpoor interest groups that benefit from the existence of each of these programs. Developers and builders support public housing; physicians are beneficiaries of medical subsidies; agriculture promotes food stamps; private businesses are eager to be subsidized to train workers they would employ anyway. The main problem with this arrangement is that the programs are not necessarily designed with poverty reduction as the primary goal. A substantial share of antipoverty funds goes to nonpoor families: administrators and social workers; businessmen, farmers and professionals who provide the specified services; and nonpoor recipients who qualify for transfers under the enabling legislation. Studies of transfer programs in the early seventies indicate that only about 30 percent of federal transfer programs contributed to a reduction in measured poverty.[13] Only 17 percent of 1973 Medicare recipients were classified as poor, and in 1970, only 17 percent of unemployment compensation was paid to families with incomes under $5000.[14] Clearly our transfer programs are not focused on the neediest people in our society.

6. WELFARE OR ILLFARE

The discussion so far has focused on antipoverty programs that rely on the services approach. However, the most visible and sensitive form of poverty program is the direct cash transfer approach, and particularly programs labeled as "welfare." The common conception of welfare is the direct transfer of cash payments from high- to low-income groups, epitomized in particular by the Aid to Families with Dependent Children (AFDC) program. This, however, is only one of several important income transfer programs, some of which, such as Social Security, are not generally viewed as welfare programs. For the purposes of poverty analysis, it is convenient that we consider all income-transfer programs under the same umbrella, whether or not they are stigmatized by the title of "welfare programs." It is also convenient that all of these programs be analyzed as special cases of a general idea called a negative income tax (NIT)—a framework that enables us to see clearly the incentive effects, degree of poverty reduction, and costs of alternative transfer programs.

We can begin our discussion of the NIT concept with an illustration of a program that provides an income guarantee of $4000 per year for a family of four and establishes a 50 percent tax rate on earnings. The essential features of this system are presented in Table 1. A family with no earnings receives a full $4000 payment or a "negative tax payment" of $4000. Positive earnings are taxed at the rate of 50 percent, meaning that this family will lose 50 cents' worth of income supplements for every dollar earned. The family earning $3000, for example, loses $1500 out of the full $4000 payment, so that its income supplement is reduced to $2500 and its income totals $5500 ($3000 in earnings plus a $2500 transfer payment). A family earning exactly $8000 has its benefits reduced to zero, and at higher levels of earnings, families are no longer covered under the plan. Therefore, $8000 is the cut-off level of income under this plan.

One can immediately see that such a program maintains incentives to work and increase earnings, since total income rises whenever earnings increase. This, of course, will hold true as long as the effective tax rate under the program is less than 100 percent. The lower the tax rate, the more that total income grows with each increase in earnings, and therefore the greater the work incentive of the program. This incentive is not, however, achieved without cost. If the tax rate were lowered to 25 percent, for example, and the guarantee left at $4000, the cut-off level of income rises to $16,000. Such a program then would include almost half of the families in the U.S., and clearly the amount of income transferred would be immense.

Table 1

Hypothetical NIT Plan: $4000 Guarantee and 50% Tax Rate

Earnings	Deduction from Basic Supplement (50% of Earnings)	Net Income Supplement ($4000 − Deduction)	Total Income (Earnings + Supplement)
0	0	$4000	$4000
1000	500	3500	4500
3000	1500	2500	5500
6000	3000	1000	7000
8000	4000	0	8000

It is also obvious that this hypothetical program reduces poverty but does not completely eliminate it. The largest transfer payments go to those families with the lowest earnings, but even so, no family covered under the program has its income raised above the poverty line of

$8380. The only way to entirely eliminate poverty would be to raise the income guarantee to the poverty line. Then if a 50 percent tax rate were maintained to retain some degree of work incentives, the cut-off income level rises to $16,760, so that again transfers are extended to nearly half of the population.

The specification of the guaranteed income level and the tax rate necessarily involves some balancing of the conflicting goals of poverty-reduction, cost minimization, and maintenance of work incentives. In addition, the definition of the group of eligible recipients has important incentive effects. If the acceptance of work, the presence of an able-bodied male in the household, or the state of residence affect a family's eligibility for benefits or size of payments, these restrictions will have obvious effects on willingness to work, family stability, and migration. One should not be surprised to learn that the poor respond to financial incentives.

The system of cash and in-kind transfer programs we are presently using to fight poverty has been effective in reducing poverty but the accompanying incentive features have aggravated several important social problems. Individual states establish criteria for eligibility and levels of support, so that a patchwork of programs comprises AFDC. The average monthly payment in 1981 to recipient families in California, for example, was $431 versus only $87.89 in Mississippi and $108.29 in Texas. Such differentials have encouraged migration of poor families to California and those states in the Northeast paying above the average level of benefits, and this migration has added to the financial burden faced by the large industrial cities of the North. Twenty-three states still limit eligibility to female-headed households, and in many states levels of benefits exceed the monthly earnings of a full-time worker receiving the minimum wage. An able-bodied male with his family's interest at heart may decide everyone will be better off financially if he leaves home, so that the family can receive welfare. AFDC recipients who work lose 67 cents for every additional dollar earned. However, in combination with other transfer programs such as food stamps and public housing in which many AFDC recipients participate, the work disincentive is even greater. Each of these other programs imposes reductions in benefit levels as earnings increase, so that the effective rate of taxation resulting from participation in all three programs is close to 80 percent.[15] When payroll and income taxes are considered, the overall rate of taxation on earnings is even higher.

A similar problem contributed to the defeat of the Family Assistance Plan, a form of NIT program proposed by the Nixon Administration. When integrated with existing housing, food stamp, and medical benefit programs, effective rates of taxation implied by the program were as high as 87 percent. Few believed this offered much in the way of work incentives, and the plan was killed in Senate committee. The creation of a welfare system with effective economic and social incentives calls for scrapping existing programs, and replacing them with a single, income transfer program with a moderate rate of taxation.

In view of the trade-offs implied in the design of any NIT program, it is not possible to design the ideal income-transfer program. The desired magnitude of an income transfer program, and hence the amount of poverty reduction, depends to a large extent on one's own ethical and social values. It is, however, possible to provide some indication of the incentive features of transfer programs incorporating alternative rates of taxation based in part upon evidence from NIT experiments conducted between 1969 and 1971 in New Jersey and Pennsylvania. Six-hundred thirty-nine families were enrolled in a temporary NIT program with tax rates ranging from 30 to 70 percent and guaranteed income support levels ranging from 50 to 125 percent of the poverty line. Labor-force participation rates, employment rates, and earnings levels for these families were compared with those of a control group. A fair summary of the wealth of information coming out of these experiments is that male heads of experimental families receiving benefits, which were taxed at a rate of 50 percent for every dollar earned, differed insignificantly from nonparticipants in their rates of labor-force participation, employment, and earnings.[16] There is some indication that tax rates exceeding 50 percent do adversely affect the decision to work,[17] and the payment of substantial transfer payments to families with working wives did reduce their labor-force participation below that of control group wives. These results are generally consistent with nonexperimental evidence on the effect of transfer payments on willingness to work.[18] Generally, this evidence indicates that a NIT program with moderate income guarantees and rates of taxation approaching 50 percent does maintain work incentives for male heads of households. In a number of respects, such a plan would be vastly superior to the existing hodgepodge of cash transfers, services, and transfers in kind, which makes up our present antipoverty policy.

7. ANTI-POVERTY POLICY: ROOM FOR REFORM

In 1979 total public expenditures on social welfare programs, excluding education, amounted to $319 billion, or $1428 for each individual.[19] This sum is equal to approximately 14 percent of this country's gross national product. Our previous discussion has indicated that the combination of all social welfare programs has reduced poverty in this country, roughly from 20 percent of the population to about 4 percent when

both cash and in-kind transfers are considered. However, this achievement comes at considerable expense, both in the disincentives to work
facing transfer recipients and in the large volume of transfers that go
to families not classified as poor. Participants in the combined AFDC,
food stamp, medicaid, and public housing programs face effective rates
of taxation on their earnings in excess of 80 percent. At the same time,
only 25 percent to 30 percent of social welfare expenditures go to persons classified as poor. A significant fraction of public welfare expenditures takes the form of in-kind transfers, which provide benefits
to the poor that fall short of their total cost.

True welfare reform may continue to be hobbled by the concern to
protect vested interest groups. The services approach has the support
of various powerful nonpoor commercial and professional interests,
and the political temptation is to build a new program on top of the
existing ones. The result would be a bigger and more expensive collection of transfer programs with reduced rather than enhanced work
incentives and questionable advances towards further poverty reduction. True reform will require the abandonment of current antipoverty
programs and their replacement with a unified system constructed so
as to preserve work incentives, focus benefits on the neediest groups in
society, and provide recipients with the freedom to make those expenditure decisions which they perceive will enhance their own welfare.

DISCUSSION QUESTIONS

1. Is Robert Charpie really 200 times as productive as a migrant farm
   worker? If there existed a million individuals with Charpie's capabilities, what would happen to his salary? What does this suggest
   about productivity being only a partial determinant of income?

2. Discuss the advantages and disadvantages of transfers-in-kind
   (housing, food, etc.) versus income supplements as alternative
   means of poverty reduction.

3. What advantages does a white, middle-class suburbanite gain from
   antipoverty programs in the black ghetto? Are private action programs of this kind likely to be underfunded? Why?

4. Pareto's law states that the overall pattern of income distribution
   has remained the same over many centuries and many societies.
   Can you offer any explanation of Pareto's law?

5. In recent years government at all levels has been spending in
   excess of $300 billion per year on social welfare programs. Use

social choice arguments to explain why government has been so willing to spend on existing social welfare programs (social security, welfare, education, job training, housing, farm programs, etc.) while the Congress was unwilling to adopt the $4.4 billion Family Assistance Plan proposed by the Nixon Administration.

6. Should the definition of a poverty level of income be the same in New York City as it is in rural Alabama? Why? Would you support a national welfare program with uniform standards?

chapter **12**

Human Capital and the Wealth of Nations

1. WHAT'S THE DIFFERENCE?

Is there a fundamental difference between education and other services provided by our economy? Why does it require government sponsorship? A hasty response might be that education is too important to be left to private profit-maximizing enterprises. But surely food production is even more important, and the private sector does a better job providing food than we would expect the government to do. Government subsidy of education can be justified if there are important social benefits beyond those that accrue to the individual or if education can be shown to achieve some of society's income redistribution goals. Otherwise, there is no reason to believe that a free market would not function as effectively in education as it does in the provision of other services or goods.

We begin this chapter with a discussion of the social benefits of education to see if, in fact, there is a justification for public expenditures on education. Next, we will examine the relation between education and incomes to determine the extent to which education can contribute to the reduction of income inequality. Finally, the specific roles of the government in both basic and higher education will be analyzed in order to see whether or not such policies are equitable and efficient.

2. HUMAN CAPITAL AND THE WEALTH OF NATIONS

If you were born in the United States, it is very likely that you will have a fairly comfortable existence without having to engage in much back-breaking toil. If, on the other hand, you happen to be a citizen of Upper Volta, you will probably suffer from severe malnutrition, be ill-clothed and unhoused, and die before you are 35. One important reason for this difference is that generations of Americans have been investing and accumulating capital, which the present generation of Americans has inherited for its own use. Railroads, highways, factories, machines, and other physical assets compose the stock of capital goods that add to the productivity of our labor force. But more important than the accumulation of physical capital has been the acquisition of knowledge, the advance of technology, and the education of the labor force.

In many ways the investment in human beings through formal education is similar to investments in factories or machines. Both of these forms of investment require a sacrifice of current consumption. To devote resources to the construction of factories or to building schools and training teachers involves reduced production of food, houses, or other consumer goods. For developing countries, where individuals live at the margin of subsistence, the sacrifice of current consumption for the sake of investment involves very high costs indeed. Any country will want to derive the most from this sacrifice by seeing that the investment is made where it will make the greatest contribution to future production. Any investment project, whether in human beings or in physical productive goods, will provide a stream of benefits—not immediately, but over some future period of time. A farmer who acquires a tractor can expect an increase in productivity for many years into the future; likewise, a farmer who has learned how to increase crop yields by the use of scientific farming methods will experience a much higher level of output for each hour worked in years to come. Since investment in the health or education of human beings shares the same characteristics as investments in physical capital goods, many economists refer to such expenditures as investments in *human capital.*

A country becomes more prosperous as the quantity and quality of its productive resources increase. Most of the increase in the productivity of the labor force comes about as the result of the accumulation of physical capital or advances in knowledge or workers' skills. Recent studies indicate that investments in human capital have historically been much more important than the accumulation of physical capital in improving the productive capability of the labor force. Only 20 percent of the increase in output per man-hour in this century can be attributed to the growth in our capital stock.[1] Most of the remainder must be due to advancement of knowledge and education of the labor force, either through formal schooling or on-the-job training. More descriptive evidence comes from the postwar rise of countries devastated by bombing during World War II. Both Japan and Germany entered the postwar period with railroads, factories, and the bulk of their physical productive capacity destroyed. In terms of physical plant, these countries were in the same position as underdeveloped nations. Yet both countries are now among the wealthiest in the world. Their successes can be largely attributed to the accumulation of human capital—the skills and knowledge of their citizens—which was not destroyed by the bombing. Their understanding of production processes, the skills and general knowledge of the labor force, and the ability to utilize basic knowledge was not lost during the war, and it was the employment of this human capital that led to the rapid recovery of these countries.

So it is apparent that investment in human capital is an important factor contributing to economic growth. But is there anything about investment in human beings that distinguishes it from investments in physical capital so as to justify public finance of education? Clearly, some education would still take place without a government subsidy, for individuals do benefit directly from an investment in their own education. But private individuals do not capture all of the benefits of their own education; there are positive "external effects" on the whole economy. Whenever this is the case, the free market will generate a less-than-desirable level of investment in that activity. Suppose, for example, that a young physicist is considering whether or not to spend an additional five years acquiring an advanced degree. The cost, including the income forgone during those five years, might amount to $50,000. He or she estimates that the advanced degree will provide an increased lifetime income valued at $45,000. If the choice is based purely on economic considerations, the physicist will not continue such an education. But society as a whole may benefit by an additional $15,000 for each Ph.D. in physics because of contributions to basic knowledge. In this case then, the total benefits to society ($60,000) exceed the costs of education, and society will be better off if physicists are subsidized to attend graduate school. In general, governmental subsidies of education at any level are justified if there are important external benefits that society can anticipate from the education of its individuals.

This is, in fact, the case. There are obvious social benefits from a literate and informed citizenry, particularly in a democracy. With the rule of the country entrusted to officials elected by the people, one sleeps a little better knowing that the electorate can read and that some might even understand a few fundamental principles of economics. There are also intangible benefits to be derived from living among an educated peer group; the educated person derives less satisfaction from books if he or she cannot share ideas with appreciative companions. Furthermore, there are likely to be significant economic advantages to a general level of literacy: markets are likely to function more smoothly, and there should be a lower incidence of crime and public-health problems. Finally, advances in basic knowledge provide benefits to society as a whole. Furthering our understanding of the atom or the nature of economic depressions is a public good—in the sense that one person's use of that knowledge does not infringe upon its value to someone else. It is generally impossible for the contributors to basic knowledge to reap rewards equal to their contributions to society, for it is not possible to own or sell exclusive rights to a piece of knowledge.

So it is safe to conclude that education offers substantial social benefits that do not accrue to the individual alone. The government does have an important role to play in subsidizing education, which promises to pay rich rewards in terms of greater prosperity, more harmonious living conditions, and more effective governmental policies. But many believe that the primary justification is that the government can use education as a means for achieving greater income equality. This possibility will be examined in the next section with reference to several important studies of the contribution of education to income equality.

3. IF YOU'RE SO SMART, WHY AREN'T YOU RICH?

One of the most cherished beliefs about education is that it will open doors to lucrative and rewarding careers. Economists have been able to point to statistics that demonstrate that those individuals with the highest levels of education tend to have substantially higher incomes than the average. From these figures, the obvious remedy for poverty seemed to be equalization of educational opportunity.

Typical of early studies was one by Herman Miller, who estimated the average lifetime earnings of males with various levels of education.[2] It was found, for example, that an 18-year-old could expect lifetime earnings of $154,114 if he completed elementary school, $257,557 if completing high school, and $435,242 if graduating from college. Such statistics have undoubtedly been a boon to parents and teachers who wished to prod their little ones into educational advancement.

A more revealing way to look at the financial benefits of education is to include in the evaluation the costs as well as the increased income levels that result from additional schooling. An additional year of schooling involves sacrifices in terms of present income forgone, as well as the explicit expenditures that the individual student or family must incur. In considering an investment of any kind, one wants to know how great a return he or she will receive for a given outlay of money. If one puts $1000 into a savings and loan account, for example, this may yield a return of $100 per year or 10 percent. Similarly, the rate of return from an additional year of education may be computed by comparing the gains in annual income from the implicit and explicit costs of education. Suppose, for example, that a 21-year-old man has a choice of completing college with one more year of education or quitting school and taking on a job which would pay $10,000 per year. The expenses of a year of college would run to, say $5000. Assume that with the completion of his degree his yearly income will be $600 greater than otherwise. The initial cost of the extra year of schooling is $15,000 (the cost of college plus the opportunity cost of the earnings forgone); an investment of $15,000 which yields $600 per year has a rate of return of 4 percent. (Notice that if the opportunity cost of earnings forgone had been ignored, one would have incorrectly computed a rate of return of 12 percent.) This percentage rate of return is a convenient summary of the financial advantages of education and can appropriately be compared with rates of return on other forms of investment. This procedure assumes that an increase in income is the only benefit to be derived from education. Since this certainly is not the case—people receive all kinds of unmeasurable psychic satisfaction from education—rate of return estimates tend to understate the true contribution of education to an individual's welfare. However, if we are mainly interested in the effects on income distribution, then increases in income are our primary concern.

Studies of the rate of return on education, such as Miller's, have found the individual return on educational investments to be 15.3 percent for high school and 11.6 percent for college.[3] In comparison with other forms of investment these returns are quite high; an implicit awareness of such figures led to a huge expansion in both private and public expenditures on education in the early sixties.

In fact, many reformers felt that our educational system held the key to social and economic equality. Inequality for minority groups was attributed to differences in educational opportunity. As part of the Civil Rights Act of 1964, the U.S. Commissioner of Education was required to conduct a survey "concerning the lack of availability of equal educational opportunities for individuals by reason of race, color, religion, or natural origin . . . ." However, the differences in educational facilities actually observed by the Coleman Commission, which carried out the survey, were considerably less than the disparities anticipated.[4] The school facilities available to blacks were by no means uniformly inferior to those available to whites. Some differences were observed, but the evidence indicated that the nation had, by 1964, already moved a considerable distance towards equality of educational opportunity.[5] Rather than confirming the widely held view that blacks were economically disadvantaged because of a lack of educational opportunities, the report initiated more critical examinations of the real contribution of education to income differentials.

The Coleman Commission discovered first of all that quantifiable differences between black and white schools were not substantial. Comparisons of school facilities (libraries, laboratories, teacher experience, and so on) available at black and white schools indicated that black students were at a minor disadvantage on "some of the facilities that seem most related to academic achievement." The evidence presented by the Coleman Commission indicated, however, that school quality made very little difference in academic performance when family background was accounted for. Using data from the Coleman study, for example, Jencks and his associates found that eliminating differences between elementary schools would reduce differences in achievement test scores of sixth graders by only three percentage points; eliminating differences in high schools would reduce differences in performance by seniors by only one percentage point.[6]

These conclusions have been the subject of controversy and criticism. Some researchers have objected to the procedures employed by Coleman and his successors.[7] Family background tends to be strongly associated with the quality of available school facilities, and controlling for family background prior to analyzing the effect of schooling can negate some of the influence that schooling actually has on academic achievement. Some contend that family background and other environmental factors are so closely associated with the quality of schooling offered that it is impossible to attribute variations in academic performance to one factor rather than the other. If good students on the average come from upper-class families and at the same time attend schools of high quality, it is not possible to say whether schooling or family background or both factors together explain the child's performance.

Later studies have attempted to separate the effects of background and school quality on academic performance without committing the procedural errors of the Coleman study. Such studies have found family background variables to be of considerably more importance than school quality variables,[8] and in this sense they have supported the findings of the Coleman Commission. Some studies have found that schools do very little to reduce differences in educational achievement; differences between pupils exist upon entrance into school, and these differences persist after years of schooling. While there is still considerable debate over these results, a blind faith in the ability of our schools to solve the problem of income inequality no longer prevails.

None of this implies that schools are not important to a child's development; certainly children do learn skills such as reading and arithmetic, which are essential to functioning in an industrial society. The Coleman Report and much subsequent research do indicate that, beyond a certain minimal level of school quality, additional expenditures on schooling do very little to improve academic achievement.

While the Coleman Commission focused mainly on the relation between schooling and academic performance, other studies have extended the analysis to effects on income inequality. Subsequent studies of the relation between ability, family background, and education on the one hand and income on the other show that earlier studies severely overestimated the contribution made by years of schooling to individual incomes. Between individuals of similar ability (measured by IQ or other aptitude test scores) and family background, differences in education are relatively unimportant in the determination of income differences. Between 30 and 40 percent of the differences in income between, say, high school and college graduates can be attributed to differences in ability and background.[9,10] This means that our previous estimates of the rate of return on education must be reduced to approximately 10 percent for high school and 7.7 percent for college. Furthermore, it appears that all of these factors—education, family background, and ability—account for only about 22 percent of observed differences in incomes.[11] This means that if we could equalize these factors for everyone, income inequalities would be reduced by 22 percent. Equalizing education would reduce income differences by only 10 percent.

The picture becomes even bleaker when we examine figures for particular groups rather than national averages. Minority groups and women can anticipate even lower rates of return on education. O. D. Duncan estimates that blacks can expect income gains from education to be only one-third as great as those of whites.[12] Studies of average earnings of blacks and whites with identical education levels indicate that income disparities actually increase with the level of education.* One researcher found, for example, that the difference between aver-

---

*Evidence, cited in Chapter 10, indicates that income equality for black college graduates is close to being realized. This is apparently a very recent phenomenon, perhaps due to affirmative-action programs.

age annual white and average nonwhite earnings in 1959 was $1519 for those with eight years of schooling, $2229 for those who completed high school, and $4567 for individuals with college degrees.[13] The rate of return on education is obviously much higher for whites than for nonwhites, and such evidence does not tend to make one optimistic about education reducing income disparities.

One conclusion from all of this is that if society desires to make incomes more equal, the problem must be attacked directly rather than through the educational system. Apparently we have been demanding too much from our education system. We have tried to make schools serve not only as a place for teaching basic skills and values but also as a vehicle for solving difficult social problems, such as income inequality. Education should be recognized as important for its own sake, and the satisfaction of other social goals should be left to policies designed specifically to meet these objectives.

4. PUBLIC HIGHER EDUCATION: SUBSIDY FOR THE RICH

Public higher education, in particular, has been advanced as a means for reducing income inequalities. Toward this goal, states have encouraged the education of all classes by the provision of free or low-cost universities and other institutions of higher learning. Throughout the fifties and sixties, governments at all levels rapidly expanded their higher education programs. State systems of higher education were enlarged to meet the goal that no qualified high school graduate should be deprived of a college education by an inability to pay. In this nationwide education boom no other state could match the vast, three-tiered system of higher education developed in California. Here access to higher education was virtually guaranteed by the system of two-year community colleges, which provided both vocational programs and academic courses preparatory for transfer to one of the colleges or universities. The system appeared to be designed to foster upward mobility of individuals who otherwise would be deprived of the opportunities afforded by a college education for reason of a low income or even a mediocre high school record.

But appearances can be deceiving. In actuality, public financing of California's system of higher education results in a transfer of benefits from the poor to the rich. For while state and local taxes as a proportion of income are at least as great for low-income groups as for the rich, the wealthier families account for a disproportionate share of the students at the heavily subsidized universities. In 1964 the richest 12 percent of

California families accounted for nearly 40 percent of the students attending the University of California. The families of university students had median incomes of $12,000 while this figure for the families of community college students was $8800, and families without children in any public institution of higher education had average incomes of $8000.

To some extent, this disparity in benefits to the various income groups is a result of the relatively strong association between parental incomes and student eligibility for university admission. Forty percent of high school graduates whose parents earned $25,000 or more were eligible to attend the University of California, while only 11 percent of those whose families earned less than the $8000 were qualified. In addition, the proportion of low-income students who were eligible but did not attend, for financial or other reasons, was larger than the comparable proportion for students from wealthier families.

Nor is this inequity offset by differences in taxation. As with most states, higher education in California is financed mainly by state and local taxes, including income, sales, and property taxes. Particularly because of these last two sources of revenue, the poor end up contributing at least as great a proportion of their incomes to the support of higher education as do higher-income groups. A comparison of total taxes paid with the annual subsidy received by each family group classified according to their children's enrollment in institutions of higher learning reveals a net income transfer from the poor to the higher-income groups. Families with children enrolled in U.C. received an annual education subsidy of $1700, while they paid state and local taxes averaging only $910. Community college students' families received benefits worth $720 and paid taxes of $680. Both of these groups received a net transfer of income from the lowest income group, namely those with no children attending public universities or colleges. The highest income group, those with children attending the U.C. system, received by far the largest net transfer of income—a net subsidy of $790. It is apparent from these figures that state higher education systems as presently financed actually do take from the poor to give it to the rich.[14]

In addition to being subsidized with tuition charges that are less than the full cost of their education, in recent years students have received large subsidies in the form of financial aid and low-cost loans. A potential advantage of such aid is that it can be given only to those students who would otherwise not be able to get a higher education because they are poor. There is also an argument for making government loans available to students regardless of their income level. We consider this argument in the next section.

5. HUMAN COLLATERAL, GUARANTEED LOANS, AND STUDENT AID

You're a smart cookie with a lot of drive. The only thing holding you back is that you don't have that sheepskin from a prestigious university decorating your wall. You would quit your lousy job selling insurance, but you have to support the wife and kids. Besides, college is expensive these days. So what do you do? You trot down to those friendly people with money to lend and tell them your situation: you need a loan for college. What about collateral? It's standing right in front of them, you reply. A fine piece of human capital—just needs a little developing. Suddenly the smiles fall from the friendly faces, and the "we're here to help" sign disappears under some papers; with their jingle still ringing in your ears, you are once again touting the latest insurance policy.

Unfortunately, no one lends on undeveloped human capital. A car, boat, or house provides adequate collateral because it is a marketable asset; a human being legally is not. The solution, of course, is to alter the law to permit indentured servitude. Then when anyone desires a loan for human capital improvements (e.g., education), he can offer himself as collateral. Failure to meet the terms of the loan will permit the loan company to repossess the defaulter for use or resale as the firm desires. The incentive to avoid default will be very great indeed.

Mild forms of indentured servitude actually do exist in this society today. Many young people enrolled in ROTC programs or in the military academies, for example, accept government finance of their education, and in return agree to relinquish their freedom for several years while serving in the armed forces. Since the agreement is voluntarily made with full information about the consequences, no one finds this example of indentured servitude particularly undesirable. In fact, the selectivity of the military academies attests to the eagerness of large numbers of men and women to commit themselves to such an arrangement. Another current example of indentured servitude is the case of sabbatical leaves granted to employees for the purpose of undertaking advanced training or study in some area related to their work. Schools will often finance advanced study for a year with the stipulation that this person will return to the school for several more years of service. In either of these arrangements, both parties benefit from the institution of indentured servitude: the individual receives financial support to make an investment in his or her own human capital, while the employer gains from the use of the services of this individual with upgraded skills. Only if the employer is certain of being able to reap these benefits—that is, only if the individual is contractually obligated to serve the employer for some period in the future—will such grants for investment in human capital be forthcoming. If such guarantees existed in other sectors of the economy, no doubt more opportunities for educational advancement or training would be financed by private firms and organizations. But laws against voluntary indentured servitude, which would be mutually beneficial to both parties, prevent the negotiation of contractual agreements.

Despite the advantages that would be available from voluntary indentured servitude, most people would be justifiably reluctant to rely on it as means of financing higher education. As an alternative means of allowing students to acquire loans, the government began a guaranteed student loan program during the 1970s. Students could borrow money from a local bank for their college education with the collateral being the federal government's guarantee that, if the student did not repay its loan, the government would. The government also allows students to borrow at below market interest rates with the government paying the difference.

There are advantages to such a student loan program. First of all, students are provided with funds to use on their education as they see fit; they are not constrained to attend a college in their state (with instate tuition) in order to receive the same subsidy as others. As will be discussed in the next section, significant benefits can come from this freedom of choice. Second, if properly structured, government loans could reduce the extent to which higher income families are subsidized. For example, all students could get a loan guarantee, but with the interest rate depending on the student's family income level.

But as with many government programs that begin with worthwhile but limited objectives, the guaranteed student loan program quickly became broader and more generous than originally intended. Until recently, very few families earning more than $25,000 could get a government-subsidized student loan. In 1978, however, Congress opened the program up, and suddenly high-income parents had an opportunity to borrow for Junior's education at low subsidized rates while receiving high interest rates on their own savings. The effect was to increase loan volume by a factor of 5.[15] Furthermore, the government has been lax in requiring the loans to be paid back. In early 1982 the default rate on subsidized loans was about 12.5 percent. The default rate on federally guaranteed, but not subsidized, loans to doctors was also running high. Reports by the General Accounting Office showed 6000 doctors defaulting on loans totalling $5.2 million dollars.[16] One doctor who had reportedly received $623,000 in Medicaid payments had not repaid his federal loan for medical school of $4750.[17]

The Reagan Administration, in an attempt to reverse this trend, wanted to reimpose more stringent limits on loan qualification. Unless need could be shown, guaranteed loans would no longer be available to families earning $30,000 or more. Also, a 5 percent loan initiation fee would be required, and the Administration wanted to raise it to 10 percent. The Reagan Administration is also hoping to reduce the Pell grants and other federally funded student-aid programs. In 1981 these aid programs cost the taxpayers over $6.2 billion dollars, and much of it went to the nonpoor.[18] Not surprisingly, students are concerned over these threatened cutbacks. On March 1, 1982, approximately 5000 students demonstrated against these cuts on the steps of the Capitol.

Even if you accept the argument that student aid has become too generous and has to a large extent subsidized those who are well-to-do, as a student you still have a legitimate complaint against cutbacks. In order to explain why, we have to ask: who benefited from student aid in the past? This may seem a silly question. Obviously, it was students who benefited from past student-aid programs. True, but students were not the only beneficiaries. Because former students had more money to spend on their education, colleges and universities also benefited. They were able to hire more professors and administrators, pay them higher salaries, build nicer facilities, and in general be less cost conscious. Why do you think college and university presidents fly to Washington to lobby against any proposed decrease in student aid? Those employed in higher education receive much of the benefits from this aid.

Having made decisions to spend more money on personnel, programs, and facilities, these decisions are difficult to reverse. Professors receive tenure, administrators have their own form of job security, and buildings are long-term commitments. Because of the generous financial aid students received in the past, commitments were made that meant higher costs for colleges and universities today. And some percentage of these costs are always passed on to students. This means that as a student today, your education costs you more because of the aid received by those who preceded you.[19]

In the long-run, cutbacks in student aid will put more pressure on colleges and universities, making them more cost-conscious and efficient. As this happens, students will benefit from lower costs. But the adjustment to lower costs and increased efficiency will take a long time. The effect of less financial aid to today's students is immediate. So if you are a student at the time aid is cut, you have a legitimate reason for complaint—even if you believe the large student-aid program was inadvisable in the first place.

The student-aid case is a particular example of a more general problem. It is difficult to eliminate government programs, even very inefficient ones, without hurting innocent people. Farm subsidies (which we discussed in Chapter 3), for example, do not help all farmers. The primary effect of agricultural price-support programs is to increase the price of farm land. Farmers who already own their land benefit, normally the wealthier farmers, but not farmers who have to buy their land after the price-support program goes into effect. The price they pay for their land offsets the advantage they expect to receive from high price supports. If the government suddenly eliminated agricultural price supports after a farmer buys land, the value of the land would drop, and the farmer would likely be wiped out financially. Just as the new student facing a cut in financial aid, the new farmer facing a cut in price supports would legitimately feel unfairly treated.

6. PUBLIC GROCERIES AND PUBLIC EDUCATION

Assume that a nationwide grocery-store chain got Congress to pass the National Nutritional Act. Under this legislation, the grocery chain would be authorized to provide the proper diet free to all through their stores, the cost of this service being paid for through increased taxes. The argument made for this law is that nutrition is too important to be left to the uninformed public, and the new arrangement would give nutritional experts more control over our diets. People could still shop at other food stores if they chose, but they would still have to pay their tax to support the provision of public food. Obviously, most people— having to pay anyway—would find it to their advantage to get their food at the local Tax Mart.

This arrangement would immediately reduce the competitive pressures on Tax Mart and its employees. If costs went up because salaries were increased, more administrators and personnel were employed, and more conferences were attended, there would be little concern that consumers would shift their patronage to other stores. Regardless, consumers would have to pay for the higher cost of Tax Mart's operation. The Tax Mart professionals would also face little pressure to stock a large variety of food to appeal to the diverse taste of consumers, to offer convenient hours, or to provide a fast and courteous checkout. Service could decline significantly before it would pay consumers to buy their food from other stores and in effect pay twice. In short, those working for Tax Mart could take it easier and devote more attention to doing the things they thought were important and less attention to satisfying the demands of the consumer.

The nutritional experts working for Tax Mart would have free rein to make sure that consumers had the type of food they should have, not necessarily the type they wanted. A consumer might want steak marbled with fat, soft drinks, white bread, ice cream, frozen pizza, and potato chips. Instead he or she would find fish, prune juice, stone-ground granola bread, unflavored yogurt, brussel sprouts, and lima beans.

If consumers wanted to have an influence on the policy of the tax-supported stores, they would have to do so through the political process. As we saw in Chapter 4, groups that feel strongly about a single issue have the advantage in exerting political influence. One group may feel strongly that tax-supported stores should not carry foods that have religious significance, since it would be felt that this violated the constitutional separation of church and state. This group may be successful in getting Kosher foods, Christmas cookies, and Easter candy banned from the stores. Another group may feel strongly that wealthier communities with larger tax bases have nicer stores than poorer communities. Also, it may be felt that allowing people to shop in their neighborhood Tax Mart promotes racial segregation. With the objective of social justice and racial balance, this group may be successful in getting a law passed requiring that many people have to use the Tax Mart on the other side of town. The only way for many people to oppose these policies would be to engage in political battle in the hope of having these laws repealed. The provision of food would become a socially divisive issue as emotional concerns dominated Tax Mart policy. The poor person who would just like a better selection of pork and beans will be completely ignored.

Service at the Tax Mart would soon decline to the point where many consumers would prefer to shop at private grocery stores. The ability of private stores, charging full price for their products, to compete successfully against the Tax Mart, giving their service away, would be undeniable evidence that the consumers' interest was being given scant consideration in the tax-supported stores.

This discussion of tax-supported food stores is, of course, fanciful. Fortunately, in most countries consumers pay directly for their food, and it is supplied by businesses that have a profit motive to take the preferences of the consumer fully into consideration. But elementary and secondary education in most countries is provided under an arrangement almost identical to that just described for food. Professional educators provide education free of charge for all children from kindergarten through 12th grade. This education is paid for through taxes that people have to pay, whether or not they send their children to public shool. The common argument for this arrangement is that education is too important to be left to the preferences of the uninformed public. Public schools give the educational experts more control over the type of education children receive, since these experts are under little competitive pressure to respond to the diverse educational preferences found in the community.

Educational professionals in the public schools also face little competitive pressures to keep their costs down. If educational costs go up, consumers do not pay this cost directly, and they cannot avoid it by taking their children out of public school and putting them in private school. This means that teachers' salaries will be higher, more administrators will be hired, and more professional conferences will be attended than would be the case with more competition. In 1979 the expenditure per pupil in public school averaged $1900.[20] This compares with a medium tuition of $552 per pupil in private schools, which depend on tuition payments to cover most of their costs.[21]

Since public schools have a largely captive clientele, single-interest groups have found that schools provide tempting opportunities for imposing their strongly held views on others. Of course, these groups prompt hostile reactions from groups with equally strong opposing views. This often turns the public schools into battlegrounds over such divisive issues as school prayer, sex education, creation versus evolution, racial balance, and censorship of books. With education policy being buffeted with such emotional issues, it is little wonder that much evidence indicates that education is being neglected in the public schools.

Not surprisingly, many parents choose to send their children to private schools, even though they continue to pay for the public schools. In the 1980-81 school year, 5,029,000 students attended private schools, according to the National Center for Educational Statistics. This amounted to 10.9 percent of the total elementary and secondary school enrollment.

7. VOUCHING FOR A BETTER EDUCATION

There is an alternative to the present government monopoly in public schooling that would satisfy the objectives of governmental activity in education. This is a system under which the government, rather than being directly involved in the provision of educational services, would simply grant each family with school-age children an educational voucher. This voucher would entitle them to, say, $1900 worth of educational services. It could be spent only on education, but the choice of school would be left entirely up to the family receiving the voucher. Schooling would be provided by private organizations or firms, which would be interested in providing the kind of educational services demanded most by their clientele so as to maximize their profits. These private schools would have the incentive to discover which facilities, instructional techniques, and teacher characteristics provide the kind of schooling most desired by the individuals in society, and to develop their curriculum and employment procedures accordingly. It is doubtful, for example, that ineffective teachers would be retained solely by virtue of seniority, as is often the case today with the tenure system. Schools offering an education considered by customers to be inferior would either change their procedures or be forced to go out of business as a result of insufficient income. Schools providing what is considered by individual families to be quality education would prosper and as a result would be imitated by others. Diversity and experimentation would be encouraged just as innovation is fostered in other sectors of the economy by the lure of higher profits.

The competitive pressure would also make schools more cost-conscious than public schools are today. Schools would not only be better, they would cost less as well. This means that the voucher could be for less than the current per-pupil education cost of $1900. Taxpayers and students would both be better off.

This does not mean that there is no opposition to the voucher approach to financing education. The real opposition to the voucher system comes from the educational professionals, who are sheltered from competition under the existing arrangement. With a voucher system operating, educators would have to pay more attention to the educational concerns of the community and less attention to their own concerns. So far, the opposition of the educational establishment has been effective. Having a concentrated interest in protecting its occupational advantages, it has more political influence than the general taxpayer and parent who would benefit from vouchers. The Reagan Administration has proposed a tuition tax-credit plan that would work much like the voucher plan. Parents who choose to send their children to private school would receive up to $500 per child in the form of a tax credit. As expected, the education lobby is vigorously opposing this plan.[22]

These critics of educational vouchers, or tax credits, argue that parents are not good judges of the kind of education their children need and that they will make decisions detrimental to the welfare of the children. This criticism contradicts a basic premise of a free society; namely, that individuals know best what is good for them or their families. The opposite view justifies control by experts, which we have encountered in other sectors of the economy (see Chapter 6). While educational authorities may have some understanding of techniques for the instruction of basic cognitive skills, it is not the case that they have expertise in the question of which values should be inculcated into the minds of our youth. We must recognize that the development of attitudes and ethical values is an important part of the educational process. The question is whether individual families or public school boards should be making this kind of decision, and it is not clear that educational experts have better judgment in these matters. The legal precedent in favor of the integrity of the family and in support of parental authority is well established. The decision about what kind of education a child should have, beyond the development of basic literacy, is no more a governmental concern than is the question of when a child should be toilet-trained.

A second objection to the voucher system is that the rich will be able to supplement their vouchers and thus purchase for their own children schooling of higher quality. No doubt the rich will be able to spend more for the education of their children, just as they now are able to buy better medical care, food, piano lessons, and baby-stimulating gewgaws. One cannot deny that the rich are better off in many ways and so are their children. But this is fundamentally an objection to the prevailing distribution of income and not to the educational voucher system. Inequities in individual incomes should be dealt with directly, rather than through the educational system.

Under the present system, a family can often provide a better education for its children only by forgoing free public education and paying for a private school, or by moving to those suburbs that provide better schooling—both costly propositions affordable only by higher-income families. If each family were provided with an educational voucher that could be supplemented with additional funds, a better education somewhat above the norm would be within reach of even low-income families. In addition, the fear that the rich will be able to advance the welfare of their children through higher expenditures on education is lessened considerably by evidence such as that from the Coleman Report that expenditures beyond a basic minimum do very little to improve academic achievement.

The criticisms of the voucher system are not sound; the advantages it would provide in terms of greater diversity, experimentation, and cost savings speak strongly in its favor. The educational establishment will naturally fight against any such proposal, but more and more citizens who are concerned about the ability of public schools to educate their children should look seriously into this idea.

8. A SECOND LOOK

In this chapter we have tried to demonstrate that while the government does have an important role to play in education at all levels, there is no reason that governmental involvement should take the particular forms that it has. State provision of educational services goes beyond the proper scope of governmental action and as a result restricts freedom of choice. Greater diversity and experimentation are to be expected under a voucher system. Second, we should recognize that we may have been asking too much of our educational system. For many years, people have assumed that equalization of educational opportunity would reduce income inequality; recent studies indicate that we should not be too optimistic on this score. Desired changes in income distribution should be achieved directly, for there is no evidence that education by itself can do much to reduce income inequities.

DISCUSSION QUESTIONS

1. To what extent does economic advancement depend on obtaining a degree rather than acquiring the education that goes with it? What does this suggest about the real contribution of education to income differences? Why do firms require high school or college degrees for certain jobs even if they have no use for the particular skills taught in the classroom? Is this rational behavior?

2. Are the external benefits from education different for different levels of education? Explain. What does this suggest about the optimal size of governmental subsidies at different levels of education?

3. If the military finds it profitable to pay for education in return for an obligation of service, why don't more firms find it profitable to do the same?

4. Yale University has recently instituted a plan whereby students are offered a tuition-free education in return for a promise to pay a certain fraction of the student's future annual income for the rest of his or her life. What advantages and disadvantages can you see from such a plan? What does such a plan do to Yale's motivation to provide an education that will yield a good income?

5. Why have many small private colleges been having financial difficulties in recent years? What, if anything, do you think should be done to improve their financial position?

6. The text contends that high levels of national income and an educated populace are highly associated with each other. Which is cause and which is effect? Explain.

7. At one time French dress designers petitioned the government to allow them to provide free dresses to those women who would most benefit from them. The cost of this service would be paid for through taxes. Given that beautiful women in beautiful dresses create positive benefits for others, do you see this proposal any less justified than public support for education? What advantages would dress designers have under the tax-supported scheme that they would not have when women paid for their dresses directly?

8. How does the plan giving tax credits for private school tuition differ from the voucher plan? Which plan would you prefer? Why?

Epilogue

It is appropriate at this point to recount some of the general principles that have been developed and applied throughout the book. Some overriding themes, principles of analysis, and policy considerations have evolved from this study of the problems of a market economy, and it should be useful to summarize them at this point.

It is important, first of all, not to lose sight of the basic value judgments that have served as the foundations for the analytical reasoning. Too often in casual discussions of policy we let our value judgments become intermingled with scientific principles to the point that it is difficult to disentangle one from the other. This can confuse discussions needlessly. In this study we have proceeded from the assumption that the individual is the best judge of his or her own welfare and can determine better than others how that welfare can be improved. There is no question that some will disagree with this position. A second related assumption is that the maximization of individual satisfaction is the primary goal of the society. Again there will be disagreement; many believe that there is some social good above and beyond the satisfaction of individuals. The common good, the community, and the state might be thought to be separate entities whose goals transcend those of the individual. Adherents of this position will undoubtedly disagree with some if not most of the positions advanced in this book.

The responsiveness of the market system to individual preferences was demonstrated in early chapters. The market mechanism is a system of information and control, which in its perfect form coordinates the activities of economic decision makers and induces responses to changing tastes, technologies, and resource scarcities in a manner consistent with the maximization of individual welfare. Divergences from the ideal market system do, of course, exist in the real world, and these departures from the ideal give rise to the economic problems described throughout the book. Unfortunately, when the market system does not perform in an ideal fashion, we cannot expect the ideal governmental agency to come to the rescue.

Many reformers assume that the alternative to the imperfect market is the perfect governmental agency. An analysis of the organizational and informational problems involved in collective action demonstrates that this is not the case. In general, these considerations suggest that government action is likely to be directed toward the interests of special groups at the expense of the general public. Direct examples of such policies were described in our examination of regulatory agencies, occupational licensing practices, and a host of specific legislative acts. The regulation of interstate trucking, federal agricultural policy, urban renewal, minimum-wage legislation, and federal regulation of the drug industry are but a few of the instances of humanely motivated policy gone awry.

Seeing this, one is led to ask how policy can be designed to minimize divergences of governmental action from society's objectives. Several recommendations are suggested by the analysis of economic policy.

As a general rule, we should attempt to make private interest and social interests coincide. For the most part, the market system operates very effectively through exactly this principle. Each individual striving to advance his or her own welfare responds to economic incentives that produce actions favorable to society as a whole. However, market imperfections do exist. In such cases social and private interest diverge, and government action may be warranted. For example, where external benefits exist (as in education), a subsidy may be desirable and recommended. And where external costs are a factor (as in pollution), a system of pollution rights could be established. Such actions tend to move the system closer to the ideal situation in which private and social costs and benefits are equal.

The principle of designing policy to make private and social interests coincide is more easily achieved in economic activities than it is in the political sphere. While the market economy employs a system of mutually advantageous exchanges, governmental action requires coercion and a conflict of interest. The influence of recurring elections and the pressure of special-interest groups encourage government officials to advance policies that are shortsighted and beneficial to particular groups at the expense of the unorganized community. The decisions of legislators and the actions of officials in regulatory agencies must be constrained by some means in order to avoid these problems. Policies that minimize the discretionary action of government officials reduce the scope for granting special favors and waivers to particular groups and are therefore more likely to lead to results that advance community rather than special interests. This is one reason for the particular policies recommended in this book: a pollution-rights system rather than direct controls, a voucher system for education rather than government provision, and so on. It is not suggested that such approaches will work flawlessly, but the principles of economics and collective action suggest that they will perform better than existing alternatives.

Designing policy to make private and social interests coincide is a compelling principle. Through its application, the power of self-interest is harnessed to work in the public interest, as is the case in properly functioning markets. The unanswered question is how to make this principle more concrete in particular problem situations. This book has presented some applications of this principle to certain policy areas, and we hope some readers will extend the analysis to the unsolved problems of the political economy of the present and the future.

Chapter Notes

CHAPTER 3

1. Mary G. Lacy, "Food Control during Forty-Six Centuries," paper presented at the meeting of the Agricultural History Society, March 16, 1922, Washington, D.C.

2. For these and other examples from the Soviet Union, see Hedrick Smith, *The Russians,* New York: Ballantine Books, 1977, chapter 2.

3. This example was reported in Thomas Sowell, *Knowledge and Decisions,* New York: Basic Books, Inc., 1980, p. 182.

4. This section is based on evidence from A. Lindbeck, "Rent Control as an Instrument of Housing Policy," in *The Economic Problems of Housing,* edited by Adela Adam Nevitt, London: MacMillan, 1967.

5. "Farmer's Golden Challenge," *Time,* September 10, 1973, p. 82.

6. These estimates come from Charles L. Schultze, *The Distribution*

of Farm Subsidies: Who Gets the Benefits, Wasinghton, D.C.: Brookings, 1971.

7. These estimates come from Bruce L. Gardner, *The Governing of Agriculture,* Lawrence: Regents Press of Kansas, 1981.

8. Ibid.

9. See Edward M. Gramlich, "Impact of Minimum Wages on Other Wages, Employment, and Family Incomes," *Brookings Papers on Economic Activity,* Vol. 2., Washington, D.C.: Brookings, 1976, pp. 409–51.

10. This table is adapted from Walter E. Williams, "Government Sanctioned Restraints That Reduce Economic Opportunities for Minorities," *Policy Review,* Fall, 1977, pp. 1–24.

CHAPTER 4

1. This quote also appears in Armen A. Alchian and William R. Allen, *Exchange and Production: Theory in Use,* Belmont, Calif.: Wadsworth, 1969, p. 83.

2. For a good discussion of this aspect of political behavior, as well as other interesting points, see Anthony Downs, "An Economic Theory of Political Action in a Democracy," *Journal of Political Economy,* April, 1957.

3. See Bruce Gardner, "Sugar Prices and the U.S.: How Sweet It Is," *Wall Street Journal,* July 10, 1981, p. 26.

CHAPTER 5

1. Adam Smith, *Wealth of Nations,* New York: Modern Library, p. 128.

2. Lee Benham, "The Effects of Advertising on the Price of Eyeglasses," *Journal of Law and Economics,* October, 1972.

3. "Effects of Restrictions on Advertising and Commercial Practice in the Professions: The Case of Optometry," staff report to the Federal Trade Commission by R. S. Bond, J. E. Kwoka, J. J. Phelan, and I. T. Whitten, April, 1980.

4. For empirical evidence on this point, see Ross D. Eckert, "The Life Cycle of Regulatory Commissioners," *Journal of Law and Economics,* April, 1981, pp. 113–20.

5. This is the conclusion of R. B. Helms, in *Natural Gas Regulation: An Evaluation of FPC Price Controls,* Washington, D.C.: American Enterprise Institute, 1975.

6. Cited in Matthew Josephson, *The Politicos,* New York: Harcourt Brace, 1938, p. 526.

7. For an excellent discussion of airline regulation that makes detailed comparisons between California intrastate airlines and the CAB-regulated airlines, see William A. Jordan, *Airline Regulation in America: Effects and Imperfections,* Baltimore: Johns Hopkins Press, 1970.

8. These data have been taken from James C. Miller, III, "Is Airline Deregulation Working?" *Wall Street Journal,* March 26, 1980, page 20.

9. Paul W. MacAvoy, *The Economic Effects of Regulation: The Trunk-Line Railroad Cartels and the Interstate Commerce Commission before 1900,* Cambridge, Mass.: M.I.T. Press, 1965.

10. Richard N. Farmer, "The Case for Unregulated Truck Transportation," *Journal of Farm Economics,* May, 1964.

11. Thomas G. Moore, "The Beneficiaries of Trucking Regulation," *Journal of Law and Economics,* Vol. 21, 1978, pp. 327–43.

12. Reported in "The Medicines We Need—But Can't Have," by Walter S. Ross, *Reader's Digest,* October, 1973, p. 101.

13. W. M. Wardell and L. Lasagna, *Regulation and Drug Development,* Washington, D.C.: American Enterprise Institute, 1975, p. 46, and L. Lasagna, "The Uncertain Future of Drug Development," *Drug Intelligence and Clinical Pharmacy,* Vol. 13, April, 1979, p. 193.

14. Ross, p. 99.

15. These figures are reported by Sam Peltzman, "An Evaluation of Consumer Protection Legislation: The 1962 Drug Amendments," *Journal of Political Economy,* October, 1973.

16. "Death and Delay," *Wall Street Journal,* July 3, 1980, p. 16.

17. W. M. Wardell, "A Close Inspection of the 'Calm Look,'" *Journal of the American Medical Association,* Vol. 239, May 12, 1978, pp. 2009–10.

18. For a review of the battle to obtain approval to market this type of drug, see "A Heart Drug's Long Road to the Marketplace," *Wall Street Journal,* January 22, 1982, p. 26.

19. R. S. Smith, *The Occupational Safety and Health Act,* Washington, D.C.: American Enterprise Institute, 1976, p. 69.

20. Sam Peltzman, *Regulation of Automobile Safety,* Washington, D.C.: American Enterprise Institute, 1975.

CHAPTER 6

1. H. G. Wells, *Anticipations,* New York: Harper, 1902, p. 208.

2. Robert Ayre, *Technological Forecasting,* New York: McGraw-Hill, 1969, p. 12.

3. Details on licensing of barbers in Arizona are given in Jonathan Rose, "Controlling Clip Joints," *Regulation,* July/August 1980, pp. 37–40.

4. Stuart Dorsey, "The Occupational Licensing Queue," *Journal of Human Resources,* Vol. 15, 1980, pp. 424–33.

5. Lawrence Shepard, "Licensing Restrictions and the Cost of Dental Care," *Journal of Law and Economics,* April, 1978, pp. 187–201.

6. A. D. Bevan, "Cooperation in Medical Education and Medical Service," *Journal of the American Medical Society,* Vol. 90, 1928, p. 1176.

7. R. A. Kessel, "The A.M.A. and the Supply of Physicians," *Law and Contemporary Problems,* Vol. 35, Spring, 1970, pp. 267–83.

8. H. E. Frech, "Occupational Licensure and Health Care Productivity: The Issues and the Literature," in John Rafferty (ed.), *Health Manpower and Productivity,* Toronto: D.C. Heath & Company, 1974, pp. 119–39.

9. Frech, "Occupational Licensure," p. 122.

10. K. B. Leffler, "Physician Licensure: Competition and Monopoly in American Medicine," *Journal of Law and Economics,* Vol. 21, 1978, pp. 165–86.

11. Frech, "Occupational Licensure," p. 130.

CHAPTER 7

1. For more on the environmentally disruptive activities of government, see John Baden and Richard Stroup (eds.), *Bureaucracy vs.*

Environment: The Environmental Cost of Bureaucratic Governance, Ann Arbor: University of Michigan Press, 1981.

2. For the percentage increase of specific pollutants from 1940–1970, see Barry Commoner, *The Closing Circle,* New York: Bantam, 1972, p. 125.

3. See "Market Booms for 'Rights' to Pollute," *Wall Street Journal,* June 12, 1981.

4. The following discussion of this case is based on an excellent article by Peter Navarro, "The Politics of Air Pollution," *Public Interest,* Spring, 1980, pp. 36–44.

5. For a discussion of some of the problems with the Clean Air Act, see Lester B. Lave and Gilbert S. Omenn, *Cleaning the Air: Reforming the Clean Air Act,* Washington, D.C.: Brookings, 1981.

6. For some specific examples, see Marshall I. Goldman, "Externalities and the Race for Economic Growth in the USSR: Will the Environment Ever Win?" *Journal of Political Economy,* March–April, 1972, pp. 314–27.

7. For these and other examples of this type, see Goldman, "Externalities."

8. This and other examples of Polish pollution come from Lloyd Timberlake, "Poland—the Most Polluted Country in the World?" *New Scientist,* October 22, 1981, p. 250. These examples are also cited in Robert J. Smith, "Privatizing the Environment," *Policy Review,* Spring, 1982, p. 11.

CHAPTER 8

1. From S. B. Pettengill, *Hot Oil,* New York: Economic Forum, 1936.

2. *The Third Annual Report of the Council on Environmental Quality,* August, 1972, p. 95.

3. Ibid., p. 97.

4. The discussion is based on John Baden and Richard Stroup, "Saving the Wilderness," *Reason,* July, 1981, pp. 28–36.

5. Thomas Malthus, *An Essay on the Principle of Population,* Baltimore: Penguin, 1971. This book went through six editions from 1798 to 1816.

6. William Jevons, *The Coal Question,* London, 1865.

7. Gifford Pinchot, *The Fight for Conservation,* New York: Double-day, Page and Co., 1910.

8. E. W. Pehrson, "The Mineral Position of the United States and the Outlook for the Future," *Mining and Metallurgy Journal,* No. 26, 1945, pp. 204–14.

9. Donella H. Meadows et al., *The Limits to Growth,* New York: New American Library, 1972.

10. William D. Nordhaus, "Resources as a Constraint on Growth," *American Economic Review,* Vol. 64, No. 2, May, 1974, pp. 22–26.

11. Ibid., p. 24.

12. The Paley Commission, "Resources for Freedom," A Report to the President's Material Policy Commission, June, 1952.

13. H. J. Barnett and Chandler Morse, *Scarcity and Growth,* Baltimore: Johns Hopkins Press, 1963.

14. Paul W. MacAvoy and Robert S. Pindyck, *Price Controls and the Natural Gas Shortage,* Washington, D.C.: American Enterprise Institute, 1975, p. 14.

15. Julian L. Simon, *The Ultimate Resource,* Princeton: Princeton University Press, 1981, pp. 153–54.

CHAPTER 9

1. John Kenneth Galbraith, *The New Industrial State,* New York: New American Library, 1968, pp. 222–23.

2. Ibid., p. 220.

3. Charles Reich, *The Greening of America,* New York: Bantam Books, 1971, p. 110.

4. Lester Telser, "Advertising and Competition," *Journal of Political Economy,* December, 1964.

5. See *Fortune* June 14, 1982, p. 64.

6. Ibid., p. 64.

7. For a full discussion of this topic, see Robert McNown and Dwight Lee, *Economics in Our Time: Macro Issue,* Chicago: Science Research Assoc., 1976, Chapter 7.

8. Quoted in David Hemenway, *Prices and Choices: Microeconomic*

Vignettes, Cambridge, Mass.: Ballinger Publishing Co., 1977, p. 26.

9. Ibid., p. 29.

10. M. Janowitz and C. C. Moskos, "Five Years of the All-Volunteer Force: 1973–1978," *Armed Forces and Society,* Vol. 5, February, 1979, pp. 171–218.

11. Ibid., pp. 198–99.

12. Ibid., p. 200.

13. P. M. Shields, "Enlistment during the Viet Nam Era and the Representation Issue of the All-Volunteer Force," *Armed Forces and Society,* Vol. 7, Fall, 1980, pp. 133–51.

14. R. W. Hunter and G. R. Nelson, "Eight Years with the All-Volunteer Armed Forces: Assessments and Prospects," in B. Scowcroft (ed.), *Military Service in the U.S.,* Englewood Cliffs, N.J.: Prentice-Hall, 1982, p. 116.

15. Ibid., pp. 93–94. One of the authors has pointed out that there is a bias in the political process against increasing military salaries. As the primary beneficiaries of military pay raises are members of a large, politically unorganized group, they do not have the influence necessary to press for a reallocation of funds away from expenditures on military hardware or other programs with a more specific constituency. See Dwight R. Lee, *Economics, Politics, and the All-Volunteer Army,* Boulder, Colorado: Economic Institute for Research and Education, 1981.

16. Ibid., p. 113.

17. J. P. White and J.R. Hosek, "The Analysis of Military Manpower Issues," in B. Scowcroft (ed.), *Military Service in the U.S.,* p. 84.

18. Hunter and Nelson, "Eight Years with the All-Volunteer Force," p. 84.

19. *55 mph Fact Book,* Washington, D.C.: U.S. Department of Transportation, NHTSA, 1979.

20. Total vehicle miles in 1978 (1,548,000 million miles) times the average number of persons per vehicle (1.8) yields total person miles of 2,786,400. When this is divided by average speeds before (60.3) and after (55.8) the speed limit, we obtain two figures for total hours. The difference between these two is 3726.5 million additional hours spent on the highways, or equivalently 425,400 years. All figures come from the *55 mph Fact Book.*

21. T. Forrester, R. McNown, and L. Singell, "A Cost-Benefit Analysis of the 55 MPH Speed Limit," mimeographed, Boulder: University of Colorado, Department of Economics, 1982.

22. The average age of persons killed in highway accidents is 33.5 years, and the life expectancy of persons of this age is 42.4 additional years. The number of lives saved times years of life expectancy yields a total saving of 316,600 years of life. Data are from the *55 mph Fact Book*.

23. R. Thaler and S. Rosen, "The Value of Saving a Life," in N. E. Terlecky (ed.), *Household Production and Consumption,* New York: National Bureau of Economic Research, 1975. Their estimates have been inflated to 1978 dollars.

CHAPTER 10

1. The following information is taken from *Money Income in 1976 of Families and Persons in the United States,* U.S. Bureau of the Census, 1977; Nancy F. Rytina, "Earnings of Men and Women: A Look At Specific Occupations," *Monthly Labor Review,* April, 1982, pp. 25–31; *Handbook of Labor Statistics,* U.S. Dept. of Labor, 1980; Nancy F. Rytina, "Tenure as a Factor in the Male-Female Earnings Gap," *Monthly Labor Review,* April, 1982, pp. 32–34.

2. Mary Corcoran and Greg Duncan, "Work History, Labor Force Attachment, and Earnings Differences between the Races and Sexes," *Journal of Human Behavior,* Vol. 14, No. 1, pp. 3–20.

3. R. S. Brown, M. Moon, and B. S. Zoloth, "Incorporating Occupational Attainment in Studies of Male-Female Earnings Differentials," *Journal of Human Resources.* Vol. 15, No. 1, pp. 3–28.

4. Thomas Sowell, *Markets and Minorities,* New York: Basic Books, 1981, p. 11, and *Statistical Abstract of the United States,* U.S. Bureau of the Census, 1980.

5. Sowell, *Markets and Minorities,* p. 12.

6. Finis Welch, "Affirmative Action and Its Enforcement," *American Economic Review,* Vol. 71, No. 2, May, 1981, pp. 127–33.

7. Edward Lazear, "The Narrowing of Black-White Wage Differentials Is Illusory," *American Economic Review,* Vol. 69, No. 4, September, 1979, pp. 553–64.

8. Victor R. Fuchs, "Differences in Hourly Earnings between Men and Women," *Monthly Labor Review,* May, 1971, pp. 9–15.

9. Sowell, *Markets and Minorities,* p. 48.

10. Ibid., p. 49.

11. O. Ashenfelter, "Racial Discrimination and Trade Unionism," *Journal of Political Economy,* Vol. 80, May/June, 1972, pp. 435–64.

CHAPTER 11

1. These and subsequent figures on the characteristics of the poor are from the *Annual Statistical Supplement* to the *Social Security Bulletin,* 1980 edition.

2. *Social Security Bulletin, Annual Statistical Supplement,* 1980, Table 2.

3. S. Danziger, R. Haveman, and R. Plotnick, "How Income Transfer Programs Affect Work, Savings, and the Income Distribution: A Critical Review," *Journal of Economic Literature,* Vol. 19, September, 1981, p. 1008.

4. B. A. Okner and A. M. Rivlin, *Income Distribution Policy in the United States,* Washington, D.C.: Brookings, 1974.

5. Danziger et al., "How Income Transfer Programs Affect Work," p. 1008.

6. E. K. Browning, *Redistribution and the Welfare System,* Washington, D.C.: American Enterprise Institute, 1975, pp. 47–48.

7. Henry M. Levin, "A Decade of Policy Developments in Improving Education and Training for Low-Income Populations," in Robert H. Haveman (ed.), *A Decade of Federal Antipoverty Programs,* New York: Academic Press, 1977, p. 140.

8. Levin, "A Decade of Policy Developments," p. 172.

9. Levin, "A Decade of Policy Developments," pp. 177–78.

10. Browning, *Redistribution and the Welfare System,* p. 43.

11. Ibid., p. 44.

12. Ibid., p. 45.

13. R. H. Haveman, "Introduction: Poverty and Social Policy in the

1960s and 1970s—An Overview and Some Speculations," in R. H. Haveman (ed.), *A Decade of Federal Antipoverty Programs,* New York: Academic Press, 1977, p. 15.

14. L. E. Lynn, Jr., "A Decade of Policy Developments in the Income Maintenance System," in Haveman, *A Decade of Federal Antipoverty Programs,* p. 101.

15. H. J. Aaron, *Why Is Welfare So Hard to Reform?* Washington D.C., Brookings, 1973, pp. 32–38.

16. A. Rees, "An Overview of the Labor Supply Results," *Journal of Human Resources,* Vol. 9, Spring, 1974, pp. 158–80.

17. Ibid., p. 173.

18. H. W. Watts et al., "The Labor Supply Response of Husbands," *Journal of Human Resources,* Vol. 9, Spring, 1974, p. 182.

19. A. K. Bixby, "Social Welfare Expenditures, Fiscal Year 1979," *Social Security Bulletin,* Vol. 44, November, 1981, pp. 3–12.

CHAPTER 12

1. W. G. Bowen, "Assessing the Economic Contribution of Education," in M. Blaug (ed.), *Economics of Education,* Vol. 1, Baltimore: Penguin, 1968, pp. 74–75.

2. H. Miller, "Annual and Lifetime Income in Relation to Education," *American Economic Review,* December, 1960.

3. W. L. Hansen, "Total and Private Rates of Return to Investment in Schooling," *Journal of Political Economy,* Vol. 81, 1963, No. 2, pp. 128–41.

4. J. S. Coleman et al., *Equality of Educational Opportunity,* Washington, D.C.: Office of Education, Department of HEW, 1966.

5. Frederick Mosteller and Daniel Moynihan, *On Equality of Educational Opportunity,* New York: Random House, 1972, pp. 3–12.

6. Christopher Jencks et al., *Inequality,* New York: Basic Books, 1972, pp. 90–91.

7. See R. W. Tyler, "The Federal Role in Education," *The Public Interest,* Winter, 1974, and S. Bowles and H. Levin, "The Determinants of Scholastic Achievement—An Appraisal of Some Recent Evidence," *The Journal of Human Resources,* Winter, 1968, pp. 3–25.

8. David Armor, "School and Family Effects on Black and White Achievement: A Reexamination of the USOE Data," in Mosteller and Moynihan, *On Equality of Educational Opportunity,* pp. 146–67.

9. Jencks, *Inequality,* p. 224.

10. J. Morgan and M. David, "Education and Income," *The Quarterly Journal of Economics,* August, 1963, pp. 423–37.

11. Jencks, *Inequality,* p. 226, n. 63.

12. Ibid., p. 223, n. 51.

13. P. M. Siegel, "On the Cost of Being a Negro," *Sociological Inquiry,* Vol. 35, No. 1, Winter, 1965, pp. 41–58.

14. Evidence on financing higher education in California is taken from W. L. Hansen and B. A. Weisbrod, *Benefits, Costs and Finance of Public Higher Education,* Chicago: Markham, 1969.

15. See Jane Bryant Quinn, "The Student Loan Scare," *Newsweek,* May 24, 1982, p. 68.

16. See Dennis P. Doyle, "The Federal Student Aid Mess," *Wall Street Journal,* May 19, 1982, p. 28.

17. Ibid.

18. See Harrison Donnelly, "Massive Lobby Campaign Derails Reagan's Proposals for College Student Aid Cuts," *Congressional Quarterly,* May 22, 1982, pp. 1167–72.

19. We thank Richard McKenzie for suggesting this connection between past student aid and current student costs.

20. 1980 Statistical Abstract, Chart #246.

21. See Harrison Donnelly, "Little Hope Seen for Tuition Tax Credit Plan," *Congressional Quarterly,* April 24, 1982, 911–13.

22. Ibid.

Index